PMP®

Project Management Professional

Practice Tests

Second Edition

PMP®
Project Management Professional

Practice Tests

Second Edition

Kim Heldman, PMP

Vanina Mangano, PMP

Acknowledgments

I am humbled to be part of such a great team who helped in developing this book, and my other Sybex books, on project management. It takes a strong, dedicated team to produce a book, and I appreciate the help and support of all the Sybex team members who made this happen.

The biggest thanks of all goes to Vanina Mangano. Without her valiant efforts, this book would not have been possible. I am so grateful to her for taking on this book project and for creating its content. To me, writing good, quality questions is by far the most difficult task an author can undertake, and Vanina did an outstanding job. I am amazed at her wealth of project management knowledge and am grateful for her willingness to share her insights and experiences. It is always a pleasure to work with Vanina, and I look forward to working with her on many more projects in the coming years.

Another big thank-you goes to Kenyon Brown, senior acquisitions editor, for giving us the opportunity to write this book. Ken is a delight to work with, and I appreciate his help and insight in making our books the best they can be.

I would also like to thank all of the instructors who use my books in their PMP® prep classes as well as all of the PMI® chapters who use my books. Thank you.

Last, but always the first on my list, is my best friend for a few decades and counting, BB. I love you, and I would never have accomplished what I have to date without your love and support. You're the best! And I'd be remiss if l didn't also thank Jason and Leah, Noelle, Amanda, and Joe, and of course the two best granddaughters on the planet, Kate and Juliette, for their support and encouragement.

—Kim Heldman

I'd like to thank the team at Sybex for the opportunity to continue developing this book. I'm always amazed at the teamwork and effort that goes into the making and editing of a book, and each role involved is a critical one.

I'd like to give a special thanks to Kim Heldman, with whom I have enjoyed collaborating for more than a decade. I'm always amazed at what a warm and personable individual she is in reality—just as she comes through in her books! Kim is truly a role model to all of us within the project management community, and I'm proud to have coauthored materials with her.

Thank you to Kenyon Brown, our senior acquisitions editor, for giving me the opportunity to continue working on this title and for moving it forward. Ken is a joy to work with, and I appreciate him keeping me in the Sybex family!

Through this edition I had an opportunity to work with Tom Dinse, who served as development editor. Tom's oversight and ongoing guidance are what made this book a success. Tom is a true delight to work with—a top-notch professional with a sharp eye. He kept things moving and helped us navigate through the process.

A special thanks to the individuals who are such a big part of my life and who have always influenced me in a magnificent way. This includes my family: Nicolas Mangano, Marysil Mangano, Nicolas Mangano, Jr., and Carina Mangano; and my beautiful nieces,

Acknowledgments

Kaylee, Alyssa, Yasmin, and Rianna—you mean everything to me! Thank you to Roshoud Brown, a brilliant and talented author; Roshoud has served as a constant source of inspiration over the past 20 years.

—Vanina Mangano

We would like to thank Kim Wimpsett, copy editor, who made sure the grammar and spelling were picture-perfect; Louise Watson, proofreader, for catching those last little "oops"; and Christine O'Connor, production editor, who made sure everything flowed through the production process. Thanks also to our compositor, Aptara Inc. of New Delhi, India, and the indexer, Johnna VanHoose Dinse. The book couldn't have happened without them.

—Kim and Vanina

About the Authors

Kim Heldman, MBA, PMP®   Kim Heldman is the senior manager/CIO of information technology for the Regional Transportation District in Denver, Colorado. Kim directs IT resource planning, budgeting, project prioritization, and strategic and tactical planning. She directs and oversees IT design and development, the IT program management office, enterprise resource planning systems, IT infrastructure, application development, cybersecurity, intelligent transportation systems, and data center operations.

Kim oversees the IT portfolio of projects ranging from projects small in scope and budget to multimillion-dollar, multiyear projects. She has more than 25 years of experience in information technology project management. Kim has served in a senior leadership role for more than 18 years and is regarded as a strategic visionary with an innate ability to collaborate with diverse groups and organizations, instill hope, improve morale, and lead her teams in achieving goals they never thought possible.

Kim is the author of the *PMP®: Project Management Professional Study Guide, Ninth Edition*. She is also the author of *Project Management JumpStart, Fourth Edition*; *CompTIA Project+, Second Edition*; and *Project Manager's Spotlight on Risk Management*. Kim has also published several articles and is currently working on a leadership book.

Kim continues to write about project management best practices and leadership topics, and she speaks frequently at conferences and events. You can contact Kim at Kim.Heldman@gmail.com. She personally answers all her email.

Vanina Mangano   Over the past decade, Vanina has specialized in working with and leading project, program, and portfolio management offices (PMOs) across various industries and companies. Currently, Vanina leads a project portfolio management office at Microsoft Corporation.

As part of her contribution to the community, Vanina devotes time to furthering the project management profession through her volunteer work at the Project Management Institute. Vanina is currently a member of PMI's Standards Insight Team, where she serves in an advisory role for all matters related to the strategic planning and management of the PMI Standards Library. She has also served as chair for *The Standard for Program Management, Fourth Edition*, and played a role in several other PMI standards and practice guides, including *A Guide to the Project Management Body of Knowledge (PMBOK® Guide), Sixth Edition*.

Vanina holds a dual bachelor's degree from the University of California, Riverside, and holds the following credentials: Project Management Professional (PMP)®, PMI® Risk Management Professional (PMI-RMP)®, PMI® Scheduling Professional (PMI-SP)®, CompTIA Project+, and ITIL Foundation v3.

You can reach Vanina through LinkedIn: https://www.linkedin.com/in/vaninam/.

Contents at a Glance

Contents

Introduction

Congratulations on your decision to pursue the Project Management Professional (PMP)® credential, one of the most globally recognized credentials within the project management industry. The PMP® credential is offered by the Project Management Institute (PMI®), a not-for-profit organization with thousands of members across the globe. PMI® has been a long-standing advocate and contributor to the project management industry and offers several credentials for those specializing in the field of project management.

This book is meant for anyone preparing for the PMP® certification exam. Whether you are in the final stages of preparation, interested in familiarizing yourself with the question formats, or simply looking for additional practice in answering exam questions, this book has you covered. Those studying for the Certified Associate in Project Management (CAPM)® exam will also benefit, since both the PMP® and CAPM® certification exams follow a similar structure and are largely based on content from *A Guide to the Project Management Body of Knowledge (PMBOK® Guide), Sixth Edition.*

When it comes to preparing for an exam, knowing the core concepts is essential, but strengthening your test-taking skills is also important. One common test-taking method is based on an old saying: "Practice makes perfect." This book complements the *PMP®: Project Management Professional Exam Review Guide, Fourth Edition*, and the *PMP®: Project Management Professional Exam Study Guide, Tenth Edition*, also published by Sybex. The Study Guide provides a summary of project management fundamentals and the core concepts included within the exam. This book tests your knowledge of the tasks covered by the exam domains with the goal of exposing you to questions formatted similarly to those you would find on the actual exam. The more questions that you expose yourself to, the better prepared you will be on exam day.

Book Structure

This book has been structured to coincide with the exam domains presented in the *PMP® Examination Content Outline*, published by PMI. Each exam domain covers a high-level knowledge area essential to carrying out project management responsibilities. The domains are as follow:

- People
- Process
- Business Environment

An explanation is provided after each practice test question to help you learn the concepts. The first three chapters align to individual exam domains, while the final three chapters contain full-length practice exams.

NOTE It's a good idea to complete at least one full length practice exam in a single timed setting. This will partially simulate the experience of exam day, when you will need to answer a set of 200 questions within a four-hour period.

Interactive Online Learning Environment and Test Bank

This book provides 1000 practice test questions, which will help you get ready to pass the PMP exam. The interactive online learning environment that accompanies the PMP Practice Tests provides a robust test bank to help you prepare for the certification exam and increase your chances of passing it the first time! By using this test bank, you can identify weak areas up front and then develop a solid studying strategy using each of the robust testing features.

The test bank also includes 3 practice exams. Take the practice exams just as if you were taking the actual exam (without any reference material). If you get more than 90 percent of the answers correct, you're ready to take the certification exam.

NOTE You can access the Sybex Interactive Online Test Bank at http://www.wiley.com/go/Sybextestprep.

Overview of PMI® Credentials

PMI® offers several credentials within the field of project management, so whether you are an experienced professional or looking to enter the project management field for the first time, you'll find something to meet your needs. You may hold one or multiple credentials concurrently.

Over the years, PMI® has contributed to the project management body of knowledge by developing global standards used by thousands of project management professionals and organizations. In total, there are four foundational standards that are supplemented by multiple practice standards and guides.

Several credentials offered by PMI® are largely based on the *PMBOK® Guide*. While the *PMBOK® Guide* is a critical resource, it is considered one of multiple resources used during the development of certification exam questions. One additional resource you may want to pay close attention to is the *Agile Practice Guide*.

As of the publication date of this book, PMI® offers eight credentials. Let's briefly go through them.

Project Management Professional (PMP)®

You are most likely familiar with the PMP® credential—after all, you purchased this book! But did you know that the PMP® certification is the most widely and globally recognized project management certification? The PMP®, along with several other credentials, validates your experience and knowledge of project management. This makes obtaining a PMP® in itself a great achievement. The following requirements are necessary to apply for the PMP® exam:

Work Experience   The following work experience must have been accrued over the past eight consecutive years:

- If you have a bachelor's degree or the global equivalent: three years (36 months) leading projects, totaling at least 4,500 hours
- If you have a high-school diploma, associate's degree, or global equivalent: five years (60 months) of leading projects, totaling at least 7,500 hours

Contact Hours   Contact hours refers to the number of qualified formal educational hours obtained that relate to project management. A total of 35 contact hours are required and must be completed before you submit your application.

Certified Associate in Project Management (CAPM)®

The CAPM® credential is ideal for someone looking to enter the project management industry. You may meet the requirements if you have a secondary degree (i.e., high-school diploma or associate's degree or global equivalent). You must also have at least 23 hours of formal project management education (contact hours).

Program Management Professional (PgMP)®

The PgMP® credential is ideal for those who specialize in the area of program management or would like to highlight their experience of program management. A PMP® is not required to obtain this or any other credential. You must meet the following requirements to apply for the PgMP® exam:

Work Experience   The following work experience must have been accrued over the past 15 consecutive years:

- If you have a bachelor's degree or global equivalent: four years of nonoverlapping project management experience, totaling at least 6,000 hours, and four years of nonoverlapping program management experience, totaling 6,000 hours
- If you have a high-school diploma, associate's degree, or global equivalent: four years of nonoverlapping project management experience, totaling at least 6,000 hours, and seven years of nonoverlapping program management experience, totaling 10,500 hours

Portfolio Management Professional (PfMP)®

The PfMP® is meant for those specializing in the area of portfolio management. It reflects several years of hands-on portfolio management experience, geared toward achieving strategic objectives. You must meet the following requirements to apply for the PfMP® exam:

Work Experience   The following work experience must have been accrued over the past 15 consecutive years:

- Eight years of professional business experience (all candidates)
- If you have a bachelor's degree or global equivalent: 6,000 hours of portfolio management experience
- If you have a high-school diploma, associate's degree, or global equivalent: 10,500 hours of portfolio management experience

PMI Risk Management Professional (PMI-RMP)®

The PMI-RMP® credential is ideal for those who specialize in the area of risk management or would like to highlight their risk management experience. The following are the requirements to apply for the PMI-RMP® exam:

Work Experience   The following work experience must have been accrued over the past five consecutive years:

- If you have a bachelor's degree or global equivalent: 3,000 hours of professional project risk management experience
- If you have a high-school diploma, associate's degree, or global equivalent: 4,500 hours of professional project risk management experience

Contact Hours

- If you have a bachelor's degree or global equivalent: 30 contact hours in the area of risk management
- If you have a high-school diploma, associate's degree, or global equivalent: 40 contact hours in the area of risk management

PMI Scheduling Professional (PMI-SP)®

The PMI-SP® credential is ideal for those who specialize in the area of project scheduling or who would like to highlight their project scheduling experience. You must meet the following requirements to apply for the PMI-SP® exam:

Work Experience   The following work experience must have been accrued over the past five consecutive years:

- If you have a bachelor's degree or global equivalent: 3,500 hours of professional project scheduling experience
- If you have a high-school diploma, associate's degree, or global equivalent: 5,000 hours of professional project scheduling experience

Contact Hours

- If you have a bachelor's degree or global equivalent: 30 contact hours in the area of project scheduling
- If you have a high-school diploma, associate's degree, or global equivalent: 40 contact hours in the area of project scheduling

PMI Agile Certified Professional (PMI-ACP)®

The PMI-ACP® credential is ideal for those who work with Agile teams or practices. The PMI-ACP® covers approaches such as Serum, Kanban, Lean, Extreme Programming (XP), and Test-Driven Development (TDD). You must meet the following requirements to apply for the PMI-ACP® exam:

Work Experience   The following work experience must have been accrued:

- 2,000 hours (12 months) working on projects teams—accrued in the last five years; current PMP or PgMP credential holders will satisfy this requirement
- 1,500 hours (8 months) working on project teams using Agile methodologies—achieved in the last three years

Contact Hours

- 21 hours of formal Agile training

PMI Professional in Business Analysis (PMI-PBA)®

The PMI-PBA® credential is meant for those specializing in business analysis. This credential is ideal for those managing requirements or product development. You must meet the following requirements to apply for the PMI-PBA® exam:

Work Experience   The following work experience must have been accrued over the past eight consecutive years:

- If you have a bachelor's degree or global equivalent: 4,500 hours of professional business analysis experience
- If you have a high-school diploma, associate's degree, or global equivalent: 7,500 hours of business analysis experience, and 2,000 hours of general project experience

Contact Hours

- 35 hours of formal training in the area of business analysis practices

For the latest information regarding the PMI® credentials and other exam information, you can visit the PMI® website at www.PMI.org.

Day of the Exam

After gaining the necessary prerequisites to sit for the exam, the PMP® exam serves as the final measure to earning your certification. You are already well ahead of the game in preparing for the exam when you purchase this book. The preparation you put forth will help you show up on the day of the exam in a calm and confident state. While you are not allowed to take anything into the exam, you are given scratch paper to work with during your exam. Using the tips in this book, before you begin the exam, you can jot down notes that will free your mind to focus fully on the questions. In the days leading up to the exam, we recommend that you practice creating your reference sheet by memorizing the mnemonics, formulas, and other information that you will need.

Clearly, standard test-taking advice is relevant here, such as getting a good night's sleep, eating a good breakfast, and going through relaxation exercises before you are called into the exam room. In addition, during the exam, do the following:

- Take the time to read through each question slowly and completely. Fully understanding what is being asked in the question can contribute greatly to getting the right answer.

- You will be given the ability to mark a question if you are unsure of your answer or are unable to come up with the answer. Take advantage of this feature, so you can move on to the next question. At the end of the exam, you can come back and review your answers and take more time to answer questions that you didn't answer earlier in the process.

You have four hours to complete an examination of 200 questions. Tell yourself that it is more important to pass than it is to go home early. If it will help, write that statement at the top of your reference scratch paper so you can remind yourself of this ideal. In a four-hour examination, it is possible to get fatigued and just want to be done with it. Make sure you keep your focus and energy on success.

It's a good idea to use scratch paper given to you for use during your exam to jot down formulas and other information memorized that you may forget if you become mentally exhausted midway through the exam. Keep in mind that you cannot use your scratch paper until the exam time officially starts.

For more information from PMI® on preparing for the exam, be sure to review www.pmi.org and search for *PMP Exam Guidance* for more valuable resources.

Project Management Professional (PMP)®: Exam Domains and Tasks

The PMP® exam is based on three exam domains: People, Process, and Business Environment. Each exam domain encompasses a series of tasks, as published by PMI within the *Project Management Professional (PMP)® Examination Content Outline*. The following table maps these exam domain tasks to the corresponding chapter that contains sample practice test questions relating to the tasks. In addition to this reference table, you will find exam domain tasks listed at the beginning of Chapters 1–3.

Exam Domain	Chapters
People (Domain 1.0)	
Manage conflict	1, 4, 5, 6
Lead a team	1, 4, 5, 6
Support team performance	1, 4, 5, 6
Empower team members and stakeholders	1, 4, 5, 6
Ensure team members/stakeholders are adequately trained	1, 4, 5, 6
Build a team	1, 4, 5, 6
Address and remove impediments, obstacles, and blockers for the team	1, 4, 5, 6
Negotiate project agreements	1, 4, 5, 6
Collaborate with stakeholders	1, 4, 5, 6
Build shared understanding	1, 4, 5, 6
Engage and support virtual teams	1, 4, 5, 6
Define team ground rules	1, 4, 5, 6
Mentor relevant stakeholders	1, 4, 5, 6
Promote team performance through the application of emotional intelligence	1, 4, 5, 6
Process (Domain 2.0)	
Execute project with the urgency required to deliver business value	2, 4, 5, 6
Manage communications	2, 4, 5, 6
Assess and manage risks	2, 4, 5, 6
Engage stakeholders	2, 4, 5, 6
Plan and manage budget and resources	2, 4, 5, 6
Plan and manage schedule	2, 4, 5, 6
Plan and manage quality of products/deliverables	2, 4, 5, 6
Plan and manage scope	2, 4, 5, 6

Process (Domain 2.0) cont'd	Chapters
Integrate project planning activities	2, 4, 5, 6
Manage project changes	2, 4, 5, 6
Plan and manage procurement	2, 4, 5, 6
Manage project artifacts	2, 4, 5, 6
Determine appropriate project methodology/methods and practices	2, 4, 5, 6
Establish project governance structure	2, 4, 5, 6
Manage project issues	2, 4, 5, 6
Ensure knowledge transfer for project continuity	2, 4, 5, 6
Plan and manage project/phase closure or transitions	2, 4, 5, 6
Business Environment (Domain 3.0)	
Plan and manage project compliance	3, 4, 5, 6
Evaluate and deliver project benefits and value	3, 4, 5, 6
Evaluate and address external business environment changes for impact on scope	3, 4, 5, 6
Support organizational change	3, 4, 5, 6

Chapter

1

People (Domain 1.0)

THE PROJECT MANAGEMENT PROFESSIONAL (PMP)® EXAM CONTENT FROM THE PEOPLE DOMAIN COVERED IN THIS CHAPTER INCLUDES THE FOLLOWING:

✓ **Task 1.1** Manage conflict

✓ **Task 1.2** Lead a team

✓ **Task 1.3** Support team performance

✓ **Task 1.4** Empower team members and stakeholders

✓ **Task 1.5** Ensure team members/stakeholders are adequately trained

✓ **Task 1.6** Build a team

✓ **Task 1.7** Address and remove impediments, obstacles, and blockers for the team

✓ **Task 1.8** Negotiate project agreements

✓ **Task 1.9** Collaborate with stakeholders

✓ **Task 1.10** Build shared understanding

✓ **Task 1.11** Engage and support virtual teams

✓ **Task 1.12** Define team ground rules

✓ **Task 1.13** Mentor relevant stakeholders

✓ **Task 1.14** Promote team performance through the application of emotional intelligence

The process names, inputs, tools and techniques, outputs, and descriptions of the project management process groups and related materials and figures in this chapter are based on content from *A Guide to the Project Management Body of Knowledge (PMBOK® Guide) – Sixth Edition* (PMI®, 2017).

1. Carina is a principal project manager of You've Got Dogs, a specialty company that creates custom dog apparel and toys. Three months into the project, she kicks off the second phase of a project that is developing high-tech dog bones. As part of her practice, she sits down with her sponsor to determine whether there are any new players that they missed in the first phase, and they hold a discussion on the direction of influence of these new stakeholders. What activity is Carina carrying out?

   A. Planning stakeholder engagement

   B. Identifying stakeholders

   C. Planning resource management

   D. Identifying risks

2. Which of the following best describes the servant leadership approach used in Agile projects?

   A. The practice of one individual directing the team to provide clear and concise direction

   B. The practice of generating work through iterations, with one leader clearly prominent

   C. The practice of installing one clear leader, with team members serving as followers

   D. The practice of focusing on understanding and addressing the needs and development of team members

3. Your project has kicked off, and you are beginning a series of overview sessions with key users to determine requirements for a new enterprise resource software implementation. One of your stakeholders is exceptionally contentious and throws obstacles up at every turn. One of the problems she has described does seem to be legitimate. There is an issue with the data from the legacy system that needs to be resolved before moving forward. Which of the following statements is not true regarding this situation?

   A. You should approach this by defining the problem and focusing on separating causes and symptoms.

   B. You should use a two-step process involving problem definition and decision-making.

   C. Your decision-making has a timing element.

   D. Your decision-making involves asking questions to determine whether the issues are internal or external to the project.

4. Nancy is a senior systems engineer who loves to work with people and can typically grasp the big picture. Because of her functional knowledge, organized nature, and ease in getting others to follow her lead, her manager decides to move her into a project manager role. Despite all of her strengths, Nancy struggles greatly with her first project. The first major milestone was missed, and the project was already over budget by $20,000. What part of the PMI Talent Triangle™ is Nancy missing?

   A. Technical project management

   B. Leadership

   C. Strategic and business management

   D. Schedule management

5. You are a project manager working on contract. The organization that's contracted with your company is not happy with the progress of the project to date. They claim that an important deliverable was overlooked and that you should halt the project and reassess how to meet this deliverable. You know that the customer has approved all phases of the project to date. Which of the following statements is true?

   A. You and your company might have to use problem-solving techniques such as arbitration and mediation to reach an agreement.

   B. You and your company might have to use communication techniques such as arbitration and mediation to reach an agreement.

   C. You and your company might have to use negotiation techniques such as arbitration and mediation to reach an agreement.

   D. You and your company might have to use influencing techniques such as arbitration and mediation to reach an agreement.

6. An Agile approach can alleviate issues that result when high uncertainty exists. Which of the following is an example of a pain point that Agile addresses under these circumstances? (Select three.)

   A. Unclear purpose

   B. Low defects

   C. Unclear requirements

   D. Technical debt

7. You're the project manager for Dream Clinics, a research organization that specializes in sleep disorders. You're working on an internal service project and are in the Executing process group. You negotiate with a manager to obtain resources for specific activities on the project that your team is not able to fulfill. These resources will roll off the project as soon as the activities are completed. Which of the following does this scenario describe?

   A. Resource requirements, which are generated when carrying out resource requirement planning activities

   B. Interpersonal and team skills, which are capabilities used by project managers to acquire resources

   C. Staffing requirements, which is information needed when acquiring resources

   D. Resource pool description, which is information needed when planning out resource requirements

8. Your colleague has reported to their manager that they passed their PMP certification exam. You know this is inaccurate, since you both took your exams at the same time and the colleague shared the results with you. What should you do?

   A. Give them an opportunity to correct their behavior and report them to PMI if they do not.

   B. Don't say anything. Since this is your friend, the code states that you must look out for each other.

   C. Give your friend a difficult time to teach them a lesson and disassociate with them.

   D. Tell their manager immediately and report the violation to PMI directly.

9. Carina is a principal project manager of You've Got Dogs, a specialty company that creates custom dog apparel and toys. As is part of her practice, she sits down with her sponsor to evaluate how the project is performing. She reviews feedback from the most recent prototype, which the team has produced successively to yield additional insight. Carina notes to the sponsor that the use of timeboxing has been helpful in reducing the uncertainty in the project. What type of life cycle is Carina using?

A. Predictive

B. Waterfall

C. Agile

D. Iterative

10. Knowledge that is difficult to express is called what?

A. Explicit knowledge

B. Tacit knowledge

C. Tangible knowledge

D. Formal knowledge

11. You are working on a project with contentious team members. You know if you resolve the conflicts, it will result in increased productivity and better working relationships. You pull the team together in a meeting to discuss the issue. You allow everyone to express their viewpoint, and as a result, some team members gain an understanding of the perspective of some of their teammates that they didn't have before this meeting. At the conclusion of the meeting, consensus is reached, and the team members thank you for taking the time to get them together and asking them to discuss this issue. Which of the following conflict-resolution techniques does this describe?

A. Compromise/reconcile

B. Force/direct

C. Smooth/accommodate

D. Collaborate/problem-solve

12. Which conflict-resolution technique does not result in a permanent resolution?

A. Withdraw/avoid

B. Force/direct

C. Collaborate/problem-solve

D. Smooth/accommodate

13. As part of establishing a new project team, a project manager chooses to create an official team charter. What will the project manager likely include within the document? (Select two.)

A. Team responsibilities

B. Team assignments

C. Team values

D. Decision-making criteria

14. You are working on a critical project for your organization. The CEO has made it clear this is a top priority. One of the key stakeholders on your project resigned, and her replacement started about three weeks ago. She does not make time for you or seem to have the same level of urgency regarding this project as the CEO. You are concerned with overall project success and want to efficiently manage the processes involved with this project. All of the following are methods referred to within this scenario except for which one?

    A. Meetings

    B. Data analysis

    C. Ground rules

    D. Decision-making

15. David is a project manager working for a prominent book publishing company. As the most senior project manager within the organization, he often gets paired with strong-willed project sponsors. During a recent project meeting, David's project sponsor began yelling in frustration at the project's status, which was blocked because of a critical resource being out ill. In frustration, the sponsor began spewing profanities at David, questioning his ability to manage effectively. In response, David calmly assured the project sponsor that a contingency plan would be implemented and requested that they speak privately to address his frustrations. David then excused the rest of the project team. What core value did David uphold during the meeting?

    A. Fairness

    B. Honesty

    C. Respect

    D. Responsibility

16. During a project status meeting, you request updates to work tasks. One of your close friends accountable for the most critical milestone on the schedule notes that they are on track. Over wine the previous evening, the friend had confided that the task was two weeks behind schedule. What should you do as the project manager?

    A. Throw your friend under the bus—after all, the wine was cheap and not worth it.

    B. Immediately report the slip, along with the source of your information.

    C. Give your friend an opportunity to report accurate status; if this does not occur, report accurately that a slippage has occurred.

    D. Do nothing. Honoring friendship is far more important, and this is an opportunity to display trust.

17. You are in the process of facilitating a change control meeting. You review a change request that would double the scope of the project but would not yield a major increase in the project's resulting benefits. You know that the submitter of the change request has a tendency to bloat a project's scope without fully thinking through the impact, but as a result of their position in the company, their changes tend to be approved. What type of power does the submitter of the change request typically use?

    A. Legitimate

    B. Expert

    C. Referent

    D. Punishment

18. You are very interested in becoming a project manager. You have mentored with other experienced project managers in your organization to learn more about how to be an effective project manager. You've been told your organizational skills and communication skills are excellent. However, you need some additional training in accounting and budgeting skills, because you are weak in these general management areas. The mentor who was honest enough to tell you this explained it which of the following ways?

A. You will not be able to sit for the exam unless you get formal training in the general management areas.

B. General management skills are likely to affect project outcomes. If you lack any of these skills, it could affect your project and your career adversely, so you should get some training in these areas.

C. The Estimating Costs and Control Costs processes are under the Planning process group, and you will not be able to pass the questions on the PMP exam that pertain to these processes if you don't get some training.

D. General management skills are important to your project outcomes, and Estimating Costs and Control Costs are two of the most important processes within the Executing phase of a project, so you should get some training in these areas.

19. A project manager following an Agile life cycle receives a request from the customer to alter a requirement. How will the project manager likely respond?

A. Blocks change

B. Welcomes change

C. Prevents change

D. Indifferent about change

20. A project manager presents a summary of project team roles and responsibilities, training needs, and recognition and rewards to the project sponsor for approval. In what activity are they engaged?

A. Developing the stakeholder engagement plan

B. Identifying resource risk

C. Developing the resource management plan

D. Estimating project costs

21. A project manager is preparing to send five engineers to Japan to install a high-security network. The engineers have never been outside of the United States before. Prior to their travel, the project manager asks the Japan-based manager to give the engineers an overview of their history, customs, and social norms. What is the project manager's motive?

A. To teach the engineers about the Japanese culture

B. To take a breather after a hard day's work

C. To ensure the engineers understand how to interact abroad

D. To prevent culture shock

22. Which of the following best describes the directing conflict-resolution technique?

   A. Pushing one's viewpoint at the expense of others

   B. Incorporating multiple viewpoints and insights

   C. Retreating from a potential conflict solution

   D. Searching for solutions that bring some degree of satisfaction

23. You've just accepted a new project management assignment. The project is for a customer in a foreign country. You've requested a business analyst and two other project team members from the country the customer resides in to participate on your team. The remaining team members are from your country. You know that the best way to ensure that the project team doesn't get bogged down in cultural differences and hold up project progress is to do which of the following?

   A. Perform team-building exercises using videoconferencing to allow team members to get to know each other and get to the performing stage of team development as soon as possible.

   B. Require project team members to read and sign the organization's diversity policy.

   C. Establish your role as project manager as the first order of business and require compliance with company policies.

   D. Provide diversity training for all the team members to make them aware of cultural differences and teach them to function effectively as a team despite these differences.

24. Carina is a principal project manager of You've Got Dogs, a specialty company that creates custom dog apparel and toys. As part of her latest project, she struggles to rein in the team, who seem to be at each other's throats. She knows everyone has good intentions, but they are not yet open and trusting with each other. What phase of the team development model is the team currently in?

   A. Norming

   B. Performing

   C. Forming

   D. Storming

25. Dr. William Ouchi developed a theory that is concerned with increasing employees' loyalty to their organizations and places emphasis on the well-being of the employees, both at work and outside of work. What is the name of this leadership theory?

   A. Theory Y

   B. Theory Z

   C. Theory X

   D. Theory Y/Z

26. You are a contract project manager and have entered into the requirements-gathering phase of your project. Two of the departments you're working with on this project have competing interests regarding this project and have done everything they can, including sabotage, to undermine the work so far. To finish up the requirements-gathering phase, you will have to exert some influence. Which of the following statements is true regarding influencing the organization? (Select three.)

A. Influencing entails the ability to get things done.

B. Influencing requires an understanding of the formal and informal structures of the organization, including the use of power and politics.

C. Politics involves getting the people in these two departments to do things they wouldn't otherwise do.

D. Power entails getting these two departments with competing interests cooperating effectively to achieve the goals of the project.

27. Match the leadership style to its corresponding attributes.

Leadership Style	Attributes
A. Laissez-faire	1. Puts other people first
B. Transactional	2. High-energy and enthusiastic
C. Servant leader	3. Management by exception
D. Transformational	4. A hands-off approach
E. Charismatic	5. Seeks to inspire and encourage innovation

28. In what ways does the servant leadership approach empower teams? (Select two.)

A. It provides greater team accountability.

B. It provides an autocratic approach to decision-making.

C. It supports the team through a single clear leader.

D. It supports the team through mentoring and encouragement.

29. You are the project manager for a large project. The initial project schedule shows the project takes approximately three years to complete. Some of the stakeholders have changed over the course of this project, and new stakeholders will become involved toward the end of the project. The project team members have also changed as the project has evolved into a new set of deliverables. You are having a difficult time motivating the new team members. The techniques you used with the previous team don't seem to be working with this team. More resources will be brought on and off the project team at various stages throughout the life cycle, so you'd like to resolve this problem soon. You know from studying the Project Resource Management Knowledge Area that you should do which of the following?

A. The processes in this Knowledge Area ensure that the human and material resources involved on the project are used in the most effective way possible.

B. The same communication style should be used throughout the life of the project.

C. You will change the techniques used to motivate, lead, and coach the human resources involved on the project as the project progresses.

D. This Knowledge Area's processes include Acquire Resources, Develop Team, and Manage Team.

30. Lewis is a marketing associate reporting to Antwon, the company's director of marketing. He pulls you aside to get your opinion about the latest project that he claims was his idea. He expresses frustration that Antwon was named sponsor of the project instead of himself. Based on the scenario presented, who is the correct project sponsor?

A. Lewis

B. Antwon

C. Neither

D. Both

31. Colocation is also known as what?

A. Tight matrix

B. Virtual teams

C. Dedicated teams

D. Effective teams

32. You are in the process of attaining and hiring resources for the project. Some of the resources can be found within the organization, but three of the resources you've identified must be hired on contract. You need to consider previous experience, personal interests, personal characteristics, availability, and the competencies and proficiency of the contractors as well as the internal staff. Which of the following statements best describes the situation?

A. The situation in this question refers to the project staff assignment, which is an output of Plan Resource Management.

B. The situation in this question refers to organizational process assets, which are an input of Plan Resource Management.

C. The situation in this question refers to the project staff assignments, which are an output of Acquire Resources.

D. The situation in this question refers to the enterprise environmental factors input to the Acquire Resources process.

33. All of the following are methods used to develop project teams except for which one?

A. Training

B. Emotional intelligence

C. Colocation

D. Negotiation

34. To whom is the theory attributed that says people are motivated by the need for power, achievement, and affiliation?

A. David McClelland

B. Victor Vroom

C. Frederick Herzberg

D. Douglas McGregor

35. Nicolas is the project manager of a project that has been described as revolutionizing the mobile fitness tracking industry. He prepares for a meeting with the project's sponsor to discuss how to approach the project. During the meeting, he tells the project sponsor that he would like to promote self-awareness, listening, and coaching versus controlling. Nicolas is promoting characteristics of what?

A. Servant leadership approach

B. Incremental approach

C. Deming approach

D. Hygiene model

36. You are a new project manager and have always been self-motivated. You are destined to achieve good things and desire to attain the coveted PMP designation. Even after attaining the designation, you will strive to apply professional knowledge to your future projects and adhere to the *PMI Code of Ethics and Professional Conduct*. Which theory is described in this question, and what area of the PMI role delineation study does this question refer to?

A. Hygiene Theory and ensure personal integrity and professionalism

B. Contingency Theory and contribute to the project management knowledge base

C. Expectancy Theory and enhance professional competence

D. Leadership Theory and responsibility

37. You hold a position that is primarily concerned with satisfying stakeholder needs as well as issues such as plans, controls, budgets, policies, procedures, and team motivation. You have signed a nondisclosure agreement, promising not to give away trade secrets, and you have signed a noncompete agreement with your current employer that says you will not go to work for a competitor any sooner than 18 months after the date of your termination. Your staff members have signed similar agreements, but their noncompete agreement is for 12 months rather than 18. You have discovered, through a friend of a friend, that one of your staff members is interviewing at a competing company, and if the position is offered and accepted, it would violate the noncompete agreement your staff member signed. Which of the following describes the type of position you hold and the domain within the *PMI Code of Ethics and Professional Conduct* that pertains to this situation?

A. Manager and Responsibility

B. Leader and Respect

C. Manager and Honesty

D. Leader and Fairness

38. Your virtual project team consists of 12 people in the same building you're located in plus 4 people from the West Coast office, 2 people from the Kansas City office, and 6 people from the London office. Your office works different hours from all the other offices. Additionally, not all of the resources in your building are available at the same times during the day. Three of those 12 team members work swing shift hours. Which of the following should you use to capture the availability information for these resources and potential future resources, as well as their capabilities and skills?

A. Activity calendar

B. Team roster

C. Project calendar

D. Resource calendar

39. Which of the following best describes the performing stage of the team development model, developed by Tuckman?

A. The phase where team members meet and learn about the project and formalize their roles and responsibilities

B. The phase where team members begin to work together and adjust their work habits and behaviors to support the team

C. The phase where the team is functioning as a well-organized unit and work through their issues smoothly

D. The phase where the team members begin to address the project work and are not yet collaborative or open with each other

40. Silvana is a junior project manager who was recently hired to work on projects supporting the networking team. Her first project is plagued with issues, mostly caused by team member conflicts. Her sponsor attempts to reassure Silvana. What fact is she likely to share with Silvana?

A. Conflict often occurs within a technical environment.

B. Conflict is inevitable in a project environment.

C. Conflict is always good.

D. Conflict is never a reflection of the project manager.

41. Yasmin is a senior project manager for a project that aims to produce a new line of medical widgets for a Fortune 100 company. The entire industry has been buzzing with excitement over this project, which was estimated to span three years and require an investment of $1.5 billion from the company. While wrapping up for the week, Yasmin receives a fifth call from a vendor that has been pursuing an active RFP for the project. The vendor notes that they have connections in the offshore company by which the product will be manufactured, and if they win the contract, they are certain that they could bypass customs, saving Yasmin's company millions of dollars in the process. What should Yasmin do?

A. Agree to discuss options with the vendor, since it would save the company millions of dollars.

B. Pass on the offer but take down the vendor's phone number to keep options open.

C. Pass on the offer and report the conversation to the company's legal department.

D. Pass on the offer and report the conversation to her colleagues.

42. You are in the process of hiring resources for a project. Some of the resources can be found within the organization, but three of the resources you've identified will be contracted from outside the organization. You need to consider previous experience, personal interests, personal characteristics, availability, and competencies and proficiency of the contractors as well as the internal staff. You have a friend who is looking for a job. He isn't qualified for the position, but you know him well enough to know he will come up to speed quickly. A couple of training classes should do the trick. What process is this question describing, and which area of the *PMI Code of Ethics and Professional Conduct* does this question refer to?

  A. Develop Team and Respect

  B. Manage Team and Honesty

  C. Plan Resource Management and Fairness

  D. Acquire Resources and Responsibility

43. You've noticed that your CIO shows all the signs of being a good leader. Which of the following statements are true regarding leaders? (Select three.)

  A. Leaders use referent power.

  B. Leaders impart vision.

  C. Leaders are concerned with strategic plans.

  D. Leaders are concerned with satisfying stakeholder needs.

44. You are working with your stakeholders and performing activities associated with the Executing process group. You are dealing with some issues involving the project objectives and are working to maintain consensus among the five stakeholders participating in this project. You have used both influencing and negotiating skills and have finally come to consensus on the issue at hand. Which of the following options best describes the contents of this question?

  A. You are using the interpersonal and team skills tool and technique of the Manage Stakeholder Engagement process.

  B. You are using the management skills tool and technique of the Control Stakeholder Engagement process.

  C. You are using the communication method tool and technique of the Plan Stakeholder Management process.

  D. You are using the meetings tool and technique of the Plan Stakeholder Management process.

45. Recognition and rewards are important parts of team interaction. They are both formal ways of recognizing and promoting desirable behavior. Which of the following statements are true regarding reward and recognition? (Select three.)

  A. They are an input of the Develop Team process.

  B. They should be proportional to the achievement.

C. Rewards can kill motivation if used improperly.

D. Rewards should be linked to performance.

46. Victor Vroom developed a theory that recognizes the belief that a positive outcome drives motivation. You are looking for a new position as a program manager. You don't have the experience for this level of responsibility, but you are rationalizing that if you have enough motivation and can fudge a bit of experience on the application, you're showing initiative, and hopefully, the outcome will be in your favor. What theory is this question describing, and what area within the Responsibility domain of the *PMI Code of Ethics and Professional Conduct* does this question refer to?

A. Hygiene Theory and Professional Demeanor

B. Achievement Theory and Ensuring Integrity

C. Expectancy Theory and Accepting Assignments

D. Self-actualization level of the Hierarchy of Needs and Conflict of Interest

47. A project manager is planning the kickoff meeting for a project that will have team members dispersed across nine countries. What can the project manager do to support an environment where diverse perspectives and views are encouraged and valued?

A. Include videoconferencing as an option.

B. Have all team members attend the kickoff in person.

C. Hold diversity training.

D. Have each team member state their name and country.

48. Your virtual project team consists of 12 people in the same building you're located in plus 4 people from the West Coast office, 2 people from the Kansas City office, and 6 people from the London office. Your office works different hours from all the other offices. Additionally, not all of the resources in your building are available at the same times during the day. Three of those 12 team members work swing shift hours. Which of the following are true? (Select three.)

A. The teams do not have the same project goals because of the differences in location. Your role is to make certain team members understand the goals and how you will be measuring their performance.

B. Team members should understand the expectations you have for them on the project, and you should make certain they understand the decision-making processes.

C. Your role is to communicate to all team members and make certain they understand the protocols for communicating with you and each other.

D. Your role is to make certain that team members are given credit for their performance and actions on the project.

49. You have accepted a position in a new company and have spent the first 30 days observing your team. Your findings, unfortunately, are not encouraging. The team exhibits a lack of motivation, poor communication among team members, a lack of respect for you and your position, and project work results that are less than satisfactory. For a fleeting moment, you think about leaving but realize that's not in keeping with the *PMI Code of Ethics and Professional Conduct*. You know all of the following are true, given the circumstances, except for which one?

A. You know that quitting would not be in keeping with the Responsibility, Respect, Fairness, or Honesty domains of the *PMI Code of Ethics and Professional Conduct*.

B. You will use interpersonal skills, training, and team-building activities, among others, to attempt to improve this dysfunctional team.

C. You are carrying out activities associated with team management and realize that since you are new, the stages of team development will start over again at the forming stage.

D. You will use ground rules, recognition and rewards, and personnel assessment tools, among others, to attempt to improve this dysfunctional team.

50. All of the following are common roles used in Agile projects except for which one?

A. Cross-functional team member

B. Project manager

C. Product owner

D. Team facilitator

51. You hold a position that is primarily concerned with satisfying stakeholder needs as well as issues such as plans, controls, budgets, policies, procedures, and team motivation. You have signed a nondisclosure agreement, promising not to give away trade secrets, and you have signed a noncompete agreement with your current employer that says you will not go to work for a competitor any sooner than 18 months after the date of your termination. You will be working with a virtual team, and during the hiring process, the members will be required to sign similar agreements, but their noncompete agreement is for 12 months rather than 18 months. Because this virtual team will have members from all over the globe, you should be concerned with one area in particular of the *PMI Code of Ethics and Professional Conduct*. Which of the following options best describes this situation?

A. You are a manager, working in the Develop Team process, and need to pay particular attention to cultural awareness and diversity training.

B. You are a manager, working in the Acquire Resources process, and need to pay particular attention to cultural awareness and diversity training.

C. You are a manager, working in the Develop Team process, and need to pay particular attention to fairness and stakeholder influence.

D. You are a manager, working in the Acquire Resources process, and need to pay particular attention to fairness and stakeholder influence.

52. Your project sponsor approaches you with a small bonus check for your excellent work keeping costs in line with the budget. You think the amount of the bonus check is fair and deserved. Which of the following statements are true? (Select two.)

    A. The reward is appropriately linked to the performance.

    B. Rewards and recognition systems are informal ways of promoting desirable behavior.

    C. Rewards and recognition systems are created as a result of the project.

    D. The reward is in line with the performance, and you should accept it.

53. At minimum, measuring stakeholder satisfaction typically occurs at what point of the project life cycle?

    A. During project initiation

    B. During project planning

    C. During project execution

    D. During project closure

54. You've decided to branch out into project management consulting and have landed your first contracting assignment. You are working on an exciting project for a midsize company that provides pet-sitting services in people's homes. The employee who is the designated project manager on this project doesn't have much experience running projects. He insists that all the stakeholders have been identified and that he alone understands their expectations so there is no need for you to meet with them. As a more experienced project manager, you know which of the following is true?

    A. He is correct. You do not need to meet with the stakeholders as long as they have been identified. His knowledge of their expectations alone is sufficient.

    B. You should meet with the stakeholders. Project Communications Management is concerned with documenting the needs and demands of the stakeholders and capturing this information in the project scope statement.

    C. You do not need to meet with the stakeholders since they have already been identified. You can meet them when you capture their requirements in the Collect Requirements process, which is part of the Project Integration Management Knowledge Area.

    D. You should meet with the stakeholders, identify them, assess their needs, and record their expectations as part of the Project Stakeholder Management Knowledge Area.

55. A project manager is interested in organizing the team based on individual team member strengths. What tool can they use to gain insights into team strengths and weaknesses, including how they make decisions, interact with others, and process information? (Select three.)

    A. Training

    B. Structured interviews

    C. Ability tests

    D. Attitudinal surveys

56. Match the following conflict-resolution techniques to their corresponding descriptions.

Technique	Description
A. Compromise	1. A resolution technique that involves withdrawing from the conflict
B. Collaborate	2. A resolution technique that partially resolves conflict by finding a solution that brings some satisfaction to all parties
C. Force	3. A resolution technique that results in a win-lose situation
D. Avoid	4. A resolution technique that often leads to consensus and commitment

57. A project manager has a reputation for leading project teams by focusing on developing team member skills, coaching them, and empowering them. What are these a characteristic of?

A. Situational leader

B. Servant leader

C. Facilitator

D. Coach

58. You are in the process of evaluating the engagement levels of stakeholders. What tool can you use to help you get started quickly?

A. Stakeholder assessment matrix

B. Alternatives analysis

C. Root-cause analysis

D. Presentations

59. Leticia is a project manager working for Dancing Apron, a company that combines cooking with simple children's cooking recipes and music. Her latest project involves the release of the company's first digital product, which parents will be able to purchase and download online. While overseeing the project, Leticia notices that recent stakeholder engagement levels have dropped significantly, and they've begun to disagree during status meetings. She decides to evaluate their engagement levels using prioritized criteria and weights that she documented in the stakeholder engagement plan so that she can share and discuss the results with the project sponsor. What primary activity is Leticia performing?

A. Strategizing how to engage stakeholders

B. Managing stakeholder engagement levels

C. Influencing stakeholder engagement levels

D. Monitoring the engagement levels of stakeholders

60. Knowledge that can be codified using images, numbers, and words is called what?

    A. Explicit knowledge

    B. Tacit knowledge

    C. Tangible knowledge

    D. Formal knowledge

61. Which of the following activities involves determining and documenting a team's effectiveness?

    A. Team performance assessments

    B. Project performance appraisals

    C. Organizational process assets updates

    D. Enterprise environmental factors updates

62. A project manager is performing closure activities for the project and meets with the project sponsor to review the final report. The report reveals that the project budget is 90 percent consumed. The project sponsor expresses concern that there may be a risk of going over budget. How is the project manager likely to respond?

    A. Assure the project sponsor that the risk of going over budget is low.

    B. Agree with the project sponsor and begin risk mitigation activities.

    C. Email the project team to express disappointment in project spending.

    D. Take offense at the project sponsor's lack of trust and confidence.

63. You are a project manager carrying out various activities that involve managing the team. At present, you are preparing for your individual team members' performance assessments. Which of the following will assist you as you carry out this activity? (Select three.)

    A. Work performance reports

    B. Project management information system

    C. Resource management plan

    D. Team performance assessments

64. Rianna is a developer who is interested in moving toward a career in project management. She takes on a small project that will implement a new security feature to protect her company's internal network. To date, she has baselined the project's scope, schedule, and budget, and she is now actively helping to resolve issues as they arise. What outcome is she looking to produce?

    A. Optimize project performance

    B. Improve competencies

    C. Improve team interaction

    D. Allocate resources appropriately

65. Which of the following best defines virtual teams? (Select two.)

   A. Groups of people with a shared goal who are dispersed across various locations

   B. Groups of colocated people with a shared goal who fulfill their roles with little or no time spent meeting face to face

   C. Groups of people with a shared goal who fulfill their roles with little or no time spent meeting face to face

   D. Groups of people with varying goals who fulfill their roles with little or no time spent meeting face to face

66. You are in the midst of some difficult procurement negotiations. The schedule, service-level agreements, and incentives have not been agreed upon. One of the parties representing the vendor lashes out at you during the negotiations. You were not expecting this outburst and are just about to stoop to their level when you remember which of the following in reference to the *PMI Code of Ethics and Professional Conduct* and the process you are currently performing?

   A. Your actions and you should maintain respect even though the other party is out of control. The Control Procurements process can be difficult when you are negotiating complex contracts.

   B. You can't control the actions of others, but you can control your actions, and you should ensure personal integrity by controlling yourself even though the other party is out of control. The Control Procurements process can be difficult when you are negotiating complex contracts.

   C. You can't control the actions of others, but you can control your actions, and you should maintain respect even though the other party is out of control. The Conduct Procurements process can be difficult when you are negotiating complex contracts.

   D. You can't control the actions of others, but you can control your actions, and you should ensure personal integrity by controlling yourself even though the other party is out of control. The Conduct Procurements process can be difficult when you are negotiating complex contracts.

67. This win-win conflict-resolution technique is the one that project managers should use most.

   A. Collaboration

   B. Compromise

   C. Withdrawal

   D. Smoothing

68. A superuser of a customer relationship management system calls the project manager for assistance in resolving a system bug recently discovered by a member of his team. What has the project manager failed to do?

   A. Provide the appropriate training to superusers to ensure they are equipped to address bugs as they arise.

   B. Publish the final report of the project, which would detail how ongoing activities are to be addressed.

   C. Release the project team back to their ongoing responsibilities, including the superuser community.

   D. Transition the ongoing support and maintenance of the system to the appropriate operational team.

69. Avoiding, accommodating, reconciling, directing, and problem-solving are all considered to be types of what?

   A. Interpersonal and team skills

   B. Communication skills

   C. Conflict resolution

   D. Power

70. Which of the following conflict-resolution techniques emphasizes areas of agreement rather than areas of difference?

   A. Smoothing

   B. Compromising

   C. Reconciling

   D. Directing

71. Your manager knocks on your door and asks whether you have time to discuss the recent draft status report you sent her for review. She knows you are interested in performing at your best, but it seems that the third paragraph of the status report may contain a misstatement. She diligently listens to your explanation and realizes that her assumptions were incorrect. She explains that if she misunderstood, others might also. She asks if you wouldn't mind taking a stab at clarifying this paragraph. Which theory does your manager practice?

   A. Achievement Theory

   B. Expectancy Theory

   C. Contingency Theory

   D. Theory Y

72. You are in the Manage Team process and preparing for your individual team members' performance assessments. You will use one of the tools and techniques of this process to determine each team member's leadership, influencing, and effective decision-making capabilities. Which tool and technique is this referring to?

   A. Interpersonal and team skills

   B. Observation and conversation

   C. Leadership skills

   D. General management skills

73. Match the decision-making technique with its description.

Term	Description
A. Autocratic	1. Uses a systematic approach to making decisions
B. Multicriteria decision analysis	2. One individual makes the decision
C. Voting	3. Uses unanimity, majority, or plurality to make decisions

74. You are a project manager working for a nonprofit organization. Your team consists of full-time employees from the same nonprofit organization, and all of you are motivated by providing a service to others in need. You have worked with these team members before and know they all have outstanding performance records. Your project concerns setting up a receiving and distribution center for new and gently used laptops to be distributed to schools in Latvia. At a recent team meeting, you reiterated the expectations for this project with all of your team members. You eagerly listened to their ideas and concerns and assured them you would support them in meeting the goals of the project no matter what it takes. Which theory do you subscribe to?

A. Theory X

B. Hygiene Theory

C. Contingency Theory

D. Theory Y

75. A junior project manager works with the procurement manager to review vendor proposals. The procurement manager decides to select a vendor who did not have the highest weighted score against the criteria that were predetermined. The project manager learns that the vendor is the procurement manager's cousin. What should the project manager do?

A. Bring this to the procurement manager's attention and report it to the appropriate department for investigation.

B. Do nothing. Project managers should respect the role and authority of each member of the team.

C. Confront the procurement manager and threaten to report their behavior to the ethics committee.

D. Overturn the procurement manager's decision and select the vendor with the highest weighted score.

76. A project manager hosted a celebration for the project team to reward them for a job well done that led to the successful completion of a major project. It was clear to the project manager that the team was relaxed and enjoying themselves, with some talking about upcoming vacation plans. What type of project ending is this?

A. Integration

B. Addition

C. Extinction

D. Starvation

77. Kaylee is a risk manager working in collaboration with Alyssa, a project manager, and both work for a top healthcare company. During a tense moment, they have a heated debate on how a risk should be treated. They decide to get the sponsor's viewpoint and reach consensus after further discussion. What conflict-resolution technique did they use?

A. Avoid

B. Collaborate

C. Direct

D. Compromise

78. Your manager requests a meeting with you. When you meet, she asks you about the third paragraph of the recent status report. She doesn't understand what it means and believes that it may cast a bad light on her and the team. She asks you to explain, listens to your response, restates what you said, and then offers suggestions regarding how to phrase this type of information on future status reports. Which style of leadership and type of power does your manager practice?

A. Transactional and punishment

B. Transformational and legitimate

C. Democratic and referent

D. Laissez-faire and reward

79. Your colleague recently accepted a job transfer that requires a PMP credential. During a recent conversation, he confided to you that he lied on his application in order to get the assignment. This is an example of what?

A. A bad friend

B. Poor judgment

C. An ethics violation

D. Unprofessional behavior

80. Reasons to Lyv is the top client of a large marketing firm. Trudy is the president of Reasons to Lyv and has decided to launch a product that leverages new GPS tracking technology. She sits down with Roy, the project manager on the project, to discuss which stakeholders are resistant, unaware, neutral, supportive, or leading within the project. What tool or technique are they using?

A. Data representation

B. Data analysis

C. Data gathering

D. Expert judgment

81. You are looking over project team assignments and see that one of your resources is overallocated. You are concerned about the future availability of this resource and also notice the resource is assigned to more than one critical activity. To keep the project on schedule, which of the following techniques should you use?

    A. Reverse resource allocation scheduling

    B. Resource leveling

    C. Resource loading

    D. Resource smoothing

82. Ralph is a project manager for Storm Health. He has struggled since joining the company, and his manager has noticed multiple gaps in critical PM skills. During a recent meeting, Ralph incorrectly claimed that the project budget had been fully approved. As a result, multiple purchase orders were processed, which alerted his manager, who knew that the budget had not yet been approved. The manager decides to confront Ralph, who admits to intentionally giving misinformation in the hopes that the budget would be approved and that all would be OK. What core value has Ralph violated as a project management practitioner?

    A. Fairness

    B. Honesty

    C. Respect

    D. Responsibility

83. Who is responsible for understanding the interests and personal agendas of stakeholders?

    A. Project sponsor

    B. Project manager

    C. Project team

    D. Executive sponsor

84. A Scrum master brings the team together at 9 a.m. sharp every morning. He asks the team the following questions: *What did you accomplish yesterday? What will you work on today? Do you have any roadblocks or issues preventing you from doing your work?* What activity is the team engaged in?

    A. A status meeting

    B. A daily roundup

    C. A sprint planning meeting

    D. A Scrum meeting

85. Many projects fail because of conflicts among stakeholders. Conflict often exists because of which of the following?

    A. Conflicting interests

    B. Human bias

    C. Varying experiences

    D. Varying personalities

86. Servant leaders tend to exhibit what characteristics? (Select three.)

    A. Helping people grow

    B. Coaching

    C. Promoting self-awareness

    D. Creating clarity by directing

87. Which of the following statements best describes stakeholders?

    A. An individual, group, or organization that may affect, be affected by, or perceive itself to be affected by a decision, activity, or outcome of a project

    B. Individuals assigned to carry out the work of the project, as defined by the project management plan

    C. The person assigned by the performing organization to lead the team that is responsible for achieving the project objectives

    D. An individual or a group that provides resources and support for the project and is accountable for enabling success

88. Sue, a project management office (PMO) leader, is interested in shifting the organization from using a predictive to an adaptive delivery model. The majority of the key stakeholders she works with have been around for more than 10 years and tend to be averse to change. What approach is Sue likely to take in shifting to an adaptive approach?

    A. Adopt Scrum

    B. Adopt a hybrid model

    C. Maintain a waterfall approach

    D. Shift toward Kanban

89. Sally and Joe are two project managers working in the corporate offices of a popular fast-food franchise. They are both studying for their PMP® certification, and they have a spirited debate over who is responsible for managing and performing project integration activities. Sally claims it is the project sponsor, while Joe adamantly insists it is the project manager. Who is correct?

    A. Both

    B. Sally

    C. Joe

    D. Neither

90. Sue is the head of an enterprise PMO. She delivers a presentation at the annual company meeting to describe her roles and responsibilities and the value of the PMO. As part of her presentation, she notes that, as practitioners, project managers should abide by four core values. In particular, Sue notes that project managers should avoid conflicts of interest. Which core value addresses conflict of interest?

    A. Responsibility

    B. Fairness

    C. Respect

    D. Honesty

91. A project manager traveled from the United Kingdom to Mexico for a project kickoff meeting. During the meeting, they became highly offended when the project sponsor attempted to welcome them by giving them a hug. The project manager noticed that many people gave a hug as part of personal introductions and decided to leave the meeting after feeling that the project team was exhibiting inappropriate behavior. What did the project manager experience?

   A. Sexual harassment

   B. An overfriendly team

   C. Culture shock

   D. Inappropriate behavior

92. Which of the following stages of the Tuckman ladder addresses the completion of the work and release of staff?

   A. Concluding

   B. Adjourning

   C. Releasing

   D. Closing

93. All of the following are characteristics of the Agile life cycle except for which one?

   A. The team typically collaborates to finish the most important feature.

   B. The team expects requirements to change.

   C. Feedback is given with the purpose of better planning the next part of the project.

   D. It combines both iterative and incremental approaches.

94. You are working on the creation of a new television series. The producer for this series has informed you that he is the final decision-maker for all questions that arise during the course of the series. He tells you that he'll set up a meeting with you to discuss the budget he's set aside for the project. Your organization has created many winning series in the past, almost all of which had the same producer as the one for this project. The producer believes this will be the best series they have produced to date and has already generated a lot of excitement about this project. No other series on the air is like the series that's being proposed. The series must be ready to debut during sweeps week in November. Which of the following is true?

   A. The producer's only involvement on the project is to provide funds.

   B. The producer is the project manager.

   C. The producer is the project sponsor.

   D. The producer is the program manager.

95. Sue is the head of an enterprise PMO. She delivers a presentation at the annual company meeting to describe her role's responsibilities and the value of the PMO. As part of her presentation, Sue stresses the critical skill sets that PMs must have in order to be effective. She stresses one in particular, which is that PMs must exhibit the knowledge, skills, and behaviors needed to guide, motivate, and direct a team. What skill set is Sue referring to?

   A. Communication skills

   B. Leadership skills

   C. Business management and strategic skills

   D. Technical project management skills

96. Agile teams favor which type of performance measurement? (Select two.)

   A. Predictive measurements

   B. Value-based measurements

   C. Cost efficiency measurements

   D. Empirical measurements

97. You are working on a project with contentious team members. You know if you resolve the conflicts, it will result in increased productivity and better working relationships. Most conflicts come about as a result of all the following except for which one?

   A. Scheduling issues

   B. Availability of resources

   C. Personal work habits

   D. Cultural differences

98. Maslow's Hierarchy of Needs is a motivational theory that notes that humans have five basic needs arranged in a hierarchical order. What is the first set of needs that must be met before a person can move to the next level of needs in the hierarchy?

   A. Social needs

   B. Safety and security needs

   C. Self-actualization

   D. Basic physical needs

99. A role delineation study can best be described as which of the following?

   A. A job analysis

   B. A credential

   C. A feasibility study

   D. A business case

100. You are a senior project manager working at a manufacturing plant that produces components used by the aviation industry. You have just finalized team assignments. What action are you likely to perform next?

   A. Manage resources by monitoring activities

   B. Develop the team by refreshing team skills

   C. Develop the training plan

   D. Review pre-assignments

101. An agile team's social contract likely addresses which of the following? (Select three.)

   A. Team values

   B. Ground rules

   C. Team assignments

   D. Group norms

102. You witness a trusted colleague violating a privacy law of the country in which you are both temporarily stationed for an assigned project. What should you do?

   A. Do nothing. This is a trusted colleague whom you assume has ethical intentions.

   B. Talk to your colleague and highlight that what they have done is wrong.

   C. Report the actions to the legal department and inform the appropriate management.

   D. Advise your colleague to talk to the legal department and give them room to take action as they see fit.

103. A project manager considers how best to navigate through the politics of the organization where most of their project team resides. What skill set is the project manager exercising?

   A. Technical project management

   B. Leadership

   C. Strategic and business management

   D. Stakeholder management

104. Which of the following best describes the role of a product owner within the Agile methodology?

   A. The product owner coordinates the work of the sprint and runs interference between the team and distractions keeping them from their work.

   B. The product owner has a vested interest in the project or the outcomes of the project and interfaces with stakeholders.

   C. The product owner represents the stakeholders and is the liaison between the stakeholders, the Scrum master, and the development team.

   D. The product owner is responsible for completing the backlog items and signing up for tasks based on priorities established.

105. Cheryl is a procurement manager assigned to a project that implemented a new system patching service. She sits down with the project manager to review the final performance of the primary vendor used, highlighting the many issues that they experienced with the vendor, including delivering three weeks late and going over budget by $5,000. Cheryl spends an additional hour with the project manager identifying what they could have done differently and what they did well in addressing the vendor issues as they occurred. What activity are Cheryl and the project manager engaged in?

   A. Finalizing an open claim with the vendor

   B. Generating a work performance report

   C. Confirming formal acceptance of the vendor's work

   D. Capturing lessons learned

106. Herzberg's Hygiene Theory notes that there are two factors that contribute to motivation, one being hygiene factors. Which of the following represents the second factor?

   A. Hygiene

   B. Motivators

   C. Self-actualization

   D. Basic needs

107. The project sponsor of a project has just met with the organization's senior executives to provide them with a summary of the latest project that is about to kick off. He introduces Yasmin, the project manager, and commits to the room of executives that the project is bound to be a success. Who assumes responsibility for the success of the project?

A. Project sponsor

B. Senior executives

C. Project team

D. Project manager

108. The project manager using a predictive delivery approach develops a project management plan to describe how the project will be executed, monitored, controlled, and closed. Which of the following is a valid tool to assist the project manager to assure the success of the project management plan?

A. Meetings

B. Enterprise environmental factors

C. Organizational process assets

D. Outputs from other processes

109. Match the Agile project charter component to the question it addresses:

Charter Component	Question Addressed
A. Project vision	1. What does "done" mean for the project?
B. Flow of work	2. How are we going to work together?
C. Release criteria	3. Who benefits and how?
D. Project purpose	4. Why are we doing this project?

110. Ralph is a project manager for Storm Health. He has struggled since joining the company, and his manager has noticed a gap in a critical PM skill. In a recent kick-off meeting, he struggled to answer questions on how the project aligns with the organization's goals, insisting it wasn't relevant. What critical skill should Ralph sharpen?

A. Business management and strategic skills

B. Technical project management skills

C. Communication skills

D. Leadership skills

111. Alfred accepts a job as a security program manager, even though he is not qualified for the role. He reasons that he can learn on the job, despite not having met the position requirements. What value did Alfred fail to uphold?

A. Honor

B. Honesty

C. Respect

D. Responsibility

112. Charles works for a prominent company within the entertainment industry as head project manager. He recently learned that a highly confidential movie deal under negotiation may feature his wife's favorite actress. Despite the confidentiality agreement he signed, he decides to reveal the information, knowing that she will keep it to herself. What core value upheld by project managers has Charles violated?

   A. Honesty

   B. Respect

   C. Honor

   D. Responsibility

113. While performing activities associated with controlling project and product scope, a project manager uncovers scope creep. The project manager learns that the scope creep was a result of a close friend, who is a prominent stakeholder of the project. What should the project manager do?

   A. Do nothing, since the scope creep is a result of a close friend and a prominent stakeholder.

   B. Reverse the changes that yielded the scope creep since the scope was unapproved.

   C. Bring the scope creep to light and address it with the change control board.

   D. Do nothing, since scope creep can yield positive changes for the project.

114. Which of the following are underlying success factors for forming Agile teams? (Select three.)

   A. Building a strong network

   B. Building a foundational trust

   C. Building a safe working environment

   D. Building an Agile mindset

115. What motivational theory is a combination of Theory Y behaviors and the Hygiene Theory?

   A. Tannenbaum and Schmidt Continuum Management Theory

   B. Situational Leadership Theory

   C. Contingency Theory

   D. Recognition and Rewards Theory

116. All of the following make up the PMI Talent Triangle™ except for which one?

   A. Communication skills

   B. Business management and strategic skills

   C. Technical project management skills

   D. Leadership skills

117. Abiding by and complying with laws and regulations, confidentiality of information, and accepting assignments for which you are qualified as a project manager are examples of upholding which value?

A. Honor

B. Honesty

C. Respect

D. Responsibility

118. Which method of analyzing stakeholders considers power, urgency, and legitimacy?

A. Stakeholder cube

B. Salience model

C. Power/interest grid

D. Power/influence grid

119. A project manager is leading a project with team members dispersed globally. Which of the following tools or methods can the project manager use to create virtual workspaces? (Select two.)

A. Establish remote pairing using video conferencing tools to allow for face-to-face meeting options.

B. Split the team in half by colocating them in two groups, using instant messaging software to connect them.

C. Create a fishbowl window through an ongoing video conferencing feed between various locations.

D. All of the above.

120. Alyssa is a project manager tasked with managing an infrastructure project that will consolidate five data centers into one. After kicking off the execution of the project work, she holds a team-building workshop with the core project team. What is she looking to achieve?

A. Address people-related corrective actions

B. Resolve existing conflicts

C. Enhance team competencies

D. Improve overall project performance

121. Your team has done an outstanding job, and you have notified their functional managers that their assignment is over. They are all reluctant to go back to their functional work group and are sorry to see the project come to an end. They enjoy working for you and say this project, and working for you, has been one of the best experiences of their career. According to the adjourning phase of team formation, you could take all of the following actions except for which one?

A. Conduct a team celebration

B. Thank your team members for their contributions

C. Guide the team through a closure process

D. Focus on closing out the project management processes

122. Your team has done an outstanding job, and you have notified their functional managers that their assignment is over. They are all reluctant to go back to their functional work group and are sorry to see the project come to an end. They enjoy working for you and say this project, and working for you, has been one of the best experiences of their career. Which of the following does this describe?

    A. The adjourning stage of team development

    B. That you are likely a Theory Y manager

    C. Maslow's performing level on the Hierarchy of Needs

    D. Recognition and rewards

123. Which of the following represents a key benefit of rapid delivery approaches?

    A. The ability to get more done

    B. The ability to flow as a team

    C. The ability to work in increments

    D. The ability to get feedback

124. During the first project kickoff meeting, Ron introduces himself to key team members, noting that he will work hard to minimize distractions that may keep them from their work at hand and will serve in more of a facilitator role. What is Ron's role?

    A. Scrum master

    B. Product owner

    C. Stakeholder

    D. Team member

125. Sue is the head of an Agile PMO. She delivers a presentation at the annual company meeting to describe her role's responsibilities and the value of the PMO. As part of her presentation, Sue delivers an award to a project manager for exhibiting strength in defining critical success factors of the project, facilitating iteration planning, and knowing when to ask for help. What skill set is she recognizing the project manager for?

    A. Communication skills

    B. Leadership skills

    C. Business management and strategic skills

    D. Technical project management skills

126. Which of the following statements is true regarding lateral thinking? (Select two.)

    A. It is a form of parallel analysis.

    B. Lateral thinking is a tool and technique of the processes used when identifying risks.

    C. Edward de Bono created this term and has done extensive research on the topic.

    D. This is a way of reasoning and thinking about problems from perspectives other than the obvious.

127. Balancing stakeholder interests and attaining customer satisfaction are important activities for project managers. One of the best things you can do to ensure customer satisfaction is to define and document which of the following?

- **A.** Estimates
- **B.** Quality
- **C.** Requirements
- **D.** Objectives

128. Your project involves the research and development of a new food additive. You're ready to release the product to your customer when you discover that a minor reaction might occur in people with certain conditions. The reactions to date have been very minor, and no known long-lasting side effects have been noted. As project manager, what should you do?

- **A.** Do nothing because the reactions are so minor that very few people will be affected.
- **B.** Inform the customer that you've discovered this condition and tell them you'll research it further to determine its impacts.
- **C.** Inform your customer that there is no problem with the additive except for an extremely small percentage of the population and release the product to them.
- **D.** Tell the customer you'll correct the reaction problems in the next batch, but you'll release the first batch of product to them now to begin using.

129. Your project has a total of 35 stakeholders. How many lines of communication exist?

- **A.** 600
- **B.** 613
- **C.** 630
- **D.** 595

130. The project manager is facilitating an exercise with the team by asking questions about the product and forming answers to describe the use, characteristics, and other relevant aspects of what will be delivered. In what activity is the team involved?

- **A.** Data analysis
- **B.** Product analysis
- **C.** Alternatives analysis
- **D.** Facilitation

131. One of the core tenants highlighted by Agile approaches is the value of flow versus focusing on how people are utilized. Which of the following reflect benefits of optimizing flow to attain value? (Select two.)

- **A.** Teams produce faster results.
- **B.** Teams waste less time.
- **C.** Teams produce value more quickly.
- **D.** Top performers stand out.

132. Diana is a newly appointed project manager. As part of onboarding to the new team, she shadows Charlie, a senior project manager. During a team meeting, she witnesses Charlie using several profanities when engaging with one engineer in particular. She cringes in her seat as she sees Charlie talk over the engineer and chastise him for challenging the schedule. Although new to the team, Diana decides to report Charlie's behavior to her manager. What core value has Charlie violated?

    A. Responsibility

    B. Fairness

    C. Respect

    D. Honesty

133. You are a project manager working in a foreign country. You observe that some of your project team members are having a difficult time adjusting to their new environment. You provided them with training on cultural differences and the customs of this country before arriving, but they still seem uncomfortable and disoriented. Which of the following statements is true?

    A. This is the result of working with teams of people from two different countries.

    B. This condition comes about when working in an unfamiliar environment or culture and is called *culture shock.*

    C. This is the result of jet lag and travel fatigue.

    D. This condition is best resolved by providing diversity training to the team.

134. A product owner calls the Scrum master and requests to see the remaining work effort for the sprint. What is the Scrum master likely to show the product owner in response?

    A. A bubble chart

    B. A status report

    C. A burndown chart

    D. A sprint summary chart

135. Reasons to Lyv is the top customer of a large marketing firm. Trudy is the president of Reasons to Lyv and has decided to launch a product that leverages new GPS tracking technology. She sits down with Roy, the project manager on the project, to discuss which stakeholders are resistant, unaware, neutral, supportive, or leading within the project. What activity are they performing?

    A. Identifying stakeholders

    B. Planning stakeholder engagement

    C. Managing stakeholder engagement

    D. Monitoring stakeholder engagement

136. You are working on a project that involves some top-secret manufacturing techniques your organization has invented and patented. One of the team members on the project has an extraordinary amount of knowledge about this technique. She is sought after by others in the organization for advice and will need to help the team with the current project. It's important that nothing involving this technique is discussed outside of this project. What type of power does this describe?

    A. Referent

    B. Situational

C. Expert

D. Punishment

137. Which of the following options explains one of the reasons that a project manager spends time developing the project team?

A. To create an open, encouraging environment in which team members can contribute

B. To create a disciplined environment in which team members can contribute

C. To create a colocated environment in which team members can contribute

D. To create a colocated, disciplined environment in which team members can contribute

138. A project manager meets with the team to increase cultural awareness by conducting training on cultural norms relating to countries they will be closely engaged with. What activity is the project manager engaged in?

A. Planning stakeholder engagement

B. Monitoring stakeholder engagement

C. Managing stakeholder engagement

D. Managing communications

139. One of your team members, Daniela, talks with you privately about a confrontation she just had with Noelle, another team member working on the same project. It seems they can't agree on a fundamental business process needed for the project. They both think they are correct in their view, and each has set up a meeting with you, independently, to convince you of her position. Which of the following statements is true?

A. This describes the storming stage of team development.

B. This describes the performing stage of team development.

C. This describes the norming stage of team development.

D. This describes the forming stage of team development.

140. You are a project manager for Dakota Software Consulting Services. You're working with a major retailer that offers its products through mail-order catalogs. It's interested in knowing customer characteristics, the amounts of first-time orders, and similar information. At one of your first project meetings, you explain to the team that quality is the number-one priority with this project and you will immediately deal with any project results (and those who caused them) that are not in keeping with this goal. The last software company that worked with this retailer was terminated because the quality of the end product was unacceptable. You tell the team there will be rewards for those who meet the quality requirements of this project. You also tell them the guidelines for escalating issues with the retailer and instruct them there are to be no deviations from this process. You want to know about anything that has the potential to become an issue. You conclude the meeting and return to your office to write the next status report. Which of the following is true regarding this question?

A. This behavior is most like the democratic leadership style.

B. This behavior is most like the transformational leadership style.

C. This behavior is most like the transactional leadership style.

D. This behavior is most like the situational leadership style.

141. Three of your stakeholders have approached you regarding the difficulty they are having with one of your team members. This team member is making inappropriate jokes, continually interrupts others, and is argumentative and unwilling to listen to the stakeholders' ideas. What is the offending team member lacking in this situation?

   A. Training

   B. Ground rules

   C. Interpersonal and team skills

   D. Team-building activities

142. You are managing a project on contract. Your bonus is contingent on the timely completion of the project. The project is behind schedule, but the remaining tasks are easy to complete and won't take more than a week. Which of the following is the most appropriate response?

   A. Invoice the customer for the full amount of the contract at the originally scheduled completion date.

   B. Invoice the customer for the amount of work as of the actual project completion date.

   C. Submit an invoice and complete the remaining tasks while the payment request is being processed because the work will be finished before the payment is made.

   D. Tell the customer about the delay and negotiate a change to the schedule and/or invoice payment date and then bill for the full amount when the work is completed.

143. Your project is running behind schedule and over budget. The account manager of a supplier you've worked with before tells you that if you select them for a contract they are bidding on, they will throw in a free resource. Later that day, you meet with the vendor selection committee and see that the vendor ranks at the bottom of the stack. You select the vendor anyway to help the budget, even though it goes against the procurement policy. How may your actions be perceived?

   A. Heroic

   B. Conflict of interest

   C. Justified

   D. Improving cost variance

144. You are a project manager with a new company. You started less than 30 days ago. Your boss has told you it's urgent that resources are attained and assigned to the project as soon as possible. This is your top priority. You have both internal and external resources. You have two internal positions that will be full-time employees, but the positions are vacant, so you need to recruit for and fill these positions. You happen to have a good friend you've known for several years who also attends your local PMI chapter. He is well qualified and looking for a new position. You call him up and hire him on the spot. You will be hiring your external resources using a work order against a contract you have with a local staffing agency. Which of the following is true regarding this situation?

   A. You have not accounted for the organization's standard processes that may impact how you build your team.

   B. Since the project is not yet underway, the new resource you hired will be considered a pre-assignment.

    C. The personal interests and characteristics of the person you hired were not considered.

    D. The resource management plan will need to be updated.

145. A project manager managing a small project has a total of 12 active stakeholders. How many lines of communication exist?

    A. 66

    B. 72

    C. 12

    D. 24

146. You are in the process of facilitating a change control meeting. You review a change request that would double the scope of the project but would not yield a major increase in the project's resulting benefits. You know that the submitter of the change request has a tendency to bloat a project's scope without fully thinking through the impact, but as a result of their position in the company, their changes tend to be approved. You invite a financial analyst to the meeting to walk the team through the negative impact of the change request, and the team votes to reject the change. What type of power did you use?

    A. Legitimate

    B. Expert

    C. Referent

    D. Punishment

147. You are a project manager for a network cabling project for your organization. Your project team consists of six full-time employees and three contractors. They have all worked together on a previous project a year ago. You are new to the team. Which of the following is true?

    A. According to Tuckman-Jensen, they will start with the storming stage of team development.

    B. According to Hersey and Blanchard, they will start with the forming stage of team development.

    C. According to Tuckman-Jensen, they will start with the forming stage of team development.

    D. According to Hersey and Blanchard, they will start with the performing stage of team development.

148. One of your project's deliverables requires skills in journalism. You have three resources working on the activities that need to be completed for this deliverable. One of the resources is beyond happy with her situation and tells you that she is finally in a project where she feels like she is performing at her peak potential. Which of the following statements best describes this situation?

    A. This team member is describing the self-actualization level of Maslow's Hierarchy of Needs.

    B. Salary is not a motivator because her basic needs have been fulfilled.

C. This team member's need has been fulfilled, and now, according to Maslow, the ability to advance, the opportunity to learn new things, and the challenges involved in the work become motivators.

D. The Expectancy Theory says that the importance of camaraderie with other team members is an important motivator.

149. A project manager working under contract for an enterprise PMO contributes to the creation of a project management handbook as part of his assignment. At the conclusion of the project, he decides to sell and market the handbook under his consulting group's brand, even though he was one of many contributors acting as agents of the organization. He reasoned that his contribution to the creation of the handbook afforded him this right. How are his actions likely to be viewed by the contracting organization?

A. As acting on his rights as a content contributor

B. As a violation of intellectual property

C. As a collaborator, given his contributions to the work

D. As operating against his agreement

150. A project team that is attempting to adopt an Agile mindset may use all of the following questions to develop an implementation strategy, except for which one?

A. What work can be avoided to focus on high-priority items?

B. How can the team act in a predictable manner?

C. What work can the team deliver rapidly to obtain early feedback?

D. How can a servant-leadership approach aid the achievement of goals?

Chapter

2

Process (Domain 2.0)

THE PROJECT MANAGEMENT PROFESSIONAL (PMP)® EXAM CONTENT FROM THE PROCESS DOMAIN COVERED IN THIS CHAPTER INCLUDES THE FOLLOWING:

- ✓ **Task 2.1** Execute project with the urgency required to deliver business value
- ✓ **Task 2.2** Manage communications
- ✓ **Task 2.3** Assess and manage risks
- ✓ **Task 2.4** Engage stakeholders
- ✓ **Task 2.5** Plan and manage budget resources
- ✓ **Task 2.6** Plan and manage schedule
- ✓ **Task 2.7** Plan and manage quality of products / deliverables
- ✓ **Task 2.8** Plan and manage scope
- ✓ **Task 2.9** Integrate project planning activities
- ✓ **Task 2.10** Manage project changes
- ✓ **Task 2.11** Plan and manage procurement
- ✓ **Task 2.12** Manage project artifacts
- ✓ **Task 2.13** Determine appropriate project methodology / methods and practices
- ✓ **Task 2.14** Establish project governance structure
- ✓ **Task 2.15** Manage project issues
- ✓ **Task 2.16** Ensure knowledge transfer for project continuity
- ✓ **Task 2.17** Plan and manage project / phase closure or transitions

The process names, inputs, tools and techniques, outputs, and descriptions of the project management process groups and related materials and figures in this chapter are based on content from *A Guide to the Project Management Body of Knowledge (PMBOK® Guide) – Sixth Edition* (PMI®, 2017).

1. Rita is a product owner responsible for the company's line of smart digital music devices. During an afternoon working session, she works with the team to review user stories in preparation for the next sprint. Her intention is to ensure the team knows enough about the stories and how large they are in relation to each other. What activity is Rita performing?

   A. Sprint planning

   B. Backlog refinement

   C. Sprint retrospective

   D. Daily stand-up

2. A project manager has just wrapped up a successful project in an environment that uses a streamlined hybrid approach to project delivery. Who is responsible for writing the project's final report?

   A. All stakeholders

   B. Project sponsor

   C. Project manager

   D. Executive sponsor

3. Risk strategy, methodology, and risk-related roles and responsibilities are all elements of what?

   A. Risk register

   B. Risk management plan

   C. Risk report

   D. Project documents

4. Kaylee has been managing projects for more than a decade and has largely used the waterfall method. She has recently taken a new job for a company that builds software for mobile devices and has begun studying the Agile method, which is largely used by this company. She begins by studying the Agile principles. What is the formalized document called that identifies 12 principles of the Agile approach?

   A. Agile Principles

   B. Agile Charter

   C. Agile Manifesto

   D. Book of Agile

5. According to the Project Management Institute (PMI)®, a good project manager spends how much time communicating?

   A. 50 percent

   B. 75 percent

   C. 90 percent

   D. 100 percent

6. Change-driven life cycles are also known by what other name?

   A. Adaptive life cycle

   B. Predictive life cycle

   C. Plan-driven life cycle

   D. Hybrid life cycle

7. Which of the following project management Knowledge Areas involve every team member and stakeholder on the project?

   A. Project Scope Management

   B. Project Communications Management

   C. Project Resource Management

   D. Project Quality Management

8. Which of the following statements are true? (Select three.)

   A. A highly predictive life cycle has reduced risk and costs due to detailed plans.

   B. A highly predictive life cycle contains requirements that are ambiguous.

   C. A highly adaptive life cycle has continuous involvement and frequent feedback from stakeholders.

   D. A highly adaptive life cycle performs Initiating activities regularly throughout the project.

9. Match the name of the Project Management Knowledge Area with its description:

Knowledge Area Name	Description
A. Project Integration Management	1. Contains the activities required to manage the timely completion of the project
B. Project Schedule Management	2. Contains the activities to identify, acquire, and manage the resources needed for the successful completion of the project
C. Project Procurement Management	3. Contains the activities required to identify the people, groups, or organizations that could impact or be impacted by the project, analyze them, and develop strategies for engaging them
D. Project Resource Management	4. Contains the activities necessary to purchase or acquire products, services, or results needed from outside the project team
E. Project Stakeholder Management	5. Contains the activities to identify, define, combine, unify, and coordinate the various processes and project management activities within the various process groups

10. You work in an environment that uses a combination of delivery approaches, namely, Agile and Predictive approaches, with one-month release cycles. The vice president of your division has told you to report the status of the project budget for the current release as on track. You have experienced three budget overruns in the past six months and know that the status of the budget for the existing release is poor. However, you also know there is a repayment coming on one of the procurement work orders that will reverse almost all of the cost overruns you've experienced for this latest release. Which of the following do you know to be true regarding this question? (Select two.)

   A. You can't control the actions of others, but you can control your actions, and you should report the truth no matter what the vice president has instructed you to do.

   B. This question describes activities associated with managing stakeholder engagement levels.

   C. Managing communications is a critical aspect of a project manager's role.

   D. You can use a burndown chart to show the potential reversal of the budget overrun.

11. Which of the following represents a benefit of using an Agile approach to manage projects?

   A. Changes can be closely monitored and controlled.

   B. A project team can adjust processes in order to meet new or modified requirements.

   C. Risks can be identified, reduced, or eliminated early on in the project life cycle.

   D. The team is not distracted by planning activities and can focus on execution.

12. David is a project manager working for a prominent book publishing company. As part of his latest project, he uses an approach that yields frequent smaller deliverables throughout the span of the project. What type of project life cycle is David using?

   A. Predictive

   B. Incremental

   C. Waterfall

   D. Agile

13. A project manager has just closed out a procurement, which produced the final deliverable of the project. What is the project manager likely to do next?

   A. Celebrate

   B. Perform administrative closure

   C. Release the remaining project resources

   D. Finalize any open claims

14. Nicolas is the project manager of a project that has been described as revolutionizing the mobile fitness tracking industry. After consulting with his team of subject-matter experts, he decides to use Scrum. Nicolas's project team continues to build on the product through two-week iterations. Iterations are also known by what other name?

   A. Phase

   B. Sprint

   C. Deliverable

   D. Stand-up

15. A project manager is in the process of assembling the final report of the project. What project document are they likely to reference to view the completion date of major project deliverables?

    A. Final report

    B. Schedule baseline

    C. Milestone report

    D. Milestone list

16. You are the project manager for a project that will produce a mobile phone application that sends alerts when the UV rays are at dangerous levels, alerting users to stay indoors. As you move into the final closing stages of the project, you review communications generated for and by stakeholders as a method of analyzing feedback. What document will you reference to review this feedback?

    A. Change log

    B. Lessons learned register

    C. Project communications

    D. Quality reports

17. A project manager works with the project team to identify lessons learned. The information captured will then be archived and summarized within the project's final report. What activity is the project team engaged in?

    A. Updating the lessons learned register

    B. Administrative closure

    C. Conducting a project meeting

    D. Capturing work performance information

18. Which of the following characteristics do all project life cycles share?

    A. Degree of uncertainty

    B. Degree of planning

    C. Degree of unfinished work

    D. Degree of work sequencing

19. Your project has kicked off, and you are beginning a series of overview sessions with key users to determine requirements for a new enterprise resource software implementation. One of your stakeholders is exceptionally contentious and throws obstacles up at every turn. One of the problems she has described does seem to be legitimate. There is an issue with the data from the legacy system that needs to be resolved before moving forward. The PMO you report to practices phase sequencing and requires closure of each phase before the next phase can begin. What is this process called? (Select all that apply.)

    A. Gate exit

    B. Phase review

    C. Phase exit

    D. Stage review

20. Which of the following best describes the purpose of the Monitoring and Controlling process group?

A. Formulating and revising project goals and objectives and creating the project management plan

B. Putting the project management plan into action

C. Measuring and analyzing project performance to determine whether the project is progressing according to the plan

D. Bringing the project or phase to a formal, orderly end

21. Agile project management can best be described as which of the following?

A. A method that focuses on defining the requirements of the project early on in the project life cycle, before moving into execution

B. An underlying concept that shows the integrative nature of the process groups that notes that each element in the life cycle is results-oriented

C. A method of managing projects through large portions of work that can be easily planned and executed to produce the overall product, service, or result of the project

D. A method of managing projects in small, incremental portions of work that can be easily assigned, easily managed, and completed within a short period of time

22. A short, time-bound period of work is also referred to as which of the following?

A. Buffer

B. Lead

C. Lag

D. Sprint

23. When is a project considered successful?

A. When the project budget is consumed, the scope is developed, and the schedule milestones are achieved

B. When the project budget is consumed and the schedule milestones are achieved

C. When project benefits are realized and the stakeholder needs and expectations are met

D. When objectives are achieved and the stakeholder needs and expectations are met

24. Yasmin is a project manager tasked with putting together the project charter for a project that will produce a new line of widgets for the company. After meeting with various key stakeholders, she sits down to draft the document. Yasmin is likely to include all of the following elements within the project charter except for which one?

A. List of detailed risks

B. Purpose of the project

    C. List of key stakeholders

    D. Preapproved budget

25. A project manager meets with the project sponsor for a weekly update. Company performance has been rocky, and the sponsor nervously asks what the chances are of the project coming to a successful closure. To date, the project has been on track and is nearing the end of Execution. How should the project manager respond?

    A. The likelihood of successful completion is high.

    B. The likelihood of successful completion is highest.

    C. The likelihood of successful completion is low.

    D. The likelihood of successful completion is lowest.

26. A project manager facilitates a meeting with the project team to review an assessment of risks recently completed. During this meeting, they evaluate options for responding to the risks. It is decided that two risks will not receive any action and that they will deal with the consequences at the time of occurrence, should they occur. What type of risk response is this?

    A. Passive acceptance

    B. Active acceptance

    C. Mitigation

    D. Avoidance

27. A project manager meets with the team to discuss how they will measure budget performance moving forward. What activity is the team engaged in?

    A. Taking corrective action

    B. Evaluating performance

    C. Developing the cost management plan

    D. Developing the project budget

28. A project manager facilitated a meeting with the product manager and project team to discuss the results of the latest iteration. As part of the meeting, the project manager also reviewed the budget consumed to date on the project, highlighting appraisal costs. Which of the following best describes appraisal costs?

    A. Costs associated with satisfying customer requirements by creating a product without defects

    B. Costs expended to examine the product or process and make certain the requirements are being met

    C. Costs when things don't go according to plan

    D. Costs that occur externally, when the customer determines that the requirements have not been met

29. You work within a project management office, and the new PMO director has adjusted project assignments to accommodate a large strategic project that the company has undertaken. You sit down with the previous project manager of your new project to review stakeholder communication requirements, escalation processes, and the list of project-related meetings. What document will you use to get this information?

    A. Stakeholder engagement plan

    B. Communications management plan

    C. Resource management plan

    D. Project management plan

30. You are a project manager for Lightning Bolt Enterprises. Your new project involves the research and development of a new type of rechargeable battery. One of your stakeholders requests a change to the product scope description. The stakeholder has filled out a change request form indicating that the change affects the project scope and that it's essential for a successful project. The change request is approved, and the project scope statement is updated to reflect this change. Which of the following statements are true? (Select three.)

    A. The product scope description, which is also a component of the project charter, is used to define the project's scope.

    B. Change requests are evaluated against the project scope statement, and if a change request is outside the bounds of the original project scope, the change should be denied.

    C. Product analysis converts the product description and objectives into deliverables and requirements.

    D. The project scope statement directs the project team's work and is the basis for future project decisions.

31. You are the director of the PMO for your organization. Terri, an employee from another department, has approached you about a new project that is being talked about in her department. Terri would like the opportunity to head up this project and wants to convince you of her knowledge of project management and that she can do this job. Terri's objective statement for the project says the following: "Convert all our distribution centers in the United States to radio frequency identification (RFID) tags. This new technology will improve inventory management by giving us a real-time view of demand for the products we sell. It will also help reduce theft and reduce stock-outs. The electronic identification stored in the tags should be fixed. This new technology will require the installation of readers at each warehouse gate." Which of the following statements are correct regarding Terri's objective statement? (Select three.)

    A. This statement describes an overview of the project, but it cannot be considered an objective statement because it's missing some important elements.

    B. Objectives describe what it is the project is trying to produce or accomplish, and requirements are specifications of the objective or deliverable.

C. This statement describes the objectives of the project adequately; however, requirements have been added into the statement.

D. Requirements have been mixed into the statement Terri wrote. One of the requirements in this statement is that "electronic identification stored in the tags should be fixed."

32. A project manager is performing quantitative risk analysis. What tangible result is likely to be produced?

A. An assessment of probability and impacts for each individual risk

B. A priority level for each individual project risk

C. An assessment of overall project risk exposure

D. A list of potential risk responses

33. A small sample of your project's PERT calculations is shown here. What is the total duration of the project?

Activity	Optimistic	Pessimistic	Likely Expected Value
1	10	14	12
2	20	30	23
3	3	3	3

A. 33

B. 38

C. 37

D. 47

34. Which quality theorist is responsible for the theory that promotes doing it right the first time?

A. Philip Crosby

B. Joseph Juran

C. W. Edwards Deming

D. Walter Shewhart

35. Carina is a principal project manager of You've Got Dogs, a specialty company that creates custom dog apparel and toys. As part of her latest project, she interviews experienced subject-matter experts to better understand what risks exist within the project. What project management process is she carrying out?

A. Plan Risk Management

B. Identify Risks

C. Perform Qualitative Risk Analysis

D. Perform Quantitative Risk Analysis

36. Kaylee is a risk manager working in collaboration with Alyssa, a project manager, and both work for a top healthcare company. They currently follow a feature-driven development approach to managing software-based projects. They work together to analyze risk, noting that of the 20 risks identified, 5 are deemed to be low priority. Where will these risks be documented?

    A. A watch list

    B. The risk report

    C. The project management plan

    D. The risk management plan

37. You are working on the communications management plan for your project and have considered the timing and need for updated information by you and your four stakeholders. Your organization has modern, up-to-date technology that your stakeholders and staff have used before, so you anticipate that supplying the information and updates to your stakeholders and team members will be a breeze. Which of the following is true?

    A. There are 10 channels of communication, which should be considered when examining communications requirements analysis.

    B. There are 5 channels of communication, which should be considered when examining communications requirements.

    C. There are 12 channels of communication, which should be considered when examining communications technology.

    D. There are 20 channels of communication, which should be considered when examining communications technology.

38. Roshoud is the VP of customer operations for Galactic Kidz and project sponsor of the latest project, called Project G. He sits down with Sally, the project manager, to discuss the current budget estimate. Roshoud expresses his concerns to Sally over the budget being far greater than originally anticipated and asks her to course-correct. What produces the greatest expense on most projects?

    A. Vendors

    B. Resources

    C. Materials

    D. Travel

39. Alyssa is a project manager tasked with managing an infrastructure project that will consolidate five data centers into one. She is currently facilitating the estimating process to calculate the duration of the project's activities. Alyssa knows that she has reliable information and is therefore planning on using an estimating technique that will yield a highly accurate estimate with minimal effort expended. What estimating technique is she planning on using?

    A. Three-point estimating

    B. Bottom-up estimating

    C. Parametric estimating

    D. Top-down estimating

40. Which of the following best describes overall project risk?

    A. An uncertain event or condition that, if it occurs, has a negative effect on one or more project objectives.

    B. An uncertain event or condition that, if it occurs, has a positive or negative effect on one or more project objectives.

    C. The effect of uncertainty on the project as a whole, arising from all sources of uncertainty.

    D. The effect of uncertainty on a project objective, arising from all sources of uncertainty.

41. You use a predictive approach to managing projects and have just completed your cost baseline. Next, you begin working on determining funding requirements. Which of the following is true?

    A. Funding requirements are derived from the activity costs.

    B. Management reserves are the difference between the funding requirements and the cost baseline.

    C. The management reserve is released in a lump sum at the beginning of the project.

    D. Funding requirements are an output of the Estimate Costs process.

42. A project manager is performing activities associated with the Plan Procurement Management process. He is attempting to determine, along with the relevant subject-matter experts, whether it makes more sense to develop internally or purchase a deliverable. What tools or methods can he use to produce a successful outcome?

    A. Market research

    B. Advertising

    C. Source selection analysis

    D. Make-or-buy analysis

43. Chu is a Scrum master working closely with Rita, the product owner, to release the latest version of a digital music device. The team is currently in their fourth sprint. Chu joins the team near the coffee machine, where their Kanban board was placed, to meet for 15 minutes and talk through what each team member completed since yesterday, what they will complete, and any obstacles that may get in the way of their commitment. What activity is Chu and the team engaged in?

    A. Sprint planning

    B. Sprint retrospective

    C. Backlog refinement

    D. Daily Scrum

44. Which of the following best describes the purpose of carrying out activities associated with planning stakeholder engagement?

A. To identify project stakeholders regularly and analyze and document relevant information regarding their interests, involvement, interdependencies, influence, and potential impact on project success

B. To communicate and work with stakeholders to meet their needs and expectations, address issues, and foster appropriate stakeholder involvement

C. To monitor project stakeholder relationships and tailor strategies for engaging stakeholders through modification of engagement strategies and plans

D. To develop approaches to involve project stakeholders based on their needs, expectations, interests, and potential impacts on the project

45. Direct and Manage Project Work, Manage Quality, and Conduct Procurements are processes belonging to what project management process group?

A. Planning

B. Executing

C. Monitoring and Controlling

D. Closing

46. A project has the highest probability of completing successfully at which stage of the project?

A. During project initiation

B. During project planning

C. During project execution

D. During project closure

47. You are a project manager for Community Trends, a nonprofit organization. Your project has come about because of a social need. You're calculating performance measurements and using actual costs to date, and you assume that ETC work will be completed at the budgeted rate. You know the following information: BAC = 900, ETC = 65, PV = 500, EV = 475, and AC = 425. Which of the following is the correct expected total cost at completion, given this situation?

A. 379

B. 804

C. 875

D. 850

48. A project manager is performing closing activities and is getting ready to release project resources. What document can they reference for guidance on how resources are to be released?

A. Project schedule

B. Project management plan

C. Release plan

D. Project documents

49. Which of the following best describes an Agile life cycle?

    A. A traditional approach where the majority of planning occurs up front, followed by execution

    B. An approach that generates finished deliverables that the customer may be able to use immediately

    C. An approach that is a blend of iterative and incremental and that refines and delivers frequently

    D. An approach that focuses on generating feedback early to improve and modify the work

50. You are a project manager working in an organization that is considered to be a weak matrix organizational type. You are two months into a four-month project when the functional manager for half of your most critical resources announces that she will be reallocating them to another project. You explain to her that this will result in early closure of your project and that resources should not be redirected. If the functional manager succeeds in reallocating the resources, what type of ending will the project experience?

    A. Extinction

    B. Starvation

    C. Integration

    D. Addition

51. All of the following are Agile and Lean frameworks except for which one?

    A. Scrumban

    B. eXtreme Programming

    C. Waterfall

    D. Crystal Methods

52. Carina is a principal project manager of You've Got Dogs, a specialty company that creates custom dog apparel and toys. As part of her practice, she sits down with her sponsor to regularly evaluate how the project is performing. In their most recent meeting, they analyze whether sufficient contingency and management reserves remain. What technique is Carina using?

    A. Forecasting

    B. Reserve analysis

    C. Earned value analysis

    D. Trend analysis

53. Earned value analysis, iteration burndown chart, performance reviews, trend analysis, variance analysis, and what-if scenario analysis are all types of what?

    A. Project management information systems

    B. Data representation tools and techniques

    C. Data analysis tools and techniques

    D. Schedule compression tools and techniques

54. Which of the following values refers to the value of the work planned to be completed?

   A. Earned value

   B. Planned value

   C. Actual cost

   D. Budget at completion

55. An Agile-based team holds monthly status review meetings with the product owner to review deliverables produced post-iteration. Following the demo, the product owner uses part of the meeting to facilitate a general status review for the project. A good status review meeting uses which type of communication method?

   A. Push

   B. Pull

   C. Interactive

   D. Public

56. Roshoud is the VP of customer operations for Galactic Kidz and is the project sponsor of the latest project, called Project G. He sits down with Sally, the project manager, to discuss resource utilization on the project. He expresses concern after recently hearing that resources have been unavailable as planned. Sally admits that this has been the case and that it has set the project back unexpectedly. What action should Sally take to remedy the situation?

   A. Review the schedule to identify what resource gaps currently exist within the project.

   B. Perform data analysis to determine what corrective action may be taken to get back on track with the plan.

   C. Procure additional resources to take the place of those who became unavailable after the project work began.

   D. Talk to the functional managers to ensure the unavailable resources receive poor performance reviews.

57. You are the project manager for a project that will produce a mobile phone application that sends alerts when UV rays are at dangerous levels, alerting users to stay indoors. You are in the process of managing the schedule and use a chart to track the work that remains to be completed within the iteration backlog. What is this chart called?

   A. Velocity chart

   B. Scrum chart

   C. Iteration burndown chart

   D. Iteration chart

58. You are using the critical chain method to construct your schedule, and there are variances in your critical path tasks. Which of the following is true?

   A. Your schedule is not at risk yet, but you should monitor both critical and noncritical path tasks for further delays or variances.

   B. You should compare the amount of buffer needed to what's remaining to help assess if the schedule is on track.

C. You should use preventive actions to get the project back on track.

D. Delays to the noncritical path tasks won't cause any further issues for the critical path.

59. While performing activities associated with controlling project and product scope, a project manager uncovers scope creep. What is scope creep?

A. The uncontrolled expansion of project or product scope

B. The controlled expansion of project or product scope

C. A team member who causes constant issues within the project

D. The delivery of scope that is behind schedule and over costs

60. A project manager is preparing to lead a project status meeting later that afternoon. The project is currently 75 percent complete and is reaching the most critical point. Since the project sponsor is planning on attending the meeting, the project manager decides to update the earned value calculations to present the latest performance updates in terms that the sponsor will want to see. The budget at completion (BAC) is set at $550,000, and the current estimate at completion (EAC) is at $525,000. How is the project performing in terms of the budget?

A. It is under the planned cost.

B. It is on the planned cost.

C. It is over the planned cost.

D. Insufficient information was provided.

61. You are the project manager for Ooh La Beauty Products. Your project concerns developing a new line of bath products. You also serve on the change control board, which has just approved a scope change. You know that which of the following statements are true? (Select three.)

A. Scope changes include modifications to the agreed-upon WBS.

B. Scope changes could result in schedule revisions.

C. Scope changes do not usually impact the project budget.

D. Scope changes should be reflected in the product scope.

62. While carrying out the Monitor and Control Project Work process, a project manager analyzes performance data to determine whether any corrective or preventive action is needed. Which of the following is a valid input that can assist the project manager in performing this activity?

A. Variance analysis

B. Work performance information

C. Work performance data

D. Expert judgment

63. Match the project life cycle with its respective description:

Life Cycle Name	Description
A. Predictive life cycle	1. A traditional approach where the majority of planning occurs up front, followed by execution of the work
B. Iterative life cycle	2. An approach that is both iterative and incremental to refine work items and deliver frequently
C. Incremental life cycle	3. An approach that provides deliverables to the customers to use immediately
D. Agile life cycle	4. An approach that allows feedback on unfinished work to improve and modify the work

64. A project manager has structured his project in a way that will allow for the planning of the project to occur during the early phases of the life cycle, with minimal changes thereafter. This approach is associated with which development life cycle?

A. Iterative

B. Predictive

C. Adaptive

D. Incremental

65. A project manager facilitates a meeting to provide updated information regarding the progress of the project. What type of meeting is this?

A. Risk review meeting

B. Status review meeting

C. Planning meeting

D. Change control meeting

66. All of the following processes belong to the Project Integration Management Knowledge Area except for which one?

A. Manage Project Knowledge

B. Identify Stakeholders

C. Monitor and Control Project Work

D. Close Project or Phase

67. Status review meetings are an important tool for informing stakeholders (and others) of the status of the project. All of the following are true regarding status review meetings except for which one?

A. They are a form of communication and include verbal and written material.

B. Verbally communicating at a status meeting is less complicated and more easily understood than written communication.

    C. You might have multiple status review meetings, each intended for different audiences.

    D. Face-to-face meetings are more effective for team members than status review meetings because you'll learn of potential risks and problems more quickly.

68. You are the project manager for an outdoor concert event scheduled for one year from today. You're working on the procurement documents for the computer software program that will control the lighting and screen projections during the concert. You've decided to contract with a professional services company that specializes in writing custom software programs. You want to minimize the risk to the organization and want a well-defined set of deliverables for a set price. You have agreed to pay the vendor a bonus if they complete the program at least 30 days earlier than scheduled, so you'll opt for which contract type?

    A. FPIF

    B. CPFF

    C. FFP

    D. CPIF

69. How are quality improvements implemented?

    A. By completing quality audits

    B. By submitting a change request and/or taking a corrective action

    C. By submitting a change request and/or implementing a preventive action

    D. By completing a quality audit and identifying gaps or shortcomings in the process

70. As part of kicking off a project, the product manager meets with the project team to review the team charter and establish team norms. The product manager also stresses the importance of quality and sets the expectation that it will be integrated into every iteration. Managing quality is sometimes called what?

    A. Quality management

    B. Quality adherence

    C. Quality assurance

    D. Plan-Do-Check-Act

71. A project manager performing Closing activities is currently focused on addressing the highest business value items first. What life cycle is she using to deliver her project?

    A. Highly predictive

    B. Adaptive

    C. Highly adaptive

    D. Waterfall

72. Marysil is an enterprise project manager for Cups on Fire. To date, she has identified risks, analyzed them, and developed risk responses for her project. Now, she and the team are executing the work and responding to risk triggers. What project management artifact will they need?

   A. Contingency plan

   B. Risk register

   C. Risk report

   D. Fallback plan

73. You are a project manager for Fly Me to Miami travel services. You need to obtain some services for your project on contract and have published an RFP. You are in the Conduct Procurements process and know that all of the following statements are true except for which one?

   A. This process is used for obtaining goods or services, whether internal or external to the organization.

   B. Several techniques can be used to evaluate proposals.

   C. Vendors may be required to be on a qualified seller list to participate in the bid.

   D. Bidder conferences are used during this process to answer questions regarding the RFP.

74. You are a project manager with a new company. You started less than 30 days ago. Your boss has told you it's urgent that resources are obtained and assigned to the project as soon as possible. This is your top priority. In addition, the quality assurance team needs to be assembled. All of the following are true regarding this situation except for which one?

   A. The project manager will have the greatest impact on quality during this process.

   B. You should follow the Acquire Project Team processes to obtain the new resources.

   C. Quality assurance is generally provided by a third party.

   D. Project team members, the project manager, and stakeholders are responsible for the quality assurance of the project.

75. You've taken over a project that's currently in trouble. You've held a meeting with the key stakeholders to demonstrate the new product prototype. They came prepared with the product requirements and upon inspection inform you that this prototype is not what the customer specified. Your boss instructs you to get the prototype corrected and make it match the requirements the customer specified before holding a demo with the customer. She also warns you to take a look at the work of the project. She's concerned that things aren't happening as planned and that the last project manager was not paying close enough attention to the project plan. Corrections might be needed. What Knowledge Area does this describe?

   A. Project Schedule Management

   B. Project Scope Management

   C. Project Integration Management

   D. Project Risk Management

76. Which of the following documents identifies 12 principles that are the focus of the Agile approach?

A. Agile Credo

B. Agile Manifesto

C. Agile Practice Guide

D. Agile Standard

77. Predictive, iterative, incremental, and Agile are all types of what?

A. Delivery methods

B. Project life cycles

C. Project management methodologies

D. Project management frameworks

78. Kaylee is a risk manager working in collaboration with Alyssa, a project manager, and both work for a top healthcare company. They partner to facilitate a session to determine how the project team can best exploit an opportunity that was recently identified. Kaylee and Alyssa are performing activities associated with what project management Knowledge Area?

A. Project Integration Management

B. Project Risk Management

C. Project Scope Management

D. Project Procurement Management

79. Which of the following best describes how Planning activities are performed in a highly adaptive (Agile) life cycle?

A. Once the plan is approved, changes that impact scope, time, or budget are controlled and minimized.

B. Progressive elaboration of scope is based on continuous feedback.

C. A high-level plan is developed and elaborated as the project progresses.

D. Work is performed as requirements are defined.

80. During a company town hall, the sponsor of your project announced that a new high-priority project will be kicking off in the next quarter. This is distressing news since resources are at a premium. You kick into preventive measures and pull together subject-matter experts to begin analyzing a way to compress the project schedule to complete the project prior to the next project launch. What activity are you and the subject-matter experts performing?

A. Agile development

B. Overlapping

C. Fast tracking

D. Iterative development

81. After concluding the sprint, the Scrum master, product owner, and team members come together to evaluate the overall progress and work completed and to review any lessons learned. This describes what type of meeting?

A. A daily stand-up

B. A sprint retrospective

C. A Scrum meeting

D. A sprint-planning meeting

82. Yasmin is the project manager of a project that will produce a new line of widgets for the company. She guides the project team in defining the project requirements in detail before moving into production. Because of compliance requirements that must be met, she maintains a rigid change control process for changing requirements. What method is Yasmin using to manage the project?

A. Waterfall

B. Agile

C. Iterative

D. Scrum

83. Using the information displayed in the following table, calculate the number of network paths.

Activity Name	Successor	Duration
A	B, C, D	5
B	E	2
C	E	10
D	E	7
E	None	2

A. 5

B. 3

C. 4

D. 0

84. Using the information displayed in the following table, identify the critical path.

Activity Name	Successor	Duration
A	B, C, D	5
B	E	2
C	E	10
D	E	7
E	None	2

A. A-B-E

B. A-C-E

C. A-D-E

D. A-E-D

85. Using the information displayed in the following table, identify the near critical path.

Activity Name	Successor	Duration
A	B, C, D	5
B	E	2
C	E	10
D	E	7
E	None	2

A. A-B-E

B. A-C-E

C. A-D-E

D. A-E-D

86. Roshoud is the VP of customer operations for Galactic Kidz and the project sponsor of the latest project, called Project G. He sits down with Sally, the project manager, to discuss how they will respond to the risks identified. For one risk in particular, he asks Sally to facilitate the purchase of insurance to protect against a liability. What type of risk response is this?

A. Avoid

B. Mitigate

C. Share

D. Transfer

87. You are a project manager for Lightning Bolt Enterprises using a hybrid model to manage projects. Your new project involves the research and development of a new type of rechargeable battery. The project objectives should include which of the following?

    A. A description of the business need that brought about this project

    B. A brief summary of the product description, including measurable, quantifiable product requirements that will help measure project success

    C. Quantifiable criteria, including elements such as cost, schedule, and quality measures

    D. Quantifiable criteria derived from value engineering, value analysis, or function analysis

88. A project manager is working with a risk manager to prioritize individual project risks. What project management process is associated with this activity?

    A. Plan Risk Management

    B. Identify Risks

    C. Perform Qualitative Risk Analysis

    D. Perform Quantitative Risk Analysis

89. Match the quality theorist with the theory they are responsible for.

Quality Theorist	Theory
A. Philip Crosby	1. Pareto Principle
B. Joseph Juran	2. Plan-Do-Check-Act
C. W. Edwards Deming	3. Total Quality Management (TQM)
D. Walter Shewhart	4. Zero Defects

90. A project manager learns of a recent issue that has been identified while running cable underground. The issue is deemed to be minor, so the project manager emails the project sponsor to ensure she is kept informed of all activities, as requested. What type of communication method did the project manager use?

    A. Interactive communication

    B. Push communication

    C. Pull communication

    D. Multidirectional communication

91. What do functional requirements describe?

- **A.** The environmental conditions or qualities required for the product to be effective
- **B.** The needs of a stakeholder or stakeholder group
- **C.** The higher-level needs of the organization as a whole
- **D.** The behaviors of the product

92. Which of the following best describes individual project risk?

- **A.** An uncertain event or condition that, if it occurs, has a negative effect on one or more project objectives
- **B.** An uncertain event or condition that, if it occurs, has a positive or negative effect on one or more project objectives
- **C.** The effect of uncertainty on the project as a whole, arising from all sources of uncertainty
- **D.** The effect of uncertainty on a project objective, arising from all sources of uncertainty

93. Which of the following methods should you use when you want to improve your estimates and account for risk and estimation uncertainty?

- **A.** Analogous estimating
- **B.** Three-point estimating
- **C.** Bottom-up estimating
- **D.** Expert judgment

94. If earned value = 500, planned value = 700, and actual costs = 450, what is the cost variance?

- **A.** −200
- **B.** 200
- **C.** −50
- **D.** 50

95. Sue leads a PMO that is in the process of shifting the organization from using predictive to more adaptive approaches to delivering project outcomes. While coaching one of her project managers on Agile practices, she explains that Agile teams focus on rapid product development. What reason is Sue likely to provide for carrying out this approach?

- **A.** Rapid product development allows for a reduced amount of change.
- **B.** Rapid product development allows for globalization of the project team.
- **C.** Rapid product development allows for early project completion.
- **D.** Rapid product development allows the team to obtain feedback.

96. You work for a company that writes billing software programs for the communication industry. Your customer is located in a country that limits the number of foreigners allowed into the country. You identify this risk in your risk management plan. The critical point during the project is installation and setup. You might do which of the following, given these circumstances?

   A. Develop a shared response strategy

   B. Develop a cause-and-effect diagram that identifies the risk and shows the cost effect of each choice on the objectives of the project

   C. Use sensitivity analysis to determine the causal influences of these risks and the time ordering of the events

   D. Develop a mitigation plan for installation and setup

97. You are working on the risk management plan for your current project and need to document how the risk activities will be recorded for the benefit of future projects. Which part of the risk management plan addresses these issues?

   A. Lessons learned

   B. Thresholds

   C. Tracking

   D. Reporting format

98. You've gathered cost estimates for the activities of your current project. Most of the activities can be completed with existing staff resources. The summary cost estimate for existing resources is $535,000. You will also need to hire contractors to perform some of the activities that require specialized skills. You've received a bid from a local vendor for $137,000 for these services. Which of the following statements are true? (Select two.)

   A. You've determined a quantitative estimate of the cost to the organization to perform the activities of the project.

   B. The cost of the vendor services to your organization is considered pricing (from the buyer's perspective), which is a business decision on their part.

   C. The procurement SOW can be prepared by either the buyer or the seller, and it should be as accurate as possible, as you will use this SOW in the contract award.

   D. You should use purchase price as the sole criterion for choosing among vendors when you have multiple qualified sellers from which to choose.

99. The project team recently participated in a working session to determine the costs associated with individual activities. To produce a more accurate estimate, they broke each activity down further into smaller chunks. What will this activity yield?

   A. Cost estimates

   B. Basis of estimates

   C. Cost baseline

   D. Project budget

100. Projects that combine elements of different life cycles to achieve a specific goal are said to use what type of project life cycle?

A. Agile

B. Hybrid

C. Predictive

D. Experimental

101. The project sponsor emails the project manager urgently requesting the latest measurement of cumulative work performed, expressed in terms of the approved budget. The sponsor notes that they must have this information by end of day to prepare for a critical meeting the next morning. What information is the sponsor looking for?

A. Earned value

B. Planned value

C. Actual cost

D. Budget at completion

102. Reasons to Lyv is the top customer of a large marketing firm. Trudy is the president of Reasons to Lyv and has decided to launch a product that leverages new GPS tracking technology. She sits down with Roy, the project manager on the project, to review and evaluate whether a sufficient amount of funds remains to address known risks. What activity are they performing?

A. Technical performance analysis

B. Audit

C. Reserve analysis

D. Risk review

103. Leticia is a project manager working for Dancing Apron, a company that combines cooking with simple children's cooking recipes and music. Her latest project involves the release of the company's first digital product that parents will be able to purchase and download online. Kip, who is the sponsor of the project, asks her to calculate the EAC assuming that the work will be accomplished at the planned rate. Leticia knows that they have spent $15,000 to date of the $20,000 budgeted and that the earned value of the project has already been calculated at $18,000. What is the EAC that she will communicate to Kip?

A. $13,000

B. $17,000

C. $20,000

D. $15,000

104. You work within a team that uses a feature-driven development approach to manage software projects. As the senior project manager on the team, you know from experience the criticality of communication. You often coach other project managers on the various elements of communication, which are incorporated within the models of communication exchange. Which of the following best explains these communication elements?

   A. The elements of communication include encode, transmit, acknowledge, and feedback/response, and the communication model includes senders, receivers, and messages.

   B. The elements of communication include senders, receivers, and messages, and the communication model includes verbal and written.

   C. The elements of communication include senders, receivers, and messages, and the communication model includes encode, transmit, acknowledge, and feedback/response.

   D. The elements of communication include encode, transmit, acknowledge, and feedback/response, and the communication model includes verbal and written.

105. Sally is a project manager who works at Galactic Kidz. While managing the execution of the project team's work, she notices that two critical activities are delayed and decides to speak to the project sponsor. What action are Sally and the project sponsor likely to take?

   A. Preventive action

   B. Defect repair

   C. Updates to the plan

   D. Corrective action

106. Roshoud is serving as the project sponsor for a high-visibility project within the Galactic Kidz corporation. During a weekly executive status meeting, he expresses concern regarding quality assurance and requests an update. Quality assurance is most concerned with what?

   A. Using processes effectively and assuring stakeholders that the end result will meet their needs

   B. Identifying quality requirements and/or standards of the project and its deliverables

   C. Documenting how the project will demonstrate compliance with quality requirements and/or standards

   D. Monitoring and recording the results of executing the quality management activities to assess project performance

107. Contract phases are closely related to the Project Procurement Management Knowledge Area processes. Which of the following are true? (Select three.)

    A. The requirement stage, which establishes the project and contract needs, is related to the Plan Procurement Management process.

    B. The requisition stage, where responses to procurement documents are reviewed, is related to the Conduct Procurements process.

    C. The award stage, where the contract is awarded, is related to the Conduct Procurements process.

    D. Two of the outputs of the Plan Procurement Management process are inputs to the Conduct Procurements process.

108. Which of the following describes who is responsible for the quality assurance of the project?

    A. Project manager

    B. Project manager and project team members

    C. Stakeholders

    D. Project team members, project manager, and stakeholders

109. You have devised some proposal evaluation criteria based on past performance, contract compliance, and quality ratings to select a seller. Your organization has used two of the three vendors that bid on this project on previous projects, so you are comfortable using whichever one is selected. Which of the following is one of the most important criteria in evaluating the responses to your proposal?

    A. Predefined performance criteria or a set of defined minimum requirements

    B. The financial records of the potential vendor to determine their fiscal ability to perform the services

    C. Determining whether the vendor has a clear understanding of what you're asking them to do

    D. Information about the seller such as past performance, delivery, contract compliance, and quality ratings

110. A Scrum master facilitates a monthly session with the team to discuss what went well in the latest sprint, what could have gone better, and what they will commit to improving in the next sprint. This meeting is referred to as a:

    A. Sprint retrospective

    B. Sprint review

    C. Sprint planning

    D. Stand-up

111. Which of the following project management documents records challenges, problems, realized risks, and opportunities?

A. Issue log

B. Lessons learned register

C. Risk register

D. Project documents

112. A project manager is carrying out activities associated with the Manage Communications process. What result will these activities produce?

A. Ensuring that the information needs of the project and its stakeholders are met

B. Developing an appropriate approach and plan for project communication activities

C. Communicating and working with stakeholders to meet their needs and expectations

D. Ensuring timely and appropriate collection, distribution, and the ultimate disposition of project information

113. You have decomposed the deliverables for your project as follows: Project Management, Design, Build, and Test. The Design deliverable is further decomposed to include these deliverables: product design document, blueprints, and prototype. Adequate cost and schedule estimates have been applied to all the deliverables. Which of the following has occurred?

A. All the steps of decomposition have been performed.

B. Steps 1, 2, and 3 of decomposition have been performed for the Design deliverable.

C. Steps 1, 2, 3, and 4 of decomposition have been performed for all the deliverables.

D. Steps 1, 2, and 3 of decomposition have been performed for all the deliverables with the exception of the Design deliverable.

114. Nicolas is the project manager of a project that has been described as revolutionizing the mobile fitness tracking industry. He recently finalized and published the scope. A key subject-matter expert on his team asks to see the list of acceptance criteria. What document will Nicolas reference to get this information?

A. Project scope statement

B. Requirements documentation

C. Business case

D. Scope management plan

115. A product owner attends a session with the team and other key stakeholders to review a demonstration of the deliverable produced. What is the frequency of this type of meeting when following an iteration-based Agile approach?

A. At the beginning of the iteration

B. At the end of the iteration

C. At the start of the project

D. At the end of the project

116. Marysil, an enterprise project manager for Cups on Fire, is in the process of sequencing activities with her team to develop the project schedule. One team member noted that when the next-generation prototype cup is cauterized, it will need to sit for a period of two days before it can be hand-painted. How will Marysil reflect this within the schedule?

   A. By adding a two-day lead between the two activities

   B. By adding a two-day lag between the two activities

   C. By adding a two-day buffer between the two activities

   D. By adding a two-day project buffer to the project

117. Which of the following statements best describes the product scope?

   A. The work performed to deliver a product, service, or results with the specified features and functions

   B. The higher-level needs of the organization as a whole and the reasons why a project has been undertaken

   C. The features and characteristics that describe the product, service, or result of the project

   D. A description of the behaviors of the product, including actions and interactions that the product should execute

118. Which of the following represents a definitive range of estimates?

   A. –25 percent to +75 percent

   B. –5 percent to +10 percent

   C. –10 percent to +10 percent

   D. –50 percent to +50 percent

119. You are a project manager for Time Will Tell, an international watch manufacturer. Your project entails developing a watch with global positioning satellite (GPS) capabilities. Kit is a junior staff member with two years of experience in GPS technology. Carrie is a senior staff member with five years of experience working with GPS technology. You are developing the activity duration estimates for the project activities. You are trying to determine an estimate for a particular activity that involves GPS skills and knowledge. Carrie has worked on activities similar to this in the past. She tells you the activity will likely take 45 days. All of the following statements are true regarding the information in this question except which one?

   A. Carrie used an analogous estimating technique to come up with the 45-day estimate for this activity.

   B. The activities are similar in fact, not just appearance, and Carrie has the needed expertise to provide this estimate, so you can rely on the estimate being reasonably accurate.

   C. Carrie used a technique that is a form of expert judgment to estimate this activity.

   D. The technique Carrie used can also be used to estimate project duration because of the amount of information available about the details of the project.

120. Your project sponsor has reviewed the initial project schedule you created for the project. She is not happy with the project end date because it doesn't match the promise date she gave the customer. You decide to use some compression techniques first. Which of the following statements should you keep in mind (and know to be true) regarding duration compression?

    A. Crashing is a compression technique that typically produces a viable alternative.

    B. Fast-tracking is a compression technique that typically results in increased costs.

    C. Schedule compression shortens the project schedule but doesn't change the project scope.

    D. Crashing is a compression technique that typically results in increased risk.

121. You are a senior project manager for a company that produces mobile phone applications. In your latest project, you have teamed up with another project manager, who will manage a subset of the project. She tells you that the work packages have been decomposed and milestones captured for her deliverables. Together, you review her list of milestones, the first of which reads "Finish GUI: 30 Days." What is wrong with this scenario?

    A. Two project managers cannot be associated with one project.

    B. A milestone cannot contain the word *GUI*.

    C. Work packages should not be decomposed.

    D. The project manager is unclear as to the definition of a milestone.

122. What action can a project manager take if the selected risk response strategy turns out not to be fully effective?

    A. Develop and implement a fallback plan

    B. Document and respond to a secondary risk

    C. Actively accept the risk

    D. Update the risk register with the outcome

123. Emma is a project manager working on a project that will require a specially engineered machine. Several manufacturers can make the machine to the specifications Emma needs. She will use purchase price as the sole criterion for choosing from among the vendors. Which of the following is true regarding this question?

    A. Emma must use purchase price alone as the sole criterion for evaluation because multiple vendors are involved.

    B. Emma will review the procurement documents and teaming agreements as some of the inputs to this process.

    C. Emma will include delivery and setup charges as part of the purchase price criterion.

    D. Emma will use the advertising tool and technique of this process to let vendors know about this opportunity.

124. Match the term with its definition.

Term	Definition
A. Story points	1. A unit-less measure used in relative user story estimation techniques
B. Burndown chart	2. A visual representation of the work completed toward the release of a product
C. Burnup charts	3. The sum of story point sizes for features actually completed during the iteration
D. Velocity	4. A visual representation of the work remaining versus the time left in a timebox

125. These processes are responsible for distributing information about the project to the stakeholders and satisfying the needs of the stakeholders by managing communications with them, respectively.

A. Manage Stakeholder Engagement and Manage Communications

B. Manage Stakeholder Engagement and Information Distribution

C. Manage Communications and Manage Stakeholder Engagement

D. Information Distribution and Manage Stakeholder Engagement

126. A risk manager convened with the project manager to discuss the progress of the project. The risk manager shared concerns about feedback received regarding the low likelihood that the team would achieve their go-live date successfully. What activity is the project manager likely to perform next?

A. Submit a change request in the form of corrective action.

B. Work with the risk manager to apply immediate changes to the plan.

C. Nothing, since a new issue or risk has not been officially raised.

D. Submit a change request in the form of preventive action.

127. Midway through the delivery of development services, a customer requested that new requirements be incorporated. When asked to submit a change request to modify the terms of the contract, the customer refused and insisted that the changes be implemented at no cost. After multiple discussions, neither party changed their stance on the situation. What technique will the project manager likely use to address this situation?

A. Claims administration

B. Alternative dispute resolution

C. Inspection

D. Conflict management

128. Julie is a product manager responsible for a line of smart water bottles that connect to a mobile app to capture data and provide suggestions regarding your drinking habits. Julie meets with the Scrum team to talk through a major issue that threatens the latest release. Together, the team decides to focus collectively on the issue at hand until it is resolved. What is this an example of?

A. Collaboration

B. Value-focused work

C. Issue management

D. Swarming

129. A project sponsor called the project manager to express concern over not seeing the latest weekly update on the progress of the project. What is the sponsor looking for?

A. Work performance data

B. Work performance report

C. Work performance information

D. Communications management plan

130. The Project Integration Management Knowledge Area is concerned with which of the following?

A. Ensuring timely and appropriate planning, collection, creation, distribution, storage, retrieval, management, control, monitoring, and ultimate disposition of project information

B. Identifying, combining, unifying, and coordinating the various processes and project management activities

C. Identifying the people, groups, or organizations that could impact or be impacted by the project to analyze stakeholder expectations and their impact on the project

D. Ensuring the project includes all the work required, and only the work required, to complete the project successfully

131. Julie is a product manager responsible for a line of smart water bottles that connect to a mobile app to capture data and provide suggestions regarding your drinking habits. As part of her usual routine, she grabs a cup of coffee in the morning, sits at her desk, and evaluates the prioritization of user stories. She considers which feature should make it into her next release. What is Julie looking at?

A. Burndown chart

B. Release backlog

C. Product schedule

D. Product backlog

132. Brad works as a project manager for a prominent law firm. His latest project involves an office move that will accommodate a 10 percent growth in staff over the next two years. Because of an unexpected increase in infrastructure costs, he calculates that he will be $2,000 over budget. What document can Brad reference to determine whether this falls within the allowable threshold for budget overages?

  A. Cost baseline

  B. Cost management plan

  C. Contingency reserve

  D. Project funding requirements

133. Using the earned-value analysis technique, a project manager calculates a schedule performance index of 0.75 and a cost performance index of 1.25. To bring the schedule back on track, the project manager decides to allocate additional resources to critical activities in order to complete them faster. What technique are they using to control the schedule?

  A. Fast tracking

  B. Leads and lags

  C. Crashing

  D. Resource optimization

134. A project manager facilitates the voting process for decision-makers who have convened to review a major deliverable that has been completed. The intent of the meeting is to vote on whether to approve and accept the deliverable. What key input will the committee need to reference to vote?

  A. Deliverables

  B. Accepted deliverables

  C. Verified deliverables

  D. Work performance information

135. Julie is a product manager responsible for a line of smart water bottles that connect to a mobile app to capture data and provide suggestions regarding your drinking habits. In preparation for the upcoming sprint, she meets with the team to ensure that stories are clear and appropriately sized. What activity is Julie performing with the team?

  A. Backlog refinement

  B. Backlog preparation

  C. Release planning

  D. Roadmap grooming

136. Grant hesitantly knocks on his project sponsor's door to notify her of a budget overage that has occurred. Because of a vendor error, he shared that a critical piece of equipment would cost $30,000 more than originally estimated. Fortunately for Grant, the sponsor understood the situation and approved the use of funds set aside for unexpected events. From where will Grant pull the funds to cover the equipment?

A. Management reserves

B. Contingency reserves

C. Funding limit reconciliation

D. Cost baseline

137. Which of the following estimate ranges represents a rough order of magnitude?

A. –5 percent to + 10 percent

B. –50 percent to + 50 percent

C. –25 percent to + 75 percent

D. –10 percent to + 25 percent

138. Sue leads a PMO that is in the process of shifting the organization from using predictive to more adaptive approaches to delivering project outcomes. During an Agile training session for her organization, a team member asks, "How many people are on a project team?" What response is Sue likely to provide?

A. 1–5.

B. 3–9.

C. 10–15.

D. There is no set number.

139. You are a project manager working on manufacturing a new product. The operational process is very detailed. One of the components of the product must measure 1 centimeter by 1 centimeter. Reliability is measured using a machine that samples one part in every hundred to assure the measurements are correct. Which of the following does this question describe?

A. This is statistical sampling, which is a tool and technique of the Control Quality process.

B. This describes a quality baseline, which is an output of the Plan Quality Management process.

C. This describes a quality audit, which is a tool and technique of the Plan Quality Management process.

D. This is a prevention cost, which is a tool and technique of the Plan Quality Management process.

140. Using the estimates provided, calculate the beta distribution: most likely estimate (ML) = 72, optimistic estimate (O) = 55, pessimistic estimate (P) = 85. *Round to one decimal point.*

A. 70.0

B. 70.7

C. 71.3

D. 72

141. Match the Agile approach with its description.

Agile Approach	Description
A. Scrum	1. Allows for continuous flow of work and value to the customer. This approach is less prescriptive and pulls single items through the process continuously.
B. Kanban	2. Used to meet the needs of a large software development project. This approach revolves around six core roles and is organized around five activities that are performed iteratively.
C. eXtreme programming	3. Used for software projects and features accelerated cycles and less heavyweight processes. This approach focuses on performing more iterative cycles across seven key disciplines and incorporates feedback before formal delivery.
D. Feature-driven development	4. A software development method based on frequent cycles. This approach attempts to distill a best practice into its simplest and purest form and then applies that practice continuously.
E. Agile unified process	5. A single-team process framework used to manage product development. This approach uses timeboxed sprints of one month or less and revolves around three core roles.

142. The characteristics of project life cycles vary and should be considered when determining which life cycle is the best fit for a project. Match the delivery life cycle approach based on where it falls on the continuum when considering frequency of delivery and degree of change.

Life Cycle	Continuum
A. Predictive	1. High frequency of delivery and low degree of change
B. Iterative	2. Low frequency of delivery and high degree of change
C. Incremental	3. Low frequency of delivery and low degree of change
D. Agile	4. High frequency of delivery and high degree of change

143. All of the following are true statements except for which one?
   A. Daily stand-ups are a critical component of planning.
   B. Daily stand-ups last no more than 15 minutes.
   C. Daily stand-ups are used to uncover problems.
   D. Daily stand-ups are used to ensure work is progressing well.

144. At the end of a sprint, the Scrum team met to talk through what went well and what could be improved. One engineer noted that the recent changes to daily stand-ups were working. Which of the following describes the actions that the Scrum team carried out? (Select two.)

A. Facilitated a collaboration session

B. Facilitated sprint planning

C. Facilitated a sprint retrospective

D. Facilitated process improvement

145. A sponsor meets with the project manager to better understand when the team will complete the project. The project manager notes that the team is completing an average of 40 story points per sprint, and as a result, they would complete the project within five iterations. She shows the sponsor a chart that reflects the projection and includes a date for each iteration. What chart is the project manager and sponsor reviewing?

A. Burndown chart

B. Burnup chart

C. Gantt chart

D. Velocity chart

146. The project processes are iterative, are results oriented, and interact with each other. Shewhart and Deming developed a concept that reflects this idea. Which of the following is the name of this cycle?

A. Plan-Do-Check-Act

B. Initiate-Requirements-Execute-Close

C. Select-Plan-Monitor-Act

D. Strategize-Justify-Choose-Execute-Control

147. After meeting with several subject-matter experts, the project manager determines that the project phases will need to occur one after the other. What project life cycle is the project manager using?

A. Sequential

B. Overlapping

C. Iterative

D. Incremental

148. Phase endings are characterized by which of the following?

A. Deliverables quality analysis and written sign-off

B. Completion, review, and approval of deliverables

C. Deliverables review and written sign-off

D. Completion, quality analysis, and approval of deliverables

149. Which of the following is true?

　　A. There are five project management process groups, and they are Initiating, Planning, Executing, Monitoring and Controlling, and Closing.

　　B. There are 55 project management processes, which can be grouped by process group or Knowledge Area.

　　C. There are 10 project management Knowledge Areas, whose processes are performed sequentially.

　　D. There are five project management process groups, and they are Initiating, Planning, Managing, Monitoring, and Closing.

150. A method of managing projects in small, incremental portions of work that can be easily assigned and completed within a short period of time describes what methodology?

　　A. Waterfall

　　B. Lean

　　C. Agile

　　D. Iterative

Chapter

3

Business Environment (Domain 3.0)

THE PROJECT MANAGEMENT PROFESSIONAL (PMP)® EXAM CONTENT FROM THE BUSINESS ENVIRONMENT DOMAIN COVERED IN THIS CHAPTER INCLUDES THE FOLLOWING:

✓ **Task 3.1   Plan and manage project compliance**

✓ **Task 3.2   Evaluate and deliver project benefits and value**

✓ **Task 3.3   Evaluate and address external business environment changes for impact on scope**

✓ **Task 3.4   Support organizational change**

The process names, inputs, tools and techniques, outputs, and descriptions of the project management process groups and related materials and figures in this chapter are based on content from *A Guide to the Project Management Body of Knowledge (PMBOK® Guide) – Sixth Edition* (PMI®, 2017).

1. A project manager has just been assigned to a newly approved project and has been tasked with developing the first draft of the project charter. To better understand the financials, the project manager decides to review the net present value and payback period calculated for the project. Which of the following can the project manager reference for this information?

   A. Project budget

   B. Business case

   C. Benefits management plan

   D. Project charter

2. What brings together a set of tools and techniques to describe, organize, and monitor the work of project activities?

   A. Projects

   B. Project management

   C. Portfolio management

   D. Programs

3. Reasons to Lyv is the top client of a large marketing firm. Trudy is the president of Reasons to Lyv and has decided to launch a product that leverages new GPS tracking technology. She has high confidence that the project will be a success and asks the marketing firm to make it their top priority by generating a unique campaign that will run in parallel with her project. Billy, a top executive from the marketing company, briefs his team about this unique situation that they have not managed before, and a project is launched shortly thereafter. Billy's project came about as a result of what?

   A. Strategic opportunity

   B. Environmental considerations

   C. Technological advance

   D. Customer request

4. All of the following statements about fairness are true except for which one?

   A. Conflicts of interest might include your associations or affiliations.

   B. Accepting vendor gifts is sometimes acceptable.

   C. Fairness includes avoiding favoritism and discrimination.

   D. Fairness encompasses diversity training and preventing culture shock.

5. All of the following are true regarding the organizational process assets updates output of the Manage Communications process except for which one?

   A. Stakeholder notifications are part of this output and go hand in hand with one of the areas covered in the Role Delineation Study in the *PMI Code of Ethics and Professional Conduct*.

   B. Project reports are part of this output and include status reports, among others, and according to the *PMI Code of Ethics and Professional Conduct*, the status of projects should always be truthful.

    C. Lessons learned documentation is part of this output, and lessons learned meetings should be conducted at the end of project phases and at the end of the project at a minimum.

    D. Feedback from stakeholders is part of this output and can improve performance on future projects, but it is too late to incorporate the feedback on the current project.

6. You have been with your company for three months. You were hired as a project manager and are anxious to get started on your first project. Your organization is considering taking on a project that has considerable risk associated with it and you don't know the outcome. The selection committee is meeting two weeks from today to decide on this project. Since you're new to the company, you want to make a good impression. Which of the following will you do?

    A. You make certain that the product description is documented, the strategic plan is considered, and historical information is researched before writing the project charter.

    B. You make certain to pass on the information you've gathered and documented to the project sponsor so that she can write the project charter.

    C. You know some of the deliverables in this project will be purchased. You will use EVM techniques to help optimize life-cycle costs when you get to the processes in the Project Cost Management Knowledge Area.

    D. You recommend a feasibility study be conducted as a separate project from this one because the outcome of the project is unknown.

7. You are the project manager of a construction company that is working on a project to build a new community of townhomes. A vendor that is bidding on the electrical contract for the project knows you are a big fan of your favorite comedian and sends you two tickets to attend a show. You know that the tickets are expensive, valued at more than $500 based on the location of the seats. What should you do?

    A. Respectfully decline the gift and send back the tickets.

    B. Accept the tickets since you already accepted another gift from a separate vendor competing for the same contract.

    C. Respectfully decline the gift but keep the tickets for evidence.

    D. Accept the tickets, but take the project sponsor, who is also a fan of the comedian.

8. Which organizational process asset should you consider when closing out a project or phase?

    A. Marketplace conditions

    B. Configuration management knowledge base

    C. Financial management and accounts payable system

    D. Procurement policies

9. Quincy and Michael are two executives of Widgets for Life, a company providing the latest cool lifestyle gadgets. As part of their annual planning process, they sit down to evaluate three projects linked to their department objectives. They decide to use benefit measurement methods to help them choose which project to select. Which of the following analysis tools are they likely to use?

   A. Linear

   B. Benefit-cost ratio

   C. Multi-objective programming

   D. Nonlinear

10. Project selection methods might include all of the following except for which one?

    A. Benefit measurement methods

    B. Constrained optimization analysis

    C. NPV calculations

    D. Alternatives analysis

11. You have just started working for a new company. Your previous project management experience made you stand out from your competitors. Your new business cards are being printed with the title of project coordinator. You discover that the project charter for the project you are working on was never written, so you volunteer to draft one, even though the work of the project has started. The vendor who is assisting with the project is already on board and is working with (and reporting to) the engineering division. You report to the construction division. Which of the following is true?

    A. You are working in a weak matrix organization and are in the Executing phase of the project.

    B. You are working in a strong matrix organization and are in the Initiating phase of the project.

    C. You are working in a strong matrix organization and are in the Executing phase of the project.

    D. You are working in a weak matrix organization and are in the Planning phase of the project.

12. Which of the following best defines business value?

    A. The explanation for how benefits will be created, maximized, and sustained by the project

    B. The net quantifiable benefit derived from a business endeavor

    C. Critical success factors of the project

    D. An outcome of actions, behaviors, products, services, or results that provide value to the organization

13. Which of the following represent components of a benefits management plan? (Select all that apply.)

  A. Strategic alignment

  B. Metrics

  C. Target benefits

  D. Business need

14. You are a project coordinator and work in an organization that is considered to be a weak-matrix organizational type. What is a disadvantage of working in this type of organization?

  A. You have little authority.

  B. You have limited funds.

  C. You can only use the waterfall methodology.

  D. You have job and role stability.

15. Which of the following are types of PMOs? (Select three.)

  A. Directive

  B. Center of Excellence

  C. Supportive

  D. Controlling

16. A portfolio manager is leading a project portfolio planning exercise to determine which projects will move forward in the new quarter that support the strategic goals of the portfolio. She decides to use a scoring model to rate projects against the following three criteria: profit potential, ease of use, marketability. Based on the table provided, which project will likely move forward?

Criteria	Weight	*Project A Score	*Project B Score	*Project C Score
Profit potential	5	5	2	1
Marketability	1	1	5	3
Ease of use	3	2	3	5
Weighted score	—	—	—	—

  A. Project A

  B. Project B

  C. Project C

  D. None

17. Which environmental factor should you pay close attention to when carrying out the Identify Stakeholders process?

   A. Lessons learned and historical repositories

   B. Company culture and organizational structure

   C. Existing policies, procedures, and guidelines

   D. Stakeholder registers from past similar projects

18. A project manager is performing activities associated with the Plan Procurement Management process. Which tool or technique can the project manager use to gather information on specific seller capabilities?

   A. Market research

   B. Advertising

   C. Source selection analysis

   D. Make-or-buy analysis

19. A functional manager hosted a celebration for the project team to reward them for a job well done that led to the successful completion of a major project. It was clear to the project manager that the team was relaxed and enjoying themselves, with some talking about upcoming vacation plans. What type of organizational structure does the project team likely work within?

   A. Strong matrix

   B. Weak matrix

   C. Project-oriented

   D. PMO

20. A PMO leader is guiding the organization through Agile adoption. What characteristics should she consider when evaluating organizational readiness of Agile approaches? (Select three.)

   A. Focus on long-term goals

   B. Management's willingness to change

   C. Willingness of the organization to shift its views

   D. Focus on short-term budgeting and metrics

21. Sue is the head of an enterprise PMO. She delivers a presentation at the annual company meeting to describe her roles and responsibilities and the value of the PMO. As part of her presentation, she notes that the PMO is responsible for ensuring that projects, programs, and portfolios are aligned and managed according to the organization's strategic business objectives. What is this referred to as?

    A. Business management

    B. PMI Talent Triangle™

    C. Organizational project management

    D. Project portfolio management

22. A project manager is putting together the project charter and is interested in referencing marketplace conditions to understand the factors surrounding the project. What is a valid input that the project manager can reference to get this information?

    A. Organizational process assets

    B. Enterprise environmental factors

    C. Project documents

    D. Lessons learned register

23. You are a senior manager overseeing projects for Fun Days Vacation Packages. You manage projects and weigh the value of each project against the business's strategic objectives. You also monitor projects to make certain they adhere to those objectives and that you get the most efficient use of resources possible. Which of the following does this scenario describe?

    A. Project and program management

    B. Project management

    C. Program management

    D. Portfolio management

24. Which of the following is true about benefit-cost ratio?

    A. It is the quickest and least precise project selection method.

    B. It uses algorithms to calculate the ratio.

    C. Benefit-cost ratio is the most difficult equation to calculate.

    D. Benefit-cost ratio is also known as cost-benefit analysis.

25. All of the following are true regarding projects except for which one?

    A. They are temporary in nature.

    B. They can be progressively elaborated.

    C. They produce unique products, services, or results.

    D. They can continue without an ending date.

26. Which of the following project selection methods is considered to be the least precise?

   A. Payback period

   B. Benefit-cost ratio

   C. Scoring models

   D. Net present value

27. Reasons to Lyv is the top client of a large marketing firm. Trudy is the president of Reasons to Lyv and has decided to launch a product that leverages new GPS tracking technology. She has high confidence that the project will be a success and asks the marketing firm to make it their top priority by generating a unique campaign that will run in parallel with her project. Billy, a top executive from the marketing company, briefs his team about this unique situation that they have not managed before, and a project is launched shortly thereafter. Trudy's project came about as a result of what?

   A. Strategic opportunity

   B. Environmental considerations

   C. Technological advance

   D. Customer request

28. A program manager working for an infectious disease nonprofit has just been assigned to a program that seeks to solve a deadly issue plaguing a third-world country. The issue involves a deadly bacteria that has entered into a major water source that branches out into multiple regions across the country. The first project will involve a feasibility study. This project came about as a result of what?

   A. Strategic opportunity

   B. Environmental considerations

   C. Regulatory requirement

   D. Social need

29. As a value upheld by the project management community, honesty entails which of the following?

   A. Ensuring integrity

   B. Truthful reporting

   C. Reporting ethics violations

   D. Avoiding conflict of interest

30. Which of the following values represents taking ownership for the decisions you make or fail to make, the actions you take or fail to take, and the consequences that result?

   A. Responsibility

   B. Fairness

   C. Respect

   D. Honesty

31. Which of the following best defines a program?

    A. A temporary endeavor undertaken to create a unique product, service, or result

    B. Related projects, subsidiary programs, and program activities managed in a coordinated manner to obtain benefits not available from managing them individually

    C. The iterative process of increasing the level of detail in a project management plan as greater amounts of information and more accurate estimates become available

    D. The series of phases that represent the evolution of a product, from concept through delivery, growth, and maturity to retirement

32. Antwon, the director of marketing, approaches you to tell you about the latest idea he had for a new phone app that he called Project UV2. Since he was the brain behind the company's top-selling app, you take him seriously. He notes that his idea involves enhancing the existing UV app by improving the backend to sit on technology that the company recently rolled out, thereby making response time faster. The backend changes would not affect the phone app functionality, nor would they require any new configurations to be made. This is considered to be which of the following?

    A. A project

    B. Ongoing operation

    C. A secondary phase of Project UV

    D. A program

33. All of the following are examples of constrained optimization methods except for which one?

    A. Economic models

    B. Integer

    C. Dynamic

    D. Multi-objective programming

34. The project manager reviews lessons learned from past similar projects to start the project off on the right foot. What input contains lessons learned and historical information from past projects?

    A. Organizational process assets

    B. Enterprise environmental factors

    C. Project documents

    D. Lessons learned register

35. All of the following are true regarding honesty as a value project managers should uphold, except for which one?

    A. Personal gain should never be a factor in any project decision.

    B. Honesty can include reporting the truth regarding project status.

    C. Honesty only involves information regarding your own background and experience.

    D. Honesty includes being honest about your own experience, not deceiving others, and not making false statements.

36. All of the following statements are true regarding NPV except which one?

A. NPV assumes reinvestment at the cost of capital.

B. Projects with NPV greater than zero should receive a go decision.

C. NPV is the discount rate when IRR equals zero.

D. Projects with high returns early on should be favored over projects with low returns early on.

37. You are the newly appointed project manager of a high-profile, critical project for your organization. The project team is structured outside your normal organizational structure, and you have full authority for this project. What type of organization does this describe?

A. Hybrid

B. Strong matrix

C. Functional

D. Balanced matrix

38. Yasmin is a senior project manager who has just taken on a project that will produce a new line of medical widgets for a Fortune 100 company. The entire industry is buzzing with excitement over this project, which is estimated to span three years and require an investment of $1.5 billion from the company. What type of project is this?

A. Megaproject

B. Strategic project

C. Program

D. Portfolio

39. You are the project manager for a company that produces mobile phone applications. Currently, the director of the consumer division is evaluating two projects. Funding exists for only one project. Project UV aims to produce a mobile phone application that sends alerts when the UV rays are at dangerous levels, alerting users to stay indoors; Project Fun aims to send alerts when it detects that users have not visited any destinations outside of their usual routine. The director asks you to calculate the payback period and NPV for both projects, and here is what you derive:

Project UV: The payback period is 12 months, and the NPV is (100).

Project Fun: The payback period is 18 months, and the NPV is 250.

Which project would you recommend to the director?

A. Project UV, because the payback period is shorter than Project Fun

B. Project Fun, because the NPV is a positive number

C. Project UV, because the NPV is a negative number

D. Project Fun, because the NPV is a higher number than Project UV

40. You are a project manager working on contract for an upscale retail toy store. Your project involves implementing a Party Event Planner department in stores in 12 locations across the country as a pilot to determine whether this will be a profitable new service all the stores should offer. You've identified two alternative methods of implementing the pilot. Alternative A's initial investment equals $598,000. The PV of the expected cash inflows is $300,000 in year 1 and $300,000 in year 2. The cost of capital is 12 percent. Alternative B's initial investment equals $625,000. The PV of Alternative B's expected cash inflows is $323,000 in year 1 and $300,000 in year 2. The cost of capital is 9 percent. Which of the following is true?

   A. Alternative A will earn a return of at least 12 percent.

   B. Alternative B will earn a return of at least 9 percent.

   C. The return is not known for either Alternative A or Alternative B.

   D. Both alternatives are viable choices.

41. Premature closure of a project phase that is managed using an Adaptive approach is likely to experience greater failure due to sunk costs versus a project managed using a Predictive approach.

   A. This is a true statement.

   B. This is a false statement.

42. Robert is a new executive hired to lead the marketing department of a telecommunications company. He sits down with his most senior project manager to review a project that he will now take sponsorship for. After discussing business value, he asks to review the requirements and how the requirements link to the project objectives. What document will the project manager share with Robert?

   A. The project management plan

   B. The product backlog

   C. The requirements traceability matrix

   D. The benefits management plan

43. A project manager is updating a presentation slide with updates on a high visibility project for a monthly customer service review. The purchase order for hardware has not been placed yet because of multiple complications in the process, which will cause the schedule to slip by a minimum of two weeks. The project manager knows that the customer will be enraged. Hoping to not cause a scene, he omits this information in the presentation update, with a plan of crashing the schedule to make up for the slip. What core value has the project manager violated?

   A. Fairness

   B. Honesty

   C. Respect

   D. Responsibility

44. Functional (centralized), matrix, and project-oriented are all types of which of the following?

   A. Communication styles

   B. Organizational cultures

   C. Organizational structures

   D. Project characteristics

45. You work in an organization that is considered to be a project-oriented organizational type. What is an advantage of working in this type of organization?

   A. You have high to almost total access to resources.

   B. You have unlimited access to funds.

   C. You are a part-time project manager and can straddle two roles.

   D. You have job and role stability.

46. You are a full-time project manager working within the customer operations organization, reporting to the VP of customer solutions. Your boss manages the project budget. Which organizational structure do you work in?

   A. Functional

   B. Hybrid

   C. Project-oriented

   D. PMO

47. Which of the following are considered factors that influence the initiation of a project? (Select three.)

   A. Compliance, legal requirements, or social requirements

   B. Stakeholder needs and requests

   C. Enhancement of existing operations

   D. Improvement of processes, services, or products

48. What is the present value of $8,000 received three years from the present using a 7 percent interest rate? Assume all options are rounded to the nearest whole dollar.

   A. $9,800

   B. $6,530

   C. $9,680

   D. $6,612

49. You are a project manager for the information technology division of a local satellite TV broadcasting company. This spring, the chief information officer for your company gave you the job of converting and upgrading all the PCs in the department to the latest release of a specific desktop application. Prior to this conversion, all manner of desktop software existed on machines throughout the company and had caused increasing problems with sharing files and information across the company. A lot of unproductive hours were spent converting information into several formats. This project came about as a result of which of the following?

   A. Business need

   B. Market demand

    C. Technological advance

    D. Social need

50. Which of the following best describes PMI?

    A. A nonprofit organization that focuses on project, program, and portfolio management

    B. A for-profit organization that focuses on project, program, and portfolio management

    C. The industry-recognized standard within the United States for project management practices

    D. The industry-recognized standard for project management practices

51. What is the ethical code you'll be required to adhere to as a PMP credential holder?

    A. *Code of Professional Conduct*

    B. *Code of Project Management Professional Standards and Ethics*

    C. *Code of Professional Ethics*

    D. *Code of Ethics and Professional Conduct*

52. Yasmin is a senior project manager for a project that aims to produce a new line of medical widgets for a Fortune 100 company. The entire industry has been buzzing with excitement over this project, which was estimated to span three years and require an investment of $1.5 billion from the company. Yasmin recently learned that her project would be placed on hold for the foreseeable future after a lawsuit against the company resulted in shareholders pulling out their investments, thereby liquidating capital needed to continue with the project. What type of project ending is this?

    A. Integration

    B. Starvation

    C. Addition

    D. Extinction

53. Which of the following typically shows the departments, work units, or teams within an organization?

    A. Work breakdown structure (WBS)

    B. Resource breakdown structure (RBS)

    C. Organization breakdown structure (OBS)

    D. Risk breakdown structure (RBS)

54. You are a project manager working in an organization that is considered to be a weak matrix organizational type. You are two months into a four-month project when the functional manager for half of your most critical resources announces that she will be reallocating them to another project. You explain to her that this will result in early closure of your project and that resources should not be redirected. What is the likely outcome of this scenario?

    A. Resources will be distributed to another project.

    B. Resources will not be distributed to another project.

    C. You will resign, and the project will end.

    D. The functional manager will pull the project budget.

55. What considerations should be given when applying organizational change management? (Select two.)

    A. A framework for achieving change

    B. A methodology for project change management

    C. A change control process facilitated by the Scrum Master

    D. Application of change management at the project, program, and portfolio levels

56. Project benefits can best be described as:

    A. Outcomes of actions, behaviors, products, services, or results that provide value to the sponsoring organization

    B. A document that describes how and when the benefits of the project will be delivered

    C. The intangible value to be gained by the implementation of the project

    D. The tangible value to be gained by the implementation of the project

57. You are a project manager and are meeting with your team. The goal of this meeting is to determine which compliance processes you should use to effectively manage the project. Which of the following describes what you're doing?

    A. Progressive elaboration

    B. Tailoring

    C. Phase sequencing

    D. Program management

58. Sue is the head of an enterprise PMO. She delivers a presentation at the annual company meeting to describe her roles, responsibilities, and the value of the PMO. As part of her presentation, she outlines the general responsibilities of a PMO. All of the following describe the types of support that PMOs typically provide except for which one?

    A. Establishing the company's strategic objectives and selecting projects that realize those objectives

    B. Providing an established project management methodology, including templates, forms, and standards

    C. Mentoring, coaching, and training project managers

    D. Facilitating communication within and across projects

59. Antwon is the director of marketing for a midsize company. You run into him while heating coffee in the office kitchenette and ask him what he's up to. He explains that he's in the process of evaluating project proposals to determine which best support the department and company's annual goals. In what activity is Antwon involved?

    A. Project management

    B. Program management

    C. Portfolio management

    D. Agile management

60. All of the following statements are true except for which one?

   A. Operations involves work that is continuous without an ending date.

   B. Projects are temporary but can extend over multiple years.

   C. Progressive elaboration refers to a deferral in planning.

   D. A project can evolve into ongoing operations.

61. All of the following describe a functional organizational structure except for which one?

   A. The functional manager manages the project budget.

   B. The role of project manager is part-time.

   C. A project manager has little or no authority.

   D. The role of project manager can be full-time.

62. What group is responsible for reviewing all change requests and approving or denying them?

   A. TCB

   B. CCB

   C. CRB

   D. ECB

63. Sally and Joe are two project managers working in the corporate offices of a popular fast-food franchise. They are both studying for their PMP certification, and as usual, they debate the latest topic on the agenda. Joe insists that when a project ends because of a lack of resources, this is referred to as *starvation*, whereas Sally insists that it is referred to as *integration*. Who is correct?

   A. Sally

   B. Joe

   C. Neither

   D. Both

64. What type of organization experiences the least amount of stress during project closeout?

   A. Project-oriented

   B. Functional

   C. Weak matrix

   D. Strong matrix

65. Robert is a new executive hired to lead the marketing department of a telecommunications company. He sits down with his most senior project manager to review a proposal that was created by one of his directors, pitching a new project. The proposal contains a business summary of market demand that justifies the need for the project, the expected outcomes, return on investment, and a comprehensive cost analysis. The proposal can also be described as:

   A. Business case

   B. Benefits management plan

   C. Feasibility study

   D. Project charter

66. Product owners are likely to prioritize work based on which of the following?

   A. Urgency

   B. Stakeholder needs

   C. Business value

   D. Business case

67. You work in the pharmaceutical industry, and your organization is considering building a new laboratory facility in the Northwest. Market demand is driving new research for diet medications, and the new lab would be dedicated to this product development project. Some stakeholders in your organization are not certain a new lab facility is needed because there is space that can be used in an existing building to host the diet medication research project. You've conducted a feasibility study, and the results show two possible ways to meet the space needs. Which of the following is true regarding this situation?

   A. Project selection methods are used by executive managers to determine things such as public perception, financial return, customer loyalty, and so on, and are used only to choose among alternative projects.

   B. Project selection methods are used before the Develop Project Charter process to choose among alternative ways of performing a project.

   C. Project selection methods are concerned with the type of things executive managers think about, such as public perception, financial return, customer loyalty, and market share.

   D. Project selection methods are an output of an Initiating group process that can be used to choose among alternative ways of doing a project. Project managers are generally involved with selecting among alternative projects.

68. You are working on the creation of a new television series. Your organization has created many winning series in the past. However, no other series on the air is like the series that's being proposed. The series must be ready to debut during sweeps week in November. Which of the following statements is true?

   A. This is a project, because the series is unique and it has a definite beginning and ending date.

   B. This is an ongoing operation, because the organization exists to create television series.

   C. This is an ongoing operation, because the series will be on the air for many years. It's not temporary.

   D. This is not a unique product, because the organization exists to create television series.

69. Sue is the head of an enterprise PMO. She has been given a high degree of authority within the company, and project managers report directly to the PMO. What type of PMO does Sue lead?

A. Supportive

B. Controlling

C. Directive

D. There isn't enough information in the question to determine an answer.

70. You've recently begun to suspect your friend, a fellow PMP credential holder, might be accepting gifts from hardware vendors who are bidding on an upcoming multimillion-dollar project that she's going to manage. She has a new LED flat-screen computer monitor at her desk, she showed off her new electronic tablet at a meeting two days ago, and today she unpacked a new ultra-thin laptop while you were in her office. Which of the following should you do?

A. You tell your friend these gifts probably aren't appropriate and leave it at that.

B. You and your friend have a long conversation about the items she's received, and she decides to return them and not accept any more items from vendors in the future.

C. You tell your friend you're concerned about the appearance of impropriety because of all the new things she's purchased lately, so you ask her directly whether these items were gifts from the vendor or whether she purchased them herself.

D. You know this is a conflict-of-interest situation, and it violates the *Code of Ethics and Professional Conduct.* You report your friend so that an investigation can take place.

71. A project manager has been reassigned to another project after her previous project evolved to ongoing operations. What type of project ending did she experience?

A. Addition

B. Extinction

C. Starvation

D. Integration

72. All of the following are true regarding the *Code of Ethics and Professional Conduct* except for which one?

A. It addresses responsibility, honesty, respect, and fairness.

B. It contains core values that project management practitioners are highly advised to uphold.

C. Values identified in the code stem from practitioners from the global project management community.

D. Adhering to the code is mandatory for PMI members.

73. A project manager is managing a project working to produce a fitness tracking device. Using an adaptive approach to managing the schedule, the project manager works with the team to update and prepare stories for the upcoming iteration, accounting for any recent changes that may have occurred. This is an example of:

A. Backlog refinement

B. Schedule management

C. Project management

D. Sprint planning

74. Match the type of PMO with its description.

PMO Type	Description
A. Supportive	1. Takes control of projects by directly managing them via project managers that report to the PMO
B. Controlling	2. Provides consultation to project teams by providing resources, training, and access to information
C. Directive	3. Provides support and requires compliance against published project management and governance frameworks

75. All of the following are true regarding phase gates except for which one?

A. Phase gates are also referred to as phase reviews, stage gates, or kill points.

B. A phase gate is held at the end of a phase to compare a project's performance against the plan.

C. At the end of a phase gate, a go/no-go decision is made to determine whether the project should continue.

D. Phase gates serve as audit functions that ensure regulatory compliance.

76. As part of project integration management activities, a project manager reports on value achieved to date against the plan. What does the project manager hope to accomplish by carrying out this activity?

A. Appraise stakeholders of the project's progress against the project management plan

B. Appraise stakeholders of the project's progress against the program management plan

C. Appraise stakeholders of the project's progress against the benefits management plan

D. Appraise stakeholders of the project's progress against the product backlog

77. Robert is a new executive hired to lead the marketing department of a telecommunications company. He sits down with his most senior project manager to review a project that he will now take sponsorship for. He asks the project manager to review the business value that the project is expected to deliver and how that value is to be measured. What document is the project manager likely to share with Robert?

A. The project management plan

B. The product backlog

C. The requirements traceability matrix

D. The benefits management plan

78. Quincy and Michael are two executives of Widgets for Life, a company providing the latest cool lifestyle gadgets. They've learned that a new federal law will be passed that regulates how personal data may be collected and used. Many of Widgets for Life's gadgets collect data, which has been made possible by advancements in technology. As a result, they decide to launch a new project that will address the requirements of the new law. This project came about as a result of what need?

A. Federal request

B. Legal requirement

C. Technological advance

D. Organizational need

79. Who is chartered with the authority to approve or deny change requests as defined by the organization?

A. Project manager

B. Project sponsor

C. Change control board

D. Executive team

80. One of your team members, a fellow PMP credential holder, is under investigation for violation of the *Code of Ethics and Professional Conduct*. What action should you take?

A. Cooperate fully with the investigation.

B. Tell the PMI investigator it would be a conflict of interest for you to cooperate in the investigation because this person is your team member.

C. Tell the PMI investigator it would be a conflict of interest for you to cooperate because they might uncover information about you during the investigation that could cause them to investigate you.

D. Cooperate with the PMI investigator by truthfully answering all their questions, but refuse to give them any written documentation.

81. You are a project manager working on contract. As your project comes to a close, your contract completes, and you find yourself out of work. What type of organizational structure did you work in?

A. Strong matrix

B. Project-oriented

C. Functional

D. Weak matrix

82. Cindy is practicing servant leadership. As the project manager, she gathers her team together to prepare them for the upcoming project. In explaining the benefits of business value, what points is she likely to stress?

A. Prioritization

B. Accountability

C. Improved quality

D. Predictability

E. A, B, C

F. A, B, C, D

83. The *Code of Ethics and Professional Conduct* applies to all of the following groups of individuals, except for which one?

A. Those holding PMI certification

B. All PMI members

C. Those volunteering through PMI

D. Project team members

84. As a value upheld by the project management community, responsibility entails which of the following?

A. Ensuring integrity

B. Maintaining professional demeanor

C. Reporting ethics violations

D. Avoiding conflict of interest

85. Which of the following influences the use of Agile approaches?

A. Knowledge of project management methodologies

B. Organization's culture

C. Existence of a PMO

D. Maturity of an organization

86. Roshoud is the VP of customer operations for Galactic Kidz and project sponsor of the latest project, called Project G. He sits down with Sally, the project manager, to evaluate whether the project is on track to deliver planned value. What document are they likely to reference during the discussion?

A. Product backlog

B. Project charter

C. Business case

D. Benefits management plan

87. Quincy and Michael are two executives of Widgets for Life, a company providing the latest cool lifestyle gadgets. They have recently decided to invest further in their organization's project management capabilities by creating a PMO. After lengthy discussions, they decide to focus on a PMO model that will drive compliance against a set of project management standards. What type of PMO are they implementing?

A. Supportive

B. Controlling

C. Directive

D. Agile

88. Kaylee is a project manager for a company that builds software for mobile devices. One of her projects involves the development of a health app that syncs with other health apps to combine and analyze the data for a comprehensive view. Most recently, she completed a review of the project's prioritized backlog with the project team to prepare for the upcoming iteration. She learns that a new regulation passed by the government may impact several features of this app. What is she likely to do?

A. Assess the impact of the new regulation on the project's scope and update the project scope statement.

B. Nothing. The project's backlog has already been prioritized.

C. Remove the features to avoid the risk of noncompliance against the new regulation passed and reprioritize the backlog.

D. Assess the impact of the new regulation on the project's scope and update the backlog to reflect the necessary changes.

89. Kaylee is a project manager for a company that builds software for mobile devices. One of her projects involves the development of a health app that syncs with other health apps to combine and analyze the data for a comprehensive view. As a result of a recent regulatory change, she works with the team to refine the backlog. Backlog refinement can best be described as:

A. Work items identified by the Scrum team to be completed during the Scrum sprint

B. A board used to manage the product and sprint backlogs

C. An ordered list of user-centric requirements that a team maintains for a product

D. The progressive elaboration of project requirements to satisfy the need of the customer request

90. Carina is a principal project manager of You've Got Dogs, a specialty company that creates custom dog apparel and toys. She has just concluded the Design phase and is scheduled to perform a phase review with the steering committee facilitated by the company's PMO. Phase reviews are also called by what other name?

A. Kill point

B. End point

C. PMO review

D. Project review

91. You are a project manager and are meeting with your team. The goal of this meeting is to determine which processes you should use to effectively manage the project. Which of the following describes what you're doing?

   A. Progressive elaboration

   B. Tailoring

   C. Phase sequencing

   D. Program management

92. A project manager is managing a project that contains a high degree of ambiguity. The project team is expected to adapt to changes as the scope of work becomes clearer over time. To better set expectations with the team, what is the project manager likely to communicate regarding the use of an iterative approach to managing the project life cycle?

   A. The work will experience short feedback loops with reprioritization of the backlog over iterations.

   B. The work will be progressively elaborated, with feedback loops inserted quarterly.

   C. Features will be prioritized up front, and the decomposition of the work will be progressively elaborated.

   D. The team will take work from the backlog bottom up to account for ongoing reprioritization of the work.

93. Projects may come about as a result of which of the following?

   A. Ideas

   B. Methods to exceed stakeholder expectations

   C. Motivated employees

   D. Needs and demands

94. As part of performing administrative closure activities, a project manager creates false responses to a stakeholder satisfaction survey. He reasons that he has received highly positive feedback throughout the entire project and didn't want to be a bother to his stakeholders after they worked so hard to successfully finish the project. The project manager's actions violated which core value addressed within the *Code of Ethics and Professional Conduct*?

   A. Respect

   B. Honor

   C. Honesty

   D. Integrity

95. Which of the following best describes honesty as a value that project management practitioners should abide by?

   A. Our duty to take ownership for the decisions we make or fail to make, the actions we take or fail to take, and the consequences that result

   B. Our duty to make decisions and act impartially and objectively

   C. Our duty to show a high regard for ourselves, others, and the resources entrusted to us

   D. Our duty to understand the truth and act in a truthful manner both in our communications and in our conduct

96. Match the term with its description.

Term	Description
A. Organizational process assets	1. Plans, processes, policies, procedures, and knowledge bases that are specific to and used by the performing organization
B. Enterprise environmental factors	2. Conditions, not under the immediate control of the team, that influence, constrain, or direct the project, program, or portfolio

97. A project manager is in the process of measuring the extent to which the project is compliant with regulatory standards by conducting an audit. What activity are they performing?

A. Quality assurance

B. Change management

C. Retrospective

D. Quality review

98. Which of the following is a valid tool or technique that aids the project manager, or other assigned organizational resource, in developing the project charter?

A. Brainstorming

B. Business case

C. Enterprise environmental factors

D. Organizational process assets

99. Robert is a new executive hired to lead the marketing department of a telecommunications company. He recently met with his project management team to review the project portfolio. Next, he sets his sights on better understanding the governance framework in place. Governance is considered to be which of the following?

A. Organizational process assets

B. Project management methodology

C. Enterprise environmental factors

D. Agile Manifesto

100. When joining a new organization, what must a new project manager do to be effective?

A. Brush up on project management skills

B. Get to know the team

C. Assess the organization's culture

D. Research the executive team

Chapter

4

Full-Length Practice Exam 1

The process names, inputs, tools and techniques, outputs, and descriptions of the project management process groups and related materials and figures in this chapter are based on content from *A Guide to the Project Management Body of Knowledge (PMBOK® Guide) – Sixth Edition* (PMI®, 2017).

1. Nicolas is the project manager of a project that has been described as revolutionizing the mobile fitness tracking industry. After a few preliminary strategy sessions, he pulls together the core team and notes that they will be defining deliverables early in the development life cycle and progressively elaborating them as the project progresses. What development life cycle is Nicolas following on the project?

   A. Predictive

   B. Iterative

   C. Incremental

   D. Hybrid

2. A project manager is providing guidance to the project team on the steps required to generate the work breakdown structure (WBS). She lists the following: 1) identify the deliverables and work, 2) organize the WBS, 3) decompose the WBS components into lower-level components, and 4) assign identification codes. What is the fifth step?

   A. Identifying and assigning codes to control accounts

   B. Decomposing the work packages into activities

   C. Determining cost estimates at the planning package level

   D. Verifying the degree of decomposition

3. Match the project manager's level of authority based on the organizational structure type.

Organizational Structure Type	Authority
A. Functional	1. High to almost total
B. Strong matrix	2. Low
C. Project-oriented	3. Little to none
D. Weak matrix	4. Moderate to high

4. Quincy and Michael are two executives of Widgets for Life, a company providing the latest cool lifestyle gadgets. They have recently selected the next big project and have assigned you as the project manager. This activity is associated with what process group?

   A. Initiating

   B. Planning

   C. Executing

   D. Monitoring and Controlling

5. The project processes are iterative, are results oriented, and interact with each other. Shewhart and Deming developed a concept that reflects this idea. Which of the following is the name of this cycle?

   A. Plan-Do-Check-Act

   B. Initiate-Requirements-Execute-Close

    C. Select-Plan-Monitor-Act

    D. Strategize-Justify-Choose-Execute-Control

6. Your customer has requested a specific color for the product your project is producing. This is an example of which of the following?

    A. Requirement

    B. Deliverable

    C. Product description

    D. Project description

7. Which of the following motivational theories states that the expectation of a positive outcome drives motivation?

    A. Expectancy Theory

    B. Achievement Theory

    C. Hygiene Theory

    D. Maslow's Hierarchy of Needs

8. Leticia is a project manager working for Dancing Apron, a company that combines cooking with simple children's cooking recipes and music. Her latest project involves the release of the company's first digital product that parents will be able to purchase and download online. While overseeing the project, Leticia notices that recent stakeholder engagement levels have dropped significantly, and they've begun to disagree during status meetings. What key input can she use to help her deal with the situation?

    A. Project management plan

    B. Work performance data

    C. Interpersonal and team skills

    D. Decision-making

9. Albert recently joined a rapidly growing technology startup company as a project manager. The approach to managing projects is different from the compliance-driven projects he is accustomed to managing in the past. He inherits a project that contains a great deal of uncertainty, with minimal requirements identified to date. To remedy this, he gathers the team and informs them that they will focus on nailing down the requirements before execution of work can continue. He is met with a high degree of resistance. What is the likely reason for this pushback from the team?

    A. They do not understand the value of defining good requirements.

    B. They do not know Albert and do not yet respect his authority and leadership.

    C. They are accustomed to using a predictive approach to managing projects.

    D. They are accustomed to using an adaptive approach to managing projects.

10. A product manager meets with the team to apprise them of changes to how the upcoming project will be managed. She notes that the focus will now shift to producing deliverables through iterations and that iterative scheduling with a backlog will be used to account for the uncertainty in requirements. What is the value of this approach?

   A. It keeps team members engaged.

   B. It is reliable and predictable.

   C. It delivers value incrementally.

   D. It allows for a reduction in planning.

11. The project manager facilitates the implementation of approved changes by following the documented change control process. Which of the following is a valid tool or technique to assist the project manager in performing this activity?

   A. Change log

   B. Project management information system

   C. Work performance data

   D. Approved change requests

12. Legitimate, expert, referent, and punishment are all types of what?

   A. Interpersonal and team skills

   B. Communication skills

   C. Conflict resolution

   D. Power

13. Ken is a product owner for a new product and is integrating smart technology into refrigerators. The latest project aimed to incorporate new features into the product. These features involved the use of facial technology to recognize members of the household as they walked by, displaying tailored recommendations on a panel within the refrigerator, such as favorite recipes or encouraging comments. Recently, Ken received the news that a competitor beat his company to market, and a window was missed. The project was cancelled. The competitor had recently showcased its technology in a key annual appliance conference, but Ken was not able to attend. What did Ken fail to do?

   A. Attend important events that impacted his product.

   B. Survey changes to the business environment that would affect his product.

   C. Incorporate a prototype into the project so that he may have demonstrated the product at the same convention.

   D. Ken did nothing wrong, and the project's cancellation is a product of circumstance.

14. A project manager is preparing to lead a project status meeting. The project is currently 75 percent complete and is reaching the most critical point. Since the project sponsor is planning on attending the meeting, the project manager decides to update the earned value calculations to present the latest performance updates in terms that the sponsor will want to see. The budget at completion (BAC) is set at $550,000, and the current estimate

at completion (EAC) is at $525,000. What variance at completion (VAC) value will the project manager communicate to the sponsor?

A. 0.10

B. 0.95

C. −25,000

D. 25,000

15. You are the project manager for the Heart of Texas casual clothing company. It's introducing a new line of clothing called Black Sheep Ranch Wear. You will outsource the production of this clothing line to a vendor. Your legal department has recommended you use a contract that reimburses the seller's allowable costs and includes a fixed fee upon completion of the contract. Which of the following contract types will you use?

A. CPIF

B. CPFF

C. CPF

D. FPIF

16. You are a project manager for Fly Me to Miami travel services. You are in the process of documenting and distributing project information. You know all of the following statements are true regarding information exchange except for which one?

A. Encoding the information involves putting it in a format the listener will understand.

B. The receiver is responsible for understanding the information correctly.

C. Receivers, not senders, filter the information through their knowledge of the subject, cultural influences, language, emotions, attitudes, and geographic location.

D. The message is the actual information being sent and received.

17. Your project selection committee is considering four projects. Project A's NPV is positive, it has an IRR of 14 percent, and the payback period is 21 months. Project B's NPV is negative, it has an IRR of 9 percent, and the payback period is 16 months. Project C's NPV is positive, it has an IRR of 16 percent, and the payback period is 18 months. Project D's NPV is negative, it has an IRR of 16 percent, and the payback period is 13 months. Which project should you choose?

A. Project A

B. Project B

C. Project C

D. Project D

18. Which of the following best describes the focus of Agile teams?

A. To deliver frequently

B. To reduce waste in planning

C. To operate using small, focused teams

D. To deliver business value often

19. Roshoud is the VP of customer operations for Galactic Kidz and project sponsor of the latest project, called Project G. He sits down with Sally, the project manager, to discuss the current budget estimate. Roshoud expresses his concerns to Sally about the budget being far greater than originally anticipated and asks her to course-correct. What produces the greatest expense on most projects?

   A. Vendors

   B. Resources

   C. Materials

   D. Travel

20. Analogous estimating is also known as what?

   A. Three-point estimating

   B. Bottom-up estimating

   C. Parametric estimating

   D. Top-down estimating

21. Which project management document provides the project manager with the authority to apply organizational resources to project activities?

   A. Project management plan

   B. Resource management plan

   C. Project charter

   D. Business case

22. Which of the following shows quality management issues escalated by the team, as well as recommendations for process, project, and product improvements?

   A. Quality management plan

   B. Quality control measurements

   C. Test and evaluation documents

   D. Quality reports

23. The project manager has just determined that three functional managers with a high interest in the project hold a particularly high degree of influence in the allocation of enterprise resources. Where is the project manager likely to document this information?

   A. Stakeholder analysis

   B. Resource management plan

   C. Stakeholder engagement plan

   D. Stakeholder register

24. Which of the following represents characteristics of the Planning process group?

   A. Costs are high.

   B. Staffing is lowest.

C. Chance for successful project completion is medium.

D. Stakeholder influence is high.

25. Your selection committee can choose only one of the following projects: Project A's original investment is $1 million, the present value of the cash inflows is $1 million, and the discount rate is 4 percent. Project B's original investment is $1.4 million, the present value of the cash inflows is $1.4 million, and the discount rate is 6 percent. Project C's original investment is $1.8 million, the present value of the cash inflows is $1.8 million, and the discount rate is 7 percent. Which project should the committee choose?

A. Project C

B. Project B

C. Project A

D. There isn't enough information in the question to determine an answer.

26. A project manager is likely to leverage the following techniques to manage stakeholder engagement except for which one?

A. Decision-making

B. Expert judgment

C. Ground rules

D. Meetings

27. Which of the following reflect principles listed in the Agile Manifesto? (Select three.)

A. The best architectures, requirements, and designs emerge from teams that are directed by strong leaders.

B. Working software is the primary measure of progress.

C. Our highest priority is to satisfy the customer through early and continuous delivery of valuable software.

D. Simplicity—the art of maximizing the amount of work not done—is essential.

28. You're a project manager for Music On Demand, and you're in the Monitor Risks process. Your project, when completed, will provide a way for owners of smartphones to purchase music on demand from the recording company you work for and download it directly to their devices. You are monitoring the risks on the project and have analyzed elements such as the risk audits, preventive actions, and corrective actions. This information might be reported in which of the following outputs of this process?

A. Work performance reports

B. Work performance information

C. Work performance data

D. Project document updates

29. Which of the following statements is true? (Select two.)

   A. A team that uses an Agile approach is more likely to produce greater business value.

   B. A team that uses a Predictive approach is more likely to produce greater business value.

   C. The goal of project management is to produce business value in the best way possible.

   D. An organization should choose the delivery method that best produces business value.

30. A project manager meets with a key set of experts within her project team. They express concerns over a recent scope change that was submitted by the customer, since the project is deep into the execution stages of the project life cycle. Which of the following is a valid technique that can aid the project manager in addressing the team's concerns?

   A. Decision-making

   B. Data analysis

   C. Meetings

   D. Change control tools

31. Several processes in the Monitoring and Controlling process group involve change requests. Which of the following is not true?

   A. Approved change requests are an input to the Control Procurements and Control Quality processes.

   B. Approved change requests are an output of the Perform Integrated Change Control and Monitor Risks processes.

   C. Inspection is a tool and technique of Control Quality.

   D. Changes are verified as part of the Control Scope process.

32. You are a project manager and are in the stage of the project where you are juggling a lot of activities at the same time. You are negotiating for resources, negotiating procurements, and monitoring risks and risk triggers. An approved change request has come your way and must be processed back through this process. This approved change will expand your project scope. You daydream of escaping the day-to-day work life and for a brief moment wonder whether you could contract this additional work through your spouse's company and take the money and run. But then the daydream bubble bursts and it's back to reality. What process does this describe, and what area within the *PMI Code of Ethics and Professional Conduct* pertains to this situation?

   A. Conduct Procurements and ensuring integrity

   B. Direct and Manage Project Work and accepting assignments

   C. Conduct Procurements and intellectual property

   D. Direct and Manage Project Work and conflict of interest

33. One of your project's deliverables requires skills in business analysis. You have three resources working on the activities that need to be completed for this deliverable. Jim and John are making more in salary than Mary is. Jim tends to spend a large majority of his time on social networking sites, John is motivated by accomplishment and capability, and Mary is looking for a sense of belonging as part of the team. Which of the following statements is true?

A. Your resources are at various levels of Maslow's Hierarchy of Needs.

B. McClelland contends that salary is a self-esteem need.

C. The Expectancy Theory says that salary isn't a motivator regardless of pay discrepancies.

D. The Achievement Theory contends that salary is tied to achievement, so large disparities in salary become a demotivator.

34. A project manager has facilitated the decomposition of work packages into activities. She next carries the team through several exercises to sequence the activities and determine what and how many resources will be needed to perform the work. What is she likely to do next?

A. Estimate how long each activity will take

B. Develop the schedule

C. Run various what-if scenarios against the schedule

D. Break down the activities into deliverables

35. During this contract life-cycle phase, the vendors are asked to compete for the contract and respond to the RFP. What contract life-cycle phase is this?

A. Requirement

B. Solicitation

C. Requisition

D. Award

36. Which of the following reflect key values listed in the Agile Manifesto? (Select all that apply.)

A. Individuals and interactions over processes and tools

B. Customer collaboration over contract negotiation

C. Responding to change over following a plan

D. Evolving software over comprehensive documentation

37. Each of the following is an example of an information management system except for which one?

A. Email

B. Electronic files

C. Voicemail

D. Websites

38. You are in the Planning stage of the project and have just begun to generate the cost baseline. In what activity are you engaged as a project manager?

   A. Performing the Plan Cost Management process

   B. Performing the Estimate Costs process

   C. Performing the Determine Budget process

   D. Performing the Control Costs process

39. The project phases together constitute which of the following?

   A. Project phases

   B. Project management plan

   C. Project life cycle

   D. Project management

40. A product owner is working on a new product that is intended to hit the Australian market in six months, just in time for the start of the holiday season. She plans for just enough features to get the product to market. The intent is to attract early adopters and gain feedback for a larger release in China the following year. The release in Australia can best be described as:

   A. A prototype

   B. The minimum viable product

   C. A preview

   D. Early market adoption

41. Which of the following reflect ideal characteristics of Agile teams? (Select three.)

   A. Dedicated 100 percent to project

   B. Colocated

   C. Range in size from three to nine team members

   D. Facilitate daily status meetings

42. The project manager is in the process of bringing the relevant parties together, along with a neutral party, to discuss a contested change to a procurement agreement. Which of the following is a valid tool or technique to assist the project manager in performing this activity?

   A. Claims administration

   B. Change control system

   C. Audit

   D. Inspection

43. While performing activities associated with controlling project and product scope, a project manager uncovers scope creep. What is the project manager likely to do next to take corrective action?

   A. Scold the individual(s) responsible

   B. Update the scope baseline

C. Submit a change request and analyze the impact

D. Notify the project team

44. You are a project manager for Rhone Valley Importers. Your buyer has found a new product that she's convinced will sell well in this country. Taking on this new product introduces considerable opportunity for the company but at the same time is also a considerable threat. The cost of this product exceeds anything your company has imported before, and if it doesn't sell as well as the buyer thinks it will, the company could go into bankruptcy. You determine that a feasibility study is in order. Which of the following statements is not true?

   A. A feasibility study should be conducted to determine the potential market, costs, risks, and other factors.

   B. One purpose of the feasibility study is to determine marketing demand for the new product that could in turn become the demand that drives the project.

   C. During the feasibility study, you could use the Project Risk Management processes to identify all opportunities and exploit their possibilities, determine the potential threats, and minimize the probability and consequences of those threats.

   D. One of the end results of the feasibility study might be to produce a project charter that will include a description of the intended outcome of the project, a budget, and a detailed project schedule for management review.

45. Kaylee is a risk manager working for a top healthcare company. She was recently brought in to support a project that has been plagued with a multitude of issues. The project sponsor informs her that the issues were a result of not implementing documented risk response plans. Kaylee clarifies to the sponsor that this is not the root cause of the issues at hand but is instead caused by the most common problem with project risk management. What problem is Kaylee referring to?

   A. Risks are not fully analyzed, and therefore, the risk responses are not effective.

   B. A full-time risk manager is often not allocated to a project, causing poor risk management to occur.

   C. Project teams spend effort in identifying, analyzing, and developing responses for risks but do not manage them.

   D. Risk triggers are not clearly documented in the risk register, causing the response plans to be ineffective.

46. Alyssa is a project manager tasked with managing an infrastructure project that will consolidate five data centers into one. Alyssa is in the process of determining whether communications-related artifacts and activities that she had planned earlier had the intended effect. She also recently launched a customer satisfaction survey to get feedback on how stakeholders feel things are progressing thus far within the project. What project management process is she performing?

   A. Manage Communications

   B. Monitor Communications

   C. Plan Communications Management

   D. Monitor and Control Project Work

47. An Agile project team builds their schedule by pulling features from the backlog reflected on a task board as capacity to take on work becomes available. In some cases, a feature may take two weeks to complete, while in others, it takes more. What type of delivery method does this describe?

    A. Waterfall

    B. Iteration-based Agile

    C. Scrum

    D. Flow-based Agile

48. Rianna is a developer who is interested in moving toward a career in project management. She takes on a small project that will implement a new security feature to protect her company's internal network. To date, she has baselined the project's scope, schedule, and budget, and she is now actively helping to resolve issues as they arise. What process is she currently performing?

    A. Plan Resource Management

    B. Develop Team

    C. Manage Team

    D. Control Resources

49. The project management plan might require changes and updates as the Planning processes proceed. These updates are decided upon and managed through which of the following?

    A. Approved change requests

    B. Perform Integrated Change Control process

    C. Control Communications process

    D. Control Scope process

50. All of the following are true regarding project life cycles except for which one?

    A. In the beginning of the project life cycle, costs are low, and few team members are assigned to the project.

    B. Toward the end of the project, stakeholders have the greatest chance of influencing a project.

    C. Risk is highest at the beginning of the project and gradually decreases over the project's life cycle.

    D. The potential of a project ending successfully is lowest at the beginning and increases as the project progresses through its life cycle.

51. A project manager has just facilitated the project change control process, which yielded 10 approved change requests. What process is he likely to perform next?

    A. Direct and Manage Project Work

    B. Perform Integrated Change Control

    C. Manage Project Knowledge

    D. Develop Project Management Plan

52. Roshoud is the VP of customer operations for Galactic Kidz and project sponsor of the latest project, called Project G. He sits down with Sally, the project manager, to discuss and document roles and responsibilities. What Knowledge Area are they engaged in?

A. Project Integration Management

B. Project Procurement Management

C. Project Resource Management

D. Project Stakeholder Management

53. Quincy and Michael are two executives of Widgets for Life, a company providing the latest cool lifestyle gadgets. They have recently selected the next big project and have assigned you as the project manager. This activity is associated with what process group?

A. Initiating

B. Planning

C. Executing

D. Monitoring and Controlling

54. Your project sponsor has asked you for a forecast of the likely cost to complete the work of the project. Which of the following statements is true?

A. You'll use the ETC calculation, which is part of the forecasting tool and technique of the Control Costs process.

B. You'll use the EAC calculation, which is part of the forecasting tool and technique of the Control Costs process.

C. You'll use the ETC calculation, which is part of the EVM tool and technique of the Control Costs process.

D. You'll use the EAC calculation, which is part of the EVM tool and technique of the Control Costs process.

55. As uncertainty and complexity increase in projects, so does which of the following?

A. The need for planning

B. The likelihood of re-planning

C. The likelihood of change

D. The need for longer iterations

56. Which of the following types of contract should a project manager choose when using a hybrid approach to manage the project?

A. Multitiered

B. Graduated time and materials

C. Master service agreement

D. Dynamic scope

E. Value driven

57. Who is responsible for determining which processes within each process group are appropriate for the project?

   A. The project manager

   B. The project team

   C. The project manager and project sponsor

   D. The project manager and project team

58. An assumption can best be described as which of the following?

   A. Actions that restrict or dictate the actions of the project team

   B. Factors expected to be in place or to be in evidence

   C. An uncertain event or condition that, if it occurs, has a positive or negative effect on one or more of the project's objectives

   D. An immediate and temporary response to an issue

59. Kaylee is a senior project manager for a fitness company that is developing a new franchise model. She has just led the team through various workshops to capture requirements. What activity is she likely to perform next?

   A. Publish the requirements management plan

   B. Define the scope of the project

   C. Develop the work breakdown structure

   D. Measure the completion of the requirements

60. You work for Star Bank as a project manager. Your project is so large and risky that you're not certain the organization should undertake it. You propose conducting a feasibility study, as its own project, to examine the benefits of the new proposed project. The feasibility study is approved and begun. Which of the following statements is not true regarding this project?

   A. The Initiating processes occur at the beginning of the project, when chances for a successful completion are high and the staffing levels are low.

   B. The Initiating processes acknowledge that the next project phase should begin. Costs are low in this process, while the risks are high.

   C. The Initiating processes is where approval is granted to undertake the project and the organization's resources are authorized to begin work.

   D. The Initiating processes acknowledge that the next project phase should begin. The stakeholders have the most influence over the product or service of the project during this process.

61. Match the term with its corresponding description.

Term	Description
A. Burnup chart	1. The total time it takes to deliver an item, measured from the time the work is committed to the time it is completed
B. Lead time	2. The time required to process a work item
C. Velocity	3. A measurement of the schedule efficiency expressed as a ratio of earned to planned value
D. Cycle time	4. A visual depiction of the work completed
E. Schedule performance index	5. The sum of story point sizes for the features completed in an iteration

62. According to the *PMBOK® Guide*, all of the following mean the same as *contract* except which one?

A. Purchase order

B. Memorandum of understanding

C. Agreement

D. Procurement order

63. Rachel is a project sponsor of a project that is developing a new innovative line of screen doors meant to attract budget-minded consumers. Most project managers cringe when assigned to a project sponsored by Rachel since she tends to hover for the details and be suspicious of every team member's behavior, causing a flurry of issues for the project manager to resolve. According to Douglas McGregor's leadership theory, what type of manager is Rachel?

A. Theory Y

B. Theory Z

C. Theory X

D. Theory Y/Z

64. Raw observations and measurements identified while carrying out activities associated with the project work describe what?

A. Work performance information

B. Work performance data

C. Work performance reports

D. Work performance analysis

65. You work for Sergio's, a golf equipment manufacturer. Your organization is installing some new manufacturing equipment, and you are managing the project. Some risk events have come to fruition on the project, and as a result, change requests have been submitted. You are in the Monitor Risks process and know that all of the following are true regarding this question except for which one?

   A. Change requests may take the form of corrective actions in the Monitor Risks process, which is part of the Monitoring and Controlling process group.

   B. Change requests will not take the form of preventive actions because you are in the Monitoring and Controlling process group and too far into the work of the project.

   C. Change requests must be processed through the Perform Integrated Change Control process, which is also in the Monitoring and Controlling process group.

   D. Change requests may take the form of workarounds in the Control Risks process, which is part of the Monitoring and Controlling process group.

66. Match the PMO type with its corresponding description.

PMO Type	Description
A. Supportive	1. Serves in a management role. Assigns project managers to projects and directly manages projects
B. Controlling	2. Serves in a consultative role. Provides templates, best practices, training, and lessons learned from other projects
C. Directive	3. Serves in a supportive and compliance role. Provides project management and governance frameworks that are followed by PMs

67. The project manager has just determined that three functional managers with a high interest in the project hold a particularly high degree of influence in the allocation of enterprise resources. In what activity is the project manager involved?

   A. Developing the resource plan

   B. Developing the stakeholder engagement plan

   C. Determining team assignments

   D. Identifying stakeholders

68. Carina is a principal project manager of You've Got Dogs, a specialty company that creates custom dog apparel and toys. She has just concluded the Design phase and is scheduled to perform a phase review with the steering committee facilitated by the company's PMO. Phase reviews are also called by what other name?

   A. Kill point

   B. Endpoint

   C. PMO review

   D. Project review

69. The project team recently participated in a working session to examine and document the effectiveness of risk responses in dealing with overall project risk. What project management process are they performing?

   A. Identify Risks

   B. Plan Risk Responses

   C. Implement Risk Responses

   D. Monitor Risks

70. A project sponsor asks the project manager to observe nonverbal feedback in the upcoming status meeting and adjust his presentation based on these observations. Which process is associated with these activities?

   A. Plan Communications Management

   B. Manage Communications

   C. Monitor Communications

   D. Control Communications

71. The difference between project deliverables and project requirements is best described in which of the following options?

   A. Deliverables are specific items that must be produced for the project or project phase to be considered complete. Each project phase has only one deliverable, which might have multiple requirements.

   B. Requirements are measurable items that must be produced for the project or project phase to be considered complete. Each project phase might have multiple deliverables with multiple requirements.

   C. Requirements are measurable items that must be produced for the project or project phase to be considered complete; deliverables are the specifications used to tell you what you are trying to produce.

   D. Deliverables are specific items that must be produced for the project or project phase to be considered complete; requirements are the specifications of the deliverables used to tell you whether the deliverables were produced successfully.

72. You are in the process of attaining and assigning resources to the project. You have both internal and external resources. You will be hiring your external resources using a work order against a contract you have with a local staffing agency. All of the following are true except for which one?

   A. The project manager is responsible for assuring the resources are skilled and available for the project and for documenting their reporting responsibilities. This is accomplished in this process and in the Plan Resource Management process.

   B. The project manager might not have the ability to hire or select all of the project team members.

   C. The team members coming from the consulting company are accounted for in the Plan Procurement Management process and Plan Resource Management process, not this process.

   D. Checking for availability and considering personal interests and characteristics are an important part of this process.

73. A project manager has been asked to calculate the payback period for her project. The project's investment is $500,000, with expected cash inflow of $50,000 for the first two quarters and $100,000 for every quarter thereafter. What is the payback period?

A. 6 months

B. 12 months

C. 18 months

D. 24 months

74. Robert is a practicing project manager who is studying for his PMP® exam. During a study session with a colleague, he insists that it is important for project managers to consider all 49 project management processes, while his colleague insists that it is not necessary and that project managers should carry out only the necessary processes. Who is correct?

A. Robert

B. Robert's colleague

C. Both

D. Neither

75. You have a very energetic project team. They are motivated by results, have good conflict-resolution skills, and are highly committed to the project, among other things. They have a solid understanding of the project goals and objectives and understand the direction the project is headed in. Which of the following does this describe?

A. The norming stage of team formation

B. The characteristics of an effective team

C. The transactional-style leadership the project manager employs

D. The Expectancy Theory

76. Nicolas is the project manager of a project that has been described as revolutionizing the mobile fitness tracking industry. He prepares for a meeting with the project's sponsor to discuss the performance of their largest vendor. What information will Nicolas need to reference to provide this information?

A. Data analysis

B. Project management plan

C. Agreement

D. Procurement documentation

77. Roshoud is the VP of customer operations for Galactic Kidz and the project sponsor of the latest project, called Project G. He sits down with Sally, the project manager, to discuss resource utilization on the project. He expresses concern after recently hearing in the hallway that planned resources have been unavailable. Sally admits that this has been the case and that it has set the project back unexpectedly. What did Sally fail to do in this scenario?

A. Properly plan the schedule

B. Keep the sponsor informed

C. Procure the right resources

D. Build the right relationships

78. The elements of communication are incorporated within the models of communication exchange. They are best explained as which of the following?

A. The elements of communication include encode, transmit, acknowledge, and feedback/response, and the communication model includes senders, receivers, and messages.

B. The elements of communication include senders, receivers, and messages and the communication model includes verbal and written.

C. The elements of communication include senders, receivers, and messages and the communication model includes encode, transmit, acknowledge, and feedback/response.

D. The elements of communication include encode, transmit, acknowledge, and feedback/response, and the communication model includes verbal and written.

79. The project manager has just determined that three functional managers with a high interest in the project hold a particularly high degree of influence in the allocation of enterprise resources. Armed with this new information, she updates her salience model and considers how it impacts the project. In what activity is the project manager engaged?

A. Stakeholder analysis

B. Resource analysis

C. Stakeholder engagement

D. Stakeholder monitoring

80. You are a project manager working on a project involving a new scientific discovery in conjunction with your local university. Because of some changes that were approved during the Monitoring and Controlling processes, you discover that the descriptions of the deliverables that make up the final product of the project are no longer accurate or complete. Which of the following will you use to track the changes to the deliverables and ensure their descriptions are accurate and complete, and what process is this associated with?

A. Scope change control system in Control Scope

B. Quality control system in Control Quality

C. Configuration management system in Perform Integrated Change Control

D. Change control system in Monitor Communications

81. You have received proposals in response to your recent RFP. The following types of information were used by your evaluation team to rate the vendors: availability, experience, and training. Experience was given the most weight, 5. Availability was assigned a weight of 3, and training was assigned a weight of 2. Vendor A scored the following: availability as 4, experience as 2, and training as 2. Vendor B scored the following: availability as 3, experience as 4, and training as 4. Which vendor won the bid, and what was the final score?

   A. Vendor B, final score 21

   B. Vendor B, final score 37

   C. Vendor A, final score 21

   D. Vendor B, final score 43

82. A project manager is preparing to obtain the resources needed to perform the work of the project. What project document is the project manager likely to reference as a guide to both acquiring and managing the project resources?

   A. Project management plan

   B. Resource management plan

   C. Staffing management plan

   D. Resource requirements

83. Which process is concerned with effectively engaging stakeholders, understanding their needs and interests, understanding the good and bad things they bring to the project, and understanding how the project will affect them?

   A. Control Stakeholder Engagement

   B. Plan Stakeholder Engagement

   C. Identify Stakeholders

   D. Manage Stakeholder Engagement

84. Your customer has decided that you cannot go forward with the project you're managing without a change to the agreed-upon WBS. A contract amendment is agreed on and signed, the change control system processes are followed, and you modify the appropriate planning documents to reflect the change. As a result of the approved change, substantial updates to the project costs and the project schedule occur as well. Which of the following is not true regarding this situation?

   A. Baselines must be adjusted to reflect the new project costs and schedule.

   B. The PMB includes management reserves and contingencies.

   C. The PMB is determined using EVM.

   D. The schedule, scope, and cost baseline together make up the PMB.

85. Plan Schedule Management, Estimate Activity Durations, and Control Schedule are processes that belong to what project management Knowledge Area?

   A. Project Time Management

   B. Project Integration Management

   C. Project Schedule Management

   D. Project Resource Management

86. Alyssa is a project manager tasked with managing an infrastructure project that will consolidate five data centers into one. She pulls together a core set of experts who have worked on similar projects to discuss how scope should be managed. What tool or technique is Alyssa using?

   A. Data analysis

   B. Expert judgment

   C. Alternatives analysis

   D. Organizational process assets

87. You have used several cash flow methods to determine alternative ways of performing your current project. Which of the following do you know is true regarding the results of your cash flow analysis?

   A. Payback period and IRR will generally give you the same accept/reject decision.

   B. NPV and discounted cash flows will generally give you the same accept/reject decision.

   C. Payback period and discounted cash flows will generally give you the same accept/reject decision.

   D. NPV and IRR will generally give you the same accept/reject decision.

88. The project sponsor has approached you with a dilemma. The CEO announced at the annual stockholders' meeting that the project you're managing will be completed by the end of this year. The problem is that this is six months prior to the scheduled completion date. It's too late to go back and correct her mistake, and stockholders are expecting implementation by the announced date. You must speed up the delivery date of this project. Your primary constraint before this occurred was the budget. What actions can you take to help speed up the project?

   A. Hire more resources to get the work completed faster.

   B. Ask for more money so that you can contract out one of the phases you had planned to do with in-house resources.

   C. Utilize negotiation and influencing skills to convince the project sponsor to speak with the CEO and make a correction to her announcement.

   D. Examine the project plan to see whether there are any phases that can be fast-tracked and then revise the project plan to reflect the compression of the schedule.

89. You are the project manager for a project that will produce a mobile phone application that sends alerts when the UV rays are at dangerous levels, alerting users to stay indoors. You are in the process of acquiring resources to staff the project and obtaining responses from bidders on work that is being outsourced. These activities are associated with what process group?

   A. Planning

   B. Executing

   C. Monitoring and Controlling

   D. Closing

90. You are a project manager for an engineering company. Your company won the bid to add ramp-metering lights to several on-ramps along a stretch of highway at the south end of the city. You subcontracted a portion of the project to another company. The subcontractor's work involves digging the holes and setting the lamp poles in concrete. You discover the end product does not meet safety standards, corrective action is needed to fix the problems and get the project back on track, and applicable standards were not followed. Which of the following is true?

A. You are in the Manage Communications process and have completed a performance review of the contractor's work.

B. You are in the Manage Quality process and have performed a quality audit.

C. You are in the Manage Quality process and have performed process analysis.

D. You are in the Validate Scope process and have performed an inspection to ensure correctness of work.

91. You are a project manager for SubZero Delights, a company that offers extraordinary experiences to travelers. Your latest project involves the development of a smartphone app that automatically picks up a customer's GPS coordinates to provide tailored resources and recommendations. While documenting the resource management plan, you decide to incorporate a RACI. What does RACI stand for? (Select four.)

A. Responsible

B. Inform

C. Accountable

D. Report

E. Consult

F. Advise

92. You are a project manager for an engineering company. Your company won the bid to add ramp-metering lights to several on-ramps along a stretch of highway at the south end of the city. You subcontracted a portion of the project to another company. The subcontractor's work involves digging the holes and setting the lamp poles in concrete. You've discovered the subcontractor's work is not correct because the poles are not buried to the correct depth. You review the work and note gaps in the process and a lack of safety standards as a result of this error. Which of the following is true?

A. You are in the Manage Quality process and have performed a quality audit and identified a need for a corrective action.

B. You are in the Validate Scope process and have performed a quality audit to ensure correctness of work.

C. You are in the Control Procurements process and have completed a contract audit to ensure that the subcontractor's performance meets the contract requirements.

D. You are in the Close Project or Phase process and have completed a performance review of the contractor's work.

93. All of the following statements are true regarding the Manage Project Knowledge process except for which one?

A. It addresses both explicit and tacit knowledge.

B. It generates the lessons learned register.

C. It is performed at the end of the Executing process group.

D. It often results in updates to the project management plan.

94. All of the following statements are true about the Project Resource Management Knowledge Area except for which one?

A. The Knowledge Area is responsible only for the identification, management, and monitoring of human resources.

B. The Knowledge Area has a total of six project management processes.

C. Estimating activity resources is an activity that occurs as part of this Knowledge Area.

D. The Knowledge Area has processes belonging to the Planning, Executing, and Monitoring and Controlling process groups.

95. Forming, storming, norming, performing, and adjourning are all phases of what?

A. Maslow's Hierarchy of Needs

B. Tuckman's team development model

C. Herzberg's Motivation-Hygiene Theory

D. Vroom's Expectancy Theory

96. Availability, experience levels, interests, cost, and abilities of project resources are considered part of which input to the Acquire Resources process?

A. Enterprise environmental factors

B. Organizational process assets

C. Interpersonal and team skills

D. Resource calendars

97. Cost plus incentive fee, cost plus award fee, cost plus percentage of cost, and cost plus fixed fee are all other names for what contract type?

A. Cost-reimbursable contract

B. Time and materials contract

C. Fixed-price contract

D. Cost plus contract

98. You are working on a critical project for your organization. The CEO has made it clear this is a top priority. One of the key stakeholders on your project resigned, and her replacement started about three weeks ago. She does not make time for you or seem to have the same level of urgency regarding this project as the CEO. You are concerned with overall project success and want to efficiently manage the processes involved with this project. Which of the following addresses this situation?

   A. Monitoring stakeholder engagement

   B. Monitoring the work of the project

   C. Monitoring communications

   D. Performing change management

99. Given the following information, is the project schedule ahead of or behind what was planned for this period? EV = 95, PV = 85, AC = 100.

   A. Ahead, because the result of the variance formula is negative.

   B. Behind, because the result of the variance formula is negative.

   C. Ahead, because the result of the variance formula is positive.

   D. Behind, because the result of the variance formula is positive.

100. Who is responsible for determining which processes within each process group are appropriate for the project?

   A. The project manager

   B. The project team

   C. The project manager and project sponsor

   D. The project manager and project team

101. A project manager meets with the project team to estimate the duration of activities identified to date. The project sponsor recently guided the project manager to present her with a duration estimate for the project that contains a high confidence level. What estimating technique is the project manager likely to use, assuming that the necessary information is available?

   A. Three-point estimating

   B. Bottom-up estimating

   C. Parametric estimating

   D. Top-down estimating

102. The project team recently participated in a working session to examine and document the effectiveness of risk responses in dealing with overall project risk. What is this working session, or meeting, called?

   A. Status meeting

   B. Technical performance assessment

   C. Risk review

   D. Brainstorming

103. All of the following are true regarding project phases except for which one?

   A. Project phases generally consist of segments of work that allow for easier management, planning, and control.

   B. PMOs may have predefined phases based on stakeholder or management needs.

   C. Phases are described by attributes, such as name, number, duration, and resource requirements.

   D. Project phases generally do not produce deliverables by the end of the phase.

104. Who developed the model that defines the stages of a team's development?

   A. Dr. Bruce Tuckman

   B. Victor Vroom

   C. David McClelland

   D. Abraham Maslow

105. There are 10 stakeholders within your project. As the project manager, you must therefore manage 45 communication channels. Two additional stakeholders have been added. How many more channels of communication must you manage?

   A. 47

   B. 45

   C. 21

   D. 66

106. According to the *PMBOK® Guide*, this output of the Manage Stakeholder Engagement process is used to promote communication with stakeholders.

   A. Project communications

   B. Issue log

   C. Project management plan updates

   D. Change requests

107. Nicolas is the project manager of a project that has been described as revolutionizing the mobile fitness tracking industry. He recently used his negotiation skills to achieve the support and agreement of two functional leads involved in his project. As part of his approach, he references the plan that outlines strategies and actions documented to manage specific stakeholders. What document did Nicolas reference to get this information?

   A. Communications management plan

   B. Stakeholder engagement plan

   C. Resource management plan

   D. Procurement management plan

108. Your project includes a new manufacturing technique that requires knowledge of chemical engineering to perform one of the services required in the project management plan. The service was performed, and as a result, an approved change request has been submitted. Which of the following statements is true?

    A. Approved change requests come about as a result of the Direct and Manage Project Work process, and the Direct and Manage Project Work process will be repeated in order to implement this change.

    B. Approved change requests are inputs to the Direct and Manage Project Work process, and the Direct and Manage Project Work process will be repeated in order to implement this change.

    C. This approved change request is external to the project and is expanding the scope of the original project. Therefore, this change request will be addressed during the Monitoring and Controlling process group.

    D. This approved change request is internal to the project and is expanding the scope of the original project. Therefore, this change request will be addressed during the Monitoring and Controlling process group.

109. You are sequencing activities and have just begun to identify dependencies. What can you use to help get you started quickly?

    A. Enterprise environmental factors

    B. Organizational process assets

    C. Milestone list

    D. Scheduling tool

110. Sally and Joe are two project managers working in the corporate offices of a popular fast-food franchise. They are both studying for their PMP® certification and are having a discussion on the WBS. Sally is confused and asks Joe to describe what the WBS contains. What is Joe likely to respond with?

    A. The WBS includes a description of the project scope, major deliverables, assumptions, and constraints.

    B. The WBS is a work package containing unique identifiers, which provide a structure for hierarchical summation of costs, schedule, and resource information.

    C. The WBS is a document that provides detailed deliverable, activity, and scheduling information about each component within the project scope statement.

    D. The WBS is a decomposition of the total scope of work to be carried out by the project team to accomplish the project objectives and create the required deliverables.

111. Carina is a principal project manager of You've Got Dogs, a specialty company that creates custom dog apparel and toys. She has just obtained approval of the project management plan and is about to publish it to the project team. What process group are the activities she is performing associated with?

    A. Initiating

    B. Planning

    C. Executing

    D. Monitoring and Controlling

112. Which type of estimating technique can have a high level of accuracy?

    A. Analogous estimating

    B. Bottom-up estimating

    C. Reserve analysis

    D. Parametric estimating

113. You are a project manager for Wedding Planners, Inc. Since every wedding is unique, your organization believes in managing each one as a project. You've come up with a great idea for a new event that you're certain customers will love and that will also profit the company. Your boss asks you to investigate alternative methods for implementing the new idea and come back with a recommendation. You discover that Alternative A could yield revenues of $21 million over the next two years, while Alternative B could yield revenues of $29 million over three years. The finance manager told you to use 5 percent as the cost of capital. Which project should you choose and why?

    A. Alternative A, because the discounted cash flows are $19,047,619 while the discounted cash flows for Alternative B are $25,051,831.

    B. Alternative B, because its yield is higher than Alternative A's yield.

    C. Alternative B, because the discounted cash flows are $26,303,854 while the discounted cash flows for Alternative A are $19,047,619.

    D. Alternative B, because the discounted cash flows are $20,000,000 for Alternative A while the discounted cash flows for Alternative B are $27,619,047.

114. Mandatory dependency is also known by what other name?

    A. Preferred logic

    B. Hard logic

    C. Soft logic

    D. External dependency

115. You are the project manager for a construction company that is building a new city and county office building in your city. Your CCB recently approved a scope change. You know that scope change might come about as a result of all of the following except which one?

    A. Schedule revisions

    B. Product scope change

    C. Changes to the agreed-upon WBS

    D. Changes to the project requirements

116. Which of the following processes are responsible for adjusting stakeholder engagement and communication strategies and plans, based on how the project is progressing and how the results compare to the plan.

 A. Monitor Communications and Monitor Stakeholder Engagement

 B. Manage Communications and Manage Stakeholder Engagement

 C. Plan Communications Management and Plan Stakeholder Engagement

 D. Direct and Manage Project Work and Monitor and Control Project Work

117. All of the following statements are true regarding trend analysis except for which one?

 A. Trend analysis is a tool and technique of the Control Costs process.

 B. Trend analysis is a mathematical formula used to forecast future outcomes.

 C. Trend analysis determines whether project performance is improving or worsening over time.

 D. Trend analysis is used to analyze how problems occur.

118. Using a triangular distribution formula, calculate the cost estimate based on the following three-point estimates: Optimistic = $2,500, Most Likely = $3,500, Pessimistic = $7,200.

 A. $4,400

 B. $3,950

 C. $13,200

 D. $3,500

119. A project team is using iterations within the project to introduce new functionality and complete the project deliverables. What development life cycle is the project team following?

 A. Predictive

 B. Iterative

 C. Incremental

 D. Hybrid

120. You have selected a vendor and are meeting with them to begin discussing the details of the final contract. They tell you that the equipment originally bid in the RFP is no longer available. They say the best solution is to buy the new equipment they're offering, which costs more than the original equipment. You have concerns that the new equipment might not be compatible with existing equipment and discuss this with them. After further investigation, it's proven the new equipment will work, and the vendor agrees to add some additional training time to help offset the difference in price. Which of the following tools and techniques of the Conduct Procurement process does this describe?

 A. Procurement negotiation

 B. Independent estimates

 C. Proposal evaluation techniques

 D. Fait accompli

121. The project management team is coordinating the decision between making or buying a product. Making the product would require an initial investment of $35,000 and has a probability of 15 percent failure and a probable impact of $15,000. Buying the product would require an initial investment of $25,000 but has a probability of 35 percent failure and $10,000 impact. What is the expected monetary value of making the product?

   A. $37,250

   B. $20,250

   C. $5,250

   D. $2,250

122. Your selection committee can choose only one of the following projects: Project A's original investment is $1 million, and the payback period is 18 months. Project B's original investment is $1.4 million, and the payback period is 18 months. Project C's original investment is $1.8 million, and the payback period is 18 months. Which project should the committee choose?

   A. Project A

   B. Project B

   C. Project C

   D. There isn't enough information in the question to determine an answer.

123. You have a very energetic project team. One of your team members has been classified by his teammates as brilliant. The team members are motivated by results, have good conflict-resolution skills, and are highly committed to the project, among other things. They have a solid understanding of the project goals and objectives and understand the direction the project is headed in. When their brilliant teammate questions the approach the team is using regarding one of the goals, you ask the team for their input and gather the facts before making a decision. You ask the team what they would do, and their conclusion is that the brilliant teammate is right and it's better to go with his solution than the one they planned. What type of power is the teammate displaying, and what leadership style does the project manager possess based on this question?

   A. Expert, democratic

   B. Referent, democratic

   C. Expert, situational

   D. Legitimate, situational

124. At what point in the project's life cycle is the risk probability of occurrence at its highest?

   A. Initiating

   B. Planning

   C. Executing

   D. Closing

125. Two project managers preparing for the PMP® exam sat and debated over the various ways that project life-cycle phases could be performed. The project managers would be covering all of the following except for which one?

A. Sequential

B. Fast-tracked

C. Iterative

D. Overlapping

126. Yazzy is a junior project manager for a fitness company that is developing a new franchise model. She is currently working under the guidance of a senior project manager over her parent project, who asks that she calculate the expected costs to finish the remaining project work. The work is proceeding as planned. She determines that the EAC is $75,000, and the cumulative actual costs to date are $50,000. What will Yazzy communicate to the senior project manager?

A. $25,000

B. -$25,000

C. $10,000

D. $15,000

127. A project manager is overseeing the execution of the team's project activities. She closes out the day, satisfied that the team is working together harmoniously and beginning to adjust their work habits and behaviors to support one another. Which stage of the Tuckman team development ladder is the team currently in?

A. Forming

B. Storming

C. Norming

D. Performing

128. If earned value = 500, planned value = 700, and actual costs = 450, what is the schedule variance?

A. −200

B. 200

C. −50

D. 50

129. You are in the Monitor Communications process. Your organization has taken on a large, complex, multiyear project. You are coming in as the new project manager (the old project manager left one day for lunch and never came back). After you've spent some time working on the project, you begin to realize that the project sponsor doesn't want to hear bad news. There is, unfortunately, some bad news related to the project, but you have a plan to get the project back on track. One of the other stakeholders on the project informed you that the sponsor had just told them that the project was proceeding as planned and was on time and on budget. You've found that the stakeholders are not communicating with each other and that since you've started working on the project, there have been no regularly scheduled meetings with stakeholders. All of the following are true regarding this question except which one?

A. Regular, timely status meetings will help prevent situations like this. Meetings, which include regularly scheduled status review meetings, are a tool and technique of this process.

B. Reporting templates and communication policies will help with the communication process. Templates and policies are part of the project communications input to this process.

C. The project manager is responsible for facilitating the status meetings and for providing honest, truthful information.

D. You may need status meetings with different groups of people for a project as complex as this one.

130. Which of the following techniques can provide the probability of a project completing on any given date?

A. Critical chain method

B. Critical path method

C. Precedence diagramming method

D. What-if scenario analysis

131. Your organization uses a predicative approach to managing projects. You have recently kicked off your project, and you are beginning a series of overview sessions with key users to determine requirements for a new enterprise resource software implementation. What process group are the activities you are performing in?

A. Initiating

B. Planning

C. Executing

D. Monitoring and Controlling

132. Carina is a principal project manager of You've Got Dogs, a specialty company that creates custom dog apparel and toys. She has just finished developing the project charter of a project that will create a new line of high-tech dog bones. What is the significance of the project charter?

A. Once the charter is approved, the project team can begin working on the project.

B. Once the charter is approved, the project manager can begin carrying out planning activities.

C. Once the charter is approved, the project sponsor can begin allocating funds to the project.

D. Once the charter is approved, it gives the project manager authority to apply resources to the project.

133. A project manager is managing a project working to produce a fitness tracking device. He has just finished getting the project authorized and analyzing stakeholder needs and expectations. What activity is he likely to perform next?

    A. Generate a project charter

    B. Put together the project management plan

    C. Collect the project and product requirements

    D. Develop a stakeholder engagement strategy

134. David is a project manager working for a prominent book publishing company. As the most senior project manager within the organization, he often gets the most complex project assignments. For this reason, the PMO manager assigns David to manage a project for a sponsor who is notorious for scope creep. Knowing this, David is likely to place greater emphasis on what project management process?

    A. Validate Scope

    B. Monitor and Control Project Work

    C. Control Quality

    D. Control Scope

135. You are using the tools and techniques of the Control Schedule process and know all of the following are true except for which one?

    A. Schedule variances are a key factor in monitoring and controlling project time.

    B. Comparing actual dates to estimated or forecast dates is one way to determine schedule variances.

    C. Delays to noncritical path activities will not cause schedule delays.

    D. Delays to critical path tasks will always cause schedule delays.

136. The project sponsor asks the project manager to validate that the product scope has been met. What will the project manager use to measure the completion of the product scope?

    A. Product requirements

    B. Project management plan

    C. Requirements documentation

    D. Project charter

137. Which of the following best describes the purpose of the project management plan?

    A. The project management plan describes how the project will be executed, monitored, controlled, and closed.

    B. The project management plan describes the requirements that must be met in order to produce the project and product scope.

    C. The project management plan documents the project success criteria, the approval requirements, and who will sign off on the project.

    D. The project management plan documents the business need and the cost-benefit analysis that justifies the project.

138. A project manager is addressing risks or potential concerns related to stakeholder management and is anticipating future issues that may be raised by stakeholders. What process is she performing?

A. Monitor Communications

B. Manage Communications

C. Manage Stakeholder Engagement

D. Monitor Stakeholder Engagement

139. You are the project manager for a pharmaceutical company. The latest project involves a new drug that will be released in six months. The project for the release is going well and closely mirrors the release of a drug that took place the previous year. With accurate historical information and quantifiable parameters in hand, what is the best type of cost estimating technique to use during the Determine Budget process?

A. Cost aggregation

B. Analogous estimating

C. Earned value

D. Parametric estimating

140. The tools and techniques of the Acquire Resources process include all of the following except for which one?

A. Multicriteria decision analysis

B. Virtual teams

C. Resource calendars

D. Negotiation

141. You are a project manager for Community Trends, a nonprofit organization. Your project has come about because of a social need. So far, the project has experienced some cost variances, but these variances are atypical and are not expected to continue. You know the following information: BAC = 900, EAC = 885, PV = 475, EV = 500, and AC = 425. Which of the following is the correct ETC given this information?

A. 400

B. 460

C. 471

D. Re-estimate

142. Which of the following power types relies on the influencer's position?

A. Legitimate

B. Expert

C. Referent

D. Punishment

143. A project manager is addressing risks or potential concerns related to stakeholder management and is anticipating future issues that may be raised by stakeholders. What process is she performing?

    A. Monitor Communications

    B. Manage Communications

    C. Manage Stakeholder Engagement

    D. Monitor Stakeholder Engagement

144. Which of the following statements are true regarding the Develop Team process? (Select three.)

    A. The outputs of the Develop Team process are team performance assessments, change requests, project management plan updates, organizational process assets updates, and enterprise environmental factors updates.

    B. This process is concerned with developing and training teams, not individuals.

    C. Team building can result in effective, functioning, coordinated performance among team members.

    D. Colocation is a technique used to help the team perform better.

145. A project manager is using a predictive approach to managing her project. Recently, she has experienced several adjustments to the project. All of the following result in a change request, except for which one?

    A. Updates to project documents

    B. Corrective actions

    C. Preventive actions

    D. Defect repairs

146. Carina is a principal project manager of You've Got Dogs, a specialty company that creates custom dog apparel and toys. She has just obtained approval of the project management plan and is about to publish it to the project team. At this point in the project life cycle, costs are likely to be which of the following?

    A. Lowest

    B. Low

    C. High

    D. Highest

147. You are the project manager for Ooh La La Beauty Products. Your project concerns developing a new line of bath products. You also serve on the CCB, which has just approved a scope change. You know that all of the following statements are true except which one?

    A. Scope changes include modifications to the agreed-upon WBS.

    B. Scope changes could result in schedule revisions.

    C. Scope changes do not usually impact the project budget.

    D. Scope changes should be reflected in the product scope.

148. During a status meeting, the project manager informs the team that the project has spent a total of $7,500 to date and that the earned value is $5,000. How is the project currently performing?

   A. Under planned cost

   B. On planned cost

   C. Over planned cost

   D. Insufficient information provided

149. All of the following are true regarding EMV analysis except for which one?

   A. EMV is a tool and technique within the Perform Quantitative Risk Analysis tools and techniques.

   B. EMV is often used in conjunction with decision-tree analysis.

   C. EMV examines risk from the perspective of the project as a whole.

   D. EMV is calculated by multiplying the probability of the occurrence by the value of each possible outcome and adding the results together.

150. You are the project manager for Kitchens Plus Inc. The latest project involves the development of an automatic dicer with unique industry features and has a project budget of $95,000. Based on the latest data, the project has a planned value of $70,200, an earned value of $59,000, and an actual cost of $65,500. How is the project currently performing according to the schedule and budget?

   A. The project is ahead of schedule and under budget.

   B. The project is ahead of schedule and over budget.

   C. The project is behind schedule and under budget.

   D. The project is behind schedule and over budget.

151. A project manager is performing quantitative risk analysis. What output is likely to be produced?

   A. An assessment of probability and impacts for each individual risk

   B. A priority level for each individual project risk

   C. An assessment of overall project risk exposure

   D. A list of potential risk responses

152. Ronald Pierce is a high-end furniture store chain. The company is in the process of developing a new renaissance style edition for release in six months. The project manager leading the development of the new edition is in the process of estimating the durations of the project activities. He uses information from the previous edition's project as the primary basis of his estimates. What estimating technique is the project manager using?

   A. Analogous estimating

   B. Parametric estimating

   C. Bottom-up estimating

   D. PERT estimating

153. Carina is a principal project manager of You've Got Dogs, a specialty company that creates custom dog apparel and toys. As part of her latest project, she interviews experienced subject-matter experts to better understand what risks exist within the project. Where will she document her findings?

A. Risk register

B. Risk management plan

C. Risk report

D. Project documents

154. A project manager has recently communicated a to-complete performance index of 1.0 to the project sponsor. What does this mean?

A. That it will be difficult to complete the project within set targets

B. That the project must continue performing at the current rate to complete within target

C. That it will be relatively easy to complete the project within set targets

D. That it will be impossible to complete the project within set targets

155. Maslow's Hierarchy of Needs is a motivational theory that notes that humans have five basic needs arranged in a hierarchical order. What is the highest set of needs of the five within the hierarchy?

A. Social needs

B. Safety and security needs

C. Self-actualization

D. Basic physical needs

156. All of the following statements about the arrow diagramming method (ADM) are true except for which one?

A. In ADM, activities are placed on the arrows, which are connected to dependent activities with nodes.

B. ADM allows for multiple types of dependencies, including finish-to-start, start-to-finish, start-to-start, and finish-to-finish.

C. ADM is also referred to as *activity on arrow (AOA)* and *activity on line (AOL)*.

D. ADM allows for more than one time estimate to determine duration.

157. If Activity A has an early start of 10, an early finish of 16, and a late start of 12, what is the total float of the activity?

A. 0

B. 6

C. 2

D. 4

158. Which of the following best describes the value of respect that project management practitioners should follow?

A. Our duty to take ownership for the decisions we make or fail to make, the actions we take or fail to take, and the consequences that result

B. Our duty to make decisions and act impartially and objectively

C. Our duty to show a high regard for ourselves, others, and the resources entrusted to us

D. Our duty to understand the truth and act in a truthful manner both in our communications and in our conduct

159. The output of the Monitor and Control Project Work process can take many forms, including issues or action item logs, status reports, project documents, dashboards, and more. Which output does this refer to?

A. Work performance information

B. Work performance data

C. Work performance reports

D. Project documents updates

160. David is a project manager working for a prominent book publishing company. As the most senior project manager within the organization, he often gets the most complex project assignments. As part of his current project, he oversees the inspection of deliverables, measuring them against documented requirements and acceptance criteria. What does he hope to achieve as part of carrying out these activities?

A. Work performance information

B. Change requests

C. Accepted deliverables

D. Updates to the plan

161. Procurement statement of work, insurance and performance bonds, vendor pricing, and payment terms are all elements of what document?

A. Agreements

B. RFP

C. Procurement management plan

D. Seller proposals

162. Which of the following statements are true regarding power types? (Select three.)

A. Punishment power is also known as coercive power.

B. Expert power comes from an individual's knowledge about the subject.

C. Referent power is also known as formal power.

D. Punishment, expert, legitimate, and referent are all power types.

163. Your project is dependent on a precise manufacturing process. You have hired trained auditors to evaluate the process and identify ineffective activities. The auditors bring a few ineffective activities to your attention, and as a result, you take a corrective action. All of the following are true regarding this situation except for which one?

A. This is a quality improvement that came about as a result of the quality audit.

B. Quality improvements are implemented by submitting change requests.

C. Quality improvements are implemented by taking corrective actions.

D. Quality audits have the same purpose as the Control Quality process.

164. You are a project manager reporting to the director of operations. You navigate to the department's PMO intranet set to download the latest project charter template. What type of PMO is this?

A. Supportive

B. Controlling

C. Directive

D. There isn't enough information in the question to determine an answer.

165. You are the project manager for Xylophone Phonics, which produces children's software programs that teach basic reading and math skills. You are performing the Plan Quality Management process and are considering the trade-offs between cost and quality. You know that it is cheaper and more efficient to prevent defects in the first place than to spend time and money fixing them later. Which of the following does this describe?

A. Cost-benefit analysis

B. Make-or-buy decisions

C. Cost of quality

D. Nonconformance costs

166. At what point in the project life cycle do costs peak?

A. Initiating

B. Planning

C. Executing

D. Closing

167. If you know that EV = 114, PV = 120, and AC = 103, what are CPI and SPI, respectively?

A. 1.1 and .95

B. 1.2 and 1.05

C. 1.05 and 1.2

D. .95 and 1.1

168. Which of the following best describe characteristics of a product backlog? (Select three.)

A. It is prioritized by a business representative.

B. It contains prioritized work to be completed in the current sprint.

    C. Work is pulled from the top of the backlog.

    D. It contains a list of prioritized work.

169. Leticia is a project manager working for Dancing Apron, a company that combines cooking with simple children's cooking recipes and music. Her latest project involves the release of the company's first digital product that parents will be able to purchase and download online. While overseeing the project, Leticia notices that recent stakeholder engagement levels have dropped significantly, and they've begun to disagree during status meetings. What key information can she use to help her deal with the situation?

    A. Project management plan

    B. Work performance data

    C. Interpersonal and team skills

    D. Decision-making

170. The project team recently participated in a working session to determine the costs associated with individual activities. To produce a more accurate estimate, they broke each activity down further into smaller chunks. What process is the team engaged in?

    A. Plan Cost Management

    B. Estimate Costs

    C. Determine Budget

    D. Control Costs

171. The processes that make up the project management process groups often interact and overlap with one another and are often performed in what way?

    A. Sequentially

    B. Singularly

    C. Iteratively

    D. Progressively

172. During a status meeting, the project sponsor made a rare appearance to address questions on project funding and asked for an update on the project's overall progress. At one point, the sponsor asked the project manager for a copy of the schedule baseline to see what work had already been accomplished. What was wrong with the sponsor's request?

    A. The sponsor should not be asking for project-specific information, particularly in regard to the schedule.

    B. What they are really looking for is the project management plan with all of the baselines.

    C. The schedule baseline provides the original schedule, plus the approved changes, but not the current schedule.

    D. Nothing. It was a valid request.

173. You have examined the problems and constraints experienced while conducting the project and identified inefficient and ineffective processes associated with process operations. Which tool and technique of the Manage Quality process have you used?

    A. Quality management and control tools

    B. Quality audits

    C. Cost-benefit analysis

    D. Process analysis

174. The following is included within the cost baseline:

    A. Management reserve

    B. Contingency reserve

    C. Cost aggregation

    D. Cash flow

175. Which of the following statements is inaccurate?

    A. Gathering three-point estimates helps generate a more accurate estimate of activity resources needed.

    B. Bottom-up estimating is a time-consuming technique that generates confident resource estimates.

    C. Resource breakdown structures are generated as part of the Estimate Activity Resources process.

    D. Project management software helps increase the level of accuracy, organization, and data accessibility.

176. You work for Writer's Block, a service that reviews and critiques manuscripts for aspiring writers. You were assigned to be the project manager for a new computer system that logs, tracks, and saves submitted manuscripts along with the editor's notes. You hired and worked with a vendor who wrote the system from scratch to your specifications. You are reviewing a report regarding certain aspects of the project's performance, and one of the measurements on the report is the expected cost of the work when completed. Which of the following does this describe?

    A. AC

    B. EV

    C. ETC

    D. EAC

177. While acquiring the project team, the project manager discovers that a key resource has just resigned from the company. This was the only resource available with the necessary skill set to perform the activity requiring the given expertise. Since hiring and getting a new resource up to speed would take up to three months, the project sponsor authorized

the procurement of a specialized contractor. Where will the project management team look to determine how resources are to be acquired externally?

A. Requirements management plan

B. Project management plan

C. Human resource management plan

D. Schedule management plan

178. A project manager has executed work, producing a key deliverable. What process is he likely to perform next?

A. Direct and Manage Project Work

B. Develop Project Management Plan

C. Perform Integrated Change Control

D. Monitor and Control Project Work

179. You are working on a communications management plan for your project. You examine elements such as the company and department organization charts, stakeholder relationships, the different departments involved on the project, the number of people associated with the project and where they work, and the government reporting needs you have because of the nature of this project. Which of the following does this question describe?

A. Communications models

B. Communications technology

C. Communication methods

D. Communications requirements analysis

180. Corrective actions are taken as a result of which of the following?

A. When comparing and monitoring project performance against the baseline

B. When deviations are discovered while coordinating and integrating the various elements of the project

C. When there is a probability of negative consequences

D. When product defects are discovered during the quality processes

181. A project manager of Cyber Channels Inc. is in the process of identifying project risks. While reviewing how the elements of a particular system interrelate, she discovers two risks relating to the cause of another risk that were both initially overlooked. Which of the following techniques is the project manager using?

A. Influence diagram

B. Flow chart

C. Cause and effect diagram

D. Control chart

182. All of the following are true regarding the Initiating process group except for which one?

- **A.** The Initiating process group is responsible for developing the document that authorizes the project.
- **B.** The Initiating process group processes are iterative in nature and often are revisited at the beginning of every phase.
- **C.** The Initiating process group is responsible for defining a new project or phase by obtaining authorization to start the project or phase.
- **D.** The Initiating process group encompasses the fewest project management processes.

183. Molly is the lead project manager for Cube Systems Plus. A project that she is managing is utilizing three different vendors to perform various components of work. Molly's customer has just requested that the delivery date be pushed up by one month. To determine whether this is possible, she sits down with the account managers of the three vendor companies to discuss availability. Where will Molly and the account managers look to view resource availability?

- **A.** Resource management plan
- **B.** Seller Gantt charts
- **C.** Contract
- **D.** Resource calendars

184. An RV rental company is launching a consignment program for private owners who are looking to rent out their vehicles. The project manager of the project has just begun carrying out risk management activities. Since the project manager is experienced in managing risk, she immediately moved into the Identify Risks process. Based on this information, which of the following is most likely to occur?

- **A.** The project manager is likely to carry out risk management activities effectively, given her level of experience.
- **B.** The project manager is unlikely to carry out risk management activities effectively, regardless of her level of experience.
- **C.** The project manager is likely to generate a useful risk register.
- **D.** The project manager is likely to identify more risks, based on her experience.

185. Robert is a project manager, and Sergio is a business analyst working on a project. As part of their project planning strategy, they have scheduled a daily team meeting. Robert and Sergio tend to have more direct conflicts with one another during the discussions that take place as part of these meetings than other attendees. Which of the following is not likely to be a source of conflict between the two?

- **A.** Personal work styles
- **B.** Personality clashes
- **C.** Scheduling priorities
- **D.** Scarce resources

186. As project manager, Jose facilitates a weekly project team meeting to review progress achieved to date. He begins each meeting by sharing the average number of story points completed over the past one-week iteration. This is referred to as:

A. Schedule performance index

B. Velocity

C. Cycle time

D. Sprint

187. Sally and Joe are two project managers working in the corporate offices of a popular fast-food franchise. They are both studying for their PMP® certification and are reviewing processes pertaining to the Project Procurement Management Knowledge Area. They disagree on which process is responsible for performing activities relating to closure of procurements. Sally insists it's the Close Project or Phase process, while Joe argues that it is the Control Procurements process. Who is right?

A. Sally

B. Joe

C. Neither

D. Both

188. A project manager is performing activities associated with monitoring and controlling the scope of the project. What key information can they use in conjunction with the plan to help them get started?

A. Project documents

B. Variance analysis

C. Trend analysis

D. Work performance data

189. You are the project manager for Lucky Stars Candies. You've identified the deliverables and requirements and documented them where?

A. In the project scope statement, which will be used as an input to the Create WBS process

B. In the project scope management document, which is used as an input to the Define Scope process

C. In the product requirements document, which is an output of the Define Scope process

D. In the project specifications document, which is an output of the Define Activities process

190. Carina is a principal project manager of You've Got Dogs, a specialty company that creates custom dog apparel and toys. As part of her practice, she sits down with her sponsor to evaluate how the project is performing by comparing the performance measurement baseline against actual schedule and cost performance. What technique is Carina using?

A. Variance analysis

B. Earned value analysis

C. Technical performance analysis

D. Trend analysis

191. You are a project manager for Lightning Bolt Enterprises. Your new project involves the research and development of a new type of rechargeable battery. The project objectives, as documented in the project charter and used in creating the project scope statement, should include which of the following?

A. A description of the business need that brought about this project

B. A brief summary of the product description, including measurable, quantifiable product requirements that will help measure project success

C. Quantifiable criteria, including elements such as cost, schedule, and quality measures

D. Quantifiable criteria derived from value engineering, value analysis, or function analysis

192. Waterfall, Agile, and PRINCE2 are all examples of what?

A. A set of project management standards

B. Methods of managing a project

C. Global practices for managing projects

D. Project management tools and techniques

193. Your project estimates have come in as follows: Most Likely is 100 days, Pessimistic is 250 days, Optimistic is 75 days. What is the expected value of this estimate?

A. 120.83 days

B. 141.66 days

C. 108.33 days

D. 195.33 days

194. All of the following represent values addressed in the *Code of Ethics and Professional Conduct*, except for which one?

A. Honor

B. Responsibility

C. Fairness

D. Respect

195. Your project selection committee is evaluating three projects. They are using a weighted scoring model that has three criteria: decrease training time, streamline customer support functions, and return on investment. The weights for these criteria are 5, 4, and 2, respectively. Your selection committee has finished scoring the three projects and has given you the scores for the three criteria. They are as follows:

Project 1: decrease training = 5, streamline support = 3, return on investment = 5

Project 2: decrease training = 3, streamline support = 5, return on investment = 5

Project 3: decrease training = 4, streamline support = 4, return on investment = 3

Which project should you choose based on the scores from the weighted scoring model?

A. Project 3

B. Project 2

C. Project 1

D. There isn't enough information in the question to determine an answer.

196. Who is responsible for managing changes within a project?

A. Project sponsor

B. Everyone

C. Project manager

D. Product owner

197. The Big Mouth grocery food chain is planning to modernize their IT department by developing a new bar coding system that will allow them to keep their shelves stocked more efficiently by using the Just in Time strategy. However, during the project chartering phase the project manager explained to them that in order to execute the Just in Time strategy, a company must have a high level of:

A. Quality

B. Resources

C. Experience

D. Financing

198. A project manager is using a hybrid approach to manage his project. He sits down with the project's sponsor to update him on progress achieved to date. To aid the discussion, the project manager displays a chart that visually shows how much work remains versus how much time is left for the project. What is the project manager displaying?

A. A burnup chart

B. A Gantt chart

C. A burndown chart

D. A radar chart

199. You are the project manager for Ooh La La Beauty Products. Your project concerns developing a new line of bath products. A quality inspection of one of the new products reveals that the product is nonconforming. Which of the following result in conforming or nonconforming measurements?

   A. Control measurements

   B. Attributes sampling

   C. Variances

   D. Common causes of variance

200. Match the project life cycle with its corresponding description of when planning occurs.

Term	Description
A. Predictive	1. Planning occurs early in the project's life. The plan is modified through each iteration, and work completed informs future work.
B. Iterative	2. Most of the planning occurs upfront. The team strives to identify as much detail about requirements as possible early on.
C. Incremental	3. Teams plan one or more subsets of the overall project. Completion of these deliveries informs the future work.

Chapter

5

Full-Length Practice Exam 2

 NOTE The process names, inputs, tools and techniques, outputs, and descriptions of the project management process groups and related materials and figures in this chapter are based on content from *A Guide to the Project Management Body of Knowledge (PMBOK® Guide) – Sixth Edition* (PMI®, 2017).

1. The president of the company has asked you to lead a large new project that links to the company's number-one strategic priority. After kicking off the project, the president stops by to inquire whether you have already begun building your team. He eagerly notes that he would like to see engagement from multiple geographies in order to leverage special expertise that exists within the company. He notes that cost should be a consideration as well, given that the company has recently experienced losses. When building the team, what options should you consider, given this information?

   A. Build multiple small teams

   B. Outsource the team

   C. Colocate the team

   D. Use virtual teams

2. Within Agile, an "I" shaped person refers to what?

   A. An individual who supplements their expertise in one area with less-developed skills in associated areas

   B. A generalist who can take on any work within the backlog, regardless of skills needed

   C. An individual who is early in their career and requires coaching in tandem with an assignment

   D. An individual who has deep specializations in one domain and rarely contributes outside of it

3. Sue is the leader of an enterprise PMO. Recently, she rolled out a quarterly project auditing process. Each quarter, 10 percent of the project portfolio would be randomly audited. What is the leading motivator and benefit of project audits? (Select two.)

   A. Disciplining project managers not adhering to published standards and policies

   B. Determining potential threats to compliance

   C. Identifying key legal and/or contractual requirements

   D. Monitoring compliance against published standards and policies

   E. Coaching, mentoring, and training project managers

4. Match the project ending with the corresponding description.

Types of Project Endings

Type	Description
A. Integration	1. When resources are cut off from the project prior to completing all requirements
B. Starvation	2. When the project comes to an end because it was completed and accepted by the stakeholders
C. Addition	3. When resources are distributed to other areas in the organization or assigned to other projects
D. Extinction	4. When a project evolves into ongoing operations

5. Which of the following measurements is the value of the work actually completed?

   A. AC

   B. EV

   C. PV

   D. EAC

6. You are the project manager for BB Tops, a nationwide toy store chain. Your new project involves creating a prototype display at several stores across the country. You are using a RACI chart to display individuals and activities. Which of the following is true regarding this type of chart?

   A. A RACI chart is part of the organization charts and position descriptions tool and technique of the Plan Resource Management process.

   B. A RACI chart is a type of matrix-based chart that is a tool and technique of the Plan Resource Management process.

   C. A RACI chart is part of the organization chart and position descriptions and is a type of hierarchical chart that is a tool and technique of the Plan Resource Management process.

   D. A RACI chart is a type of RAM chart that is a tool and technique of the Plan Resource Management process.

7. Which of the following best describes the role of a cross-functional team member within an Agile team?

   A. The individual who guides and coaches the team, sometimes referred to as Scrum master, project manager, or team coach

   B. The individual responsible for guiding the direction of the product

   C. Individuals who possess the skills necessary to produce a working product

   D. The individual with decision-making authority who authorizes and releases team member assignments

8. Which of the following statements is true regarding diversity and inclusion?

   A. Inclusion ensures all team members can participate and have a voice on the team.

   B. Inclusion encompasses hiring project team members from a variety of religious backgrounds, cultures, ethnicities, and experiences.

   C. Diverse teams can explore new ideas and identify ideas to clear challenges and issues.

   D. Generational sensitivity involves understanding differences across the generations in the workforce today.

   E. A, B, C, D

9. Your selection committee is considering two projects. They can choose only one or the other. Project A's expected cash inflows are $14,000. It has a payback period of 14 months, and IRR equals 4 percent. Project B expects cash inflows of $5,000 per quarter for the first 16 months, and its IRR is 2. Which project should the selection committee choose and why?

    A. Project A, because its payback period is shorter than Project B's

    B. Project B, because its IRR value is less than Project A's

    C. Project B, because the payback period is shorter than Project A's

    D. Project A, because its IRR value is higher than Project B's

10. The following statements are true except for which one?

    A. It is necessary for all team members to possess emotional intelligence skills.

    B. Emotional intelligence skills include collaboration, humility, and willingness to communicate.

    C. It is critical for a project manager to possess emotional intelligence skills.

    D. It is not necessary for all team members to possess emotional intelligence skills.

11. You are in the midst of performing cost management activities. You discover there are two competing alternatives to decide between: you can hire a contractor to build one of the project's deliverables, or you can buy the deliverable from an overseas supplier. Both options require acquisition, operating, and disposal costs that you compare between the two alternatives to make a decision. What technique are you using?

    A. Value engineering

    B. Life-cycle costing

    C. Earned value management

    D. Financial analysis

12. An organization interested in shifting the organizational culture to adopt new practices, such as Agile, must create an environment that enables which of the following? (Select two.)

    A. Safe, honest work environment

    B. Checks and balances

    C. Flexible environment

    D. Transparent environment

13. The president of the company has asked you to lead a large new project that links to the company's number-one strategic priority. Shortly after learning about this news, you receive a visit from a principal architect who notes that he will also be working on the project. The project has not formally kicked off yet. What has likely occurred?

    A. The principal architect has gotten ahead of himself.

    B. A misunderstanding, since the project has not yet begun.

    C. The principal architect has been preassigned.

    D. The principal architect is expressing his interest.

14. Match the conflict resolution technique with its synonym.

Categories of Project Influence

Examples	Category
A. Accommodate	1. Reconcile
B. Withdraw	2. Avoid
C. Compromise	3. Direct
D. Collaborate	4. Problem solve
E. Force	5. Smooth

15. Alyssa is a project manager tasked with managing an infrastructure project that will consolidate five data centers into one. To date, she has completed and received sign-off of the project charter and identified her stakeholders. Currently, she is in the process of defining and documenting which processes she will use to manage the project. What output will this activity produce?

    A. The project charter

    B. The stakeholder register

    C. The project management plan

    D. The scope management plan

16. Which of the following are components that make up the scope baseline? (Select three.)

    A. Project scope statement

    B. Activities list

    C. WBS

    D. WBS Dictionary

17. Which quality theorist is known as the grandfather of Total Quality Management (TQM)?

    A. Philip Crosby

    B. Joseph Juran

    C. W. Edwards Deming

    D. Walter Shewhart

18. A project manager interested in gaining insight into areas of team strengths and weaknesses may use which of the following tools?

    A. Training

    B. Personality assessments

    C. Meetings

    D. Individual and team assessments

19. A project manager works within a department that has a PMO. The primary purpose of the PMO organization is to ensure that the department receives the support needed to deliver successful project outcomes, as well as remain compliant with published project governance requirements. What type of PMO is this?

A. Agile PMO

B. Supportive

C. Controlling

D. Directive

20. All of the following are true regarding the Perform Integrated Change Control process except for which one?

A. This process is carried out as part of executing the project work.

B. This process is performed throughout the project life cycle.

C. This process addresses changes that encompass corrective actions, preventive actions, and defect repair.

D. This process belongs to the Project Integration Management Knowledge Area.

21. Gabriela is responsible for leading project delivery efforts within her department. Currently, she is managing a project that will add a series of new features to a smartphone application that offers users an interactive "virtual friend." She is managing the beginning and end of the project using a waterfall approach and executing the work by following Scrum practices. At the onset of the project, Gabriela documents how the project will be executed, monitored, and closed. What document is Gabriela creating?

A. Release backlog

B. The project management plan

C. Agile Manifesto

D. Stakeholder engagement plan

22. You are using a control chart for quality control purposes. Which of the following statements are true regarding control charts? (Select three.)

A. Common causes of variance include random, known, or predictable, and variances that are always present in the process and common causes of variance are plotted on a control chart.

B. Control charts measure variances to determine whether process variances are in control or out of control.

C. Common causes of variance that are outside of the acceptable range may require the project manager to approve changes to or reorganization of the process.

D. Control charts are used in conjunction with the rule of seven.

23. A project manager is facilitating a meeting to further define user stories for the upcoming iteration. Two team members involved, Bob and Jenny, are very vocal during the start of the meeting, with Jenny passionately noting that the second user story should be punted to the next iteration. She moves on to the next user story, ignoring Bob's opposing views on the topic. Bob accepts the decision hesitantly and remains quiet for the remainder of the meeting, accepting other decisions made by Jenny and the rest of the team. At the end of the meeting, the project manager notes to Bob that she will prioritize user story #2 at the top of the backlog, to be pulled into the iteration should capacity allow. Which of the following conflict-resolution techniques did the project manager use in this scenario?

A. Smoothing

B. Compromising

C. Directing

D. Collaborating

24. You are a lead project manager for a company that develops and manufactures healthcare devices. Your team has recently begun to adopt Agile practices after receiving the directive from the division president. What power type is at play in this scenario?

A. Legitimate

B. Referent

C. Expert

D. Punishment

25. Availability, cost, and ability are examples of what?

A. Ongoing project assumptions

B. Ongoing project constraints

C. Team member selection criteria

D. Project selection criteria

26. A project manager is in the process of developing the project charter and is using a hybrid project management approach. Almost immediately, he identifies several constraints. Where is he likely to document the constraints and maintain regular updates as they change throughout the project?

A. Product vision

B. Sprint backlog

C. Risk register

D. Assumption log

27. Which contract type can incorporate incentives for meeting or exceeding certain contract deliverables above a firm price for the goods or services rendered?

   A. Cost-reimbursable contract

   B. Time and materials contract

   C. Fixed-price contract

   D. Cost plus contract

28. Contract phases are closely related to the Project Procurement Management Knowledge Area processes. All of the following are true except for which one?

   A. The requirement stage, which establishes the project and contract needs, is related to the Plan Procurement Management process.

   B. The requisition stage, where responses to procurement documents are reviewed, is related to the Conduct Procurements process.

   C. The award stage, where the contract is awarded, is related to the Conduct Procurements process.

   D. Two of the outputs of the Plan Procurement Management process are inputs to the Conduct Procurements process.

29. Match the levels of stakeholder engagement with their descriptions.

Levels of Stakeholder Engagement

Name	Description
A. Unaware	1. Stakeholders are not supportive of the project and may actively resist engaging.
B. Resistant	2. Stakeholders have positive expectations of the project and are supportive and engaged.
C. Neutral	3. Stakeholders are neutral, neither supporting nor resisting the project, and may be minimally engaged.
D. Supportive	4. Stakeholders are actively engaged in the project and helping to ensure its success.
E. Leading	5. Stakeholders are not engaged in the project.

30. A project manager of a large manufacturing company is working on a new system that will reduce the bolt manufacturing process by 30 seconds, saving the company 2 percent in annual operating costs. This project will touch all departments and engage senior leadership. The project manager knows stakeholder engagement will be critical to success and spends time developing a strategy for engaging stakeholders. In what activity is the project manager involved?

   A. Developing the communications management plan

   B. Developing the stakeholder register

    C. Developing the stakeholder engagement plan

    D. Developing the project management plan

31. Which of the following best describes the role of a product owner within an Agile team?

    A. The individual who guides and coaches the team, sometimes referred to as Scrum master, project manager, or team coach

    B. The individual responsible for guiding the direction of the product

    C. Individuals who possess the skills necessary to produce a working product

    D. The individual with decision-making authority who authorizes and releases team member assignments

32. Diana is a project manager for a small technology startup. One of her first projects involves shifting data hosting from an on-premise solution to a cloud-based one. With work now fully underway, she begins generating status reports so that they can later be distributed to the project team and other relevant stakeholders. Which process group does this activity—creation of status reports—belong to?

    A. Planning

    B. Executing

    C. Monitoring and Controlling

    D. Closing

33. You are a project manager for SubZero Delights, a company that offers extraordinary experiences to travelers. You have experience working at other companies that have adopted Agile practices and see opportunities to apply these practices within your new role. To ease into the transition, you choose a hybrid approach. While the team has embraced the changes, you receive strong pushback at the executive level, who prefer to see detailed project schedules with minimal change. What can you do to gain support from the executive team?

    A. Push for colocated teams

    B. Demonstrate transparency

    C. Modify the terms so they feel more familiar

    D. Provide education and training

34. Which of the following should you consider when selecting a life-cycle methodology? (Select three.)

    A. The sponsor's preferences

    B. The organization's culture

    C. The project team

    D. The project itself

35. Which of the following scheduling methods does Kanban use?

    A. Critical path method

    B. Critical chain method

    C. Iterative scheduling

    D. On-demand scheduling

36. When working in the Conduct Procurements process, you might consider asking the vendor to supply you with an ink sample for a project on which you're working. The ink must have special qualities (they were outlined in the RFQ), and before making a selection, you want to test the ink in the printers that will be used at project deployment. All of the following statements are true except for which one?

    A. This is an example of a proposal evaluation technique, which is a tool and technique of this process.

    B. This is an example of source selection criteria, which are inputs of this process.

    C. This is an example of a proposal evaluation technique, which is an output of this process.

    D. Source selection criteria might also include financial capacity and technical capability.

37. You are a project manager working within a division that recently experienced a reorganization. Your new manager will now step in as the sponsor of your existing project. She asks for a briefing on the timeline of outcomes yielded by the project that will provide value to the department. What is she describing?

    A. Benefits

    B. Milestones

    C. Net present value

    D. Internal rate of return

38. Why is assessing risk probability in the Perform Qualitative Risk Analysis process difficult?

    A. Because it relies on historical data

    B. Because the values are cardinal

    C. Because the values are ordinal

    D. Because it relies on expert judgment

39. Manfrit and Frank are two project managers who have supported one another throughout their careers. Lately, Frank has sought Manfrit's advice on getting his team to adopt eXtreme Programming practices. While wrapping up their latest lunch session, Frank asks Manfrit how he can create an open, encouraging environment in which team members can contribute. What advice can Manfrit give Frank to achieve this outcome?

    A. Spend time establishing ground rules for the project team

    B. Spend time rewarding the project team

    C. Spend time disciplining the project team

    D. Spend time developing the project team

40. Oreste is managing a project release using the Scrum model and has decided to colocate the team for the duration of the project. What benefits will Oreste realize by using this approach? (Select three.)

    A. Increase the effectiveness of team dynamics

    B. Create a continuous learning environment at a reduced cost

    C. Increase knowledge sharing

    D. Expand the pool of available resources

41. You are a lead project manager for a company that develops and manufactures healthcare devices. Your team has recently begun to adopt Agile practices after receiving the directive from the division president. While the team has complied, you know from experience that hybrid is the best path forward. You request and are granted a meeting with the division president, where you present your case advocating for a hybrid approach. At the close of the meeting, she agrees to your recommendation, crediting your experience and background. What power type is at play in this scenario?

   A. Legitimate

   B. Referent

   C. Expert

   D. Punishment

42. You have selected a predictive approach to manage your project and will use the project management plan as the project baseline. You plan to continuously collect performance data and implement approved corrective actions as soon as necessary. Which of the following process groups does this activity relate to?

   A. Planning

   B. Monitoring and Controlling

   C. Executing

   D. Initiating

43. You have just been hired into a new organization. You are working on an RFP and have discovered that the qualified sellers list for this organization includes a company owned by someone who attended college with you. You have performed a make-or-buy analysis and decided it is best to procure the product needed for this project. You are helping the procurement group prepare for the upcoming bidder conference and are determining the criteria to use to evaluate proposals. You schedule a meeting with your manager and the procurement officer to explain your association with one of the vendors. Since you haven't seen your college friend in many years, you are certain this won't be a problem. What area of the *PMI Code of Ethics and Professional Conduct* does this question refer to, and which process are you conducting?

   A. Conflict of interest and the Control Procurements process

   B. Ensuring integrity and the Conduct Procurements process

   C. Ensuring integrity and the Control Procurements process

   D. Conflict of interest and the Conduct Procurements process

44. Sue is leading the transformation of her PMO from a directive PMO to an Agile PMO. What characteristics is Sue likely to highlight when describing the Agile PMO to the company's leadership team? (Select three.)

   A. The Agile PMO is invitation-oriented.

   B. The Agile PMO is value-driven.

   C. The Agile PMO is solution-oriented.

   D. The Agile PMO is multidisciplinary.

45. When building a team, a project manager may need to negotiate with which of the following roles? (Select three.)

A. Team members

B. Functional managers

C. Other project managers

D. Vendors

46. All of the following are benefits of virtual teams except for which one?

A. Costs are dispersed across regions.

B. Less travel will be required.

C. The pool of skilled resources widens.

D. The team will be closer to customers and suppliers.

47. You are a senior project manager working at a manufacturing plant that produces components used by the aviation industry. You are using a combination of lean and waterfall to manage a project and are in the process of implementing approved changes. What process group do these process activities belong to?

A. Initiating process group

B. Planning process group

C. Executing process group

D. Monitoring and Controlling process group

48. You have been assigned a new project and meet with your manager to discuss it further. The PMO organization has been on a journey over the past six months to become an Agile PMO. Your manager shares that the new project should be managed using an adaptive approach to support the direction of the team. He further clarifies that the project will be highly constraint-driven with a strong focus on quality and time and that the executive team expects incremental builds. Which of the following adaptive approaches should you use to manage this project?

A. Crystal Clear

B. Agile Unified Process

C. Dynamic Systems Development Method

D. Feature Driven Development

49. The lowest level of the WBS is referred to as which of the following?

A. WBS dictionary

B. Work package

C. Planning package

D. Control account

50. Kristin has recently joined a growing startup company as a project manager in the medical device industry, reporting to the head of research and development. During her first week, she spends time familiarizing herself with the organization and her responsibilities. She is pleasantly surprised to learn that she will be directly responsible for managing her own project budgets. What type of organizational structure does Kristin work within?

    A. Functional

    B. Project-oriented

    C. Weak matrix

    D. Strong matrix

51. You are using the data representation tool and technique of the Manage Quality process with one of the product deliverables to organize potential causes of defects into groups. Which tool and technique does this describe?

    A. Interrelationship digraphs

    B. Matrix diagrams

    C. Affinity diagrams

    D. Process decision program charts

52. People, interaction, community, communication, skills, and talents are all core values of what family of methodologies?

    A. Agile UP

    B. Crystal Methods

    C. Disciplined Agile

    D. Kanban

53. The purpose of this process is concerned with satisfying the needs of the stakeholders, managing communications with them, resolving issues, managing their expectations, and more, and this process also relates to this area of the *PMI Code of Ethics and Professional Conduct*.

    A. Manage Stakeholder Engagement and the Role Delineation Study

    B. Control Stakeholder Engagement and the Role Delineation Study

    C. Control Stakeholder Engagement and Professional Responsibility

    D. Manage Stakeholder Engagement and Professional Responsibility

54. You are a project manager for SubZero Delights, a company that offers extraordinary experiences to travelers. Your latest project involves the development of a smartphone app that automatically picks up a customer's GPS coordinates to provide tailored resources and recommendations. You chose a hybrid approach to managing the project, and the team is now well into executing the project work using one-month iterations. Since execution activities began, the project has been riddled with issues among team members—from disagreements to poor meeting etiquette. What is likely causing these issues?

    A. There are personality clashes among team members.

    B. The team remains in the forming stages.

    C. Ground rules have not been established.

    D. The hybrid approach does not work for the team.

55. You are a project manager working within a division that recently experienced a reorganization. Your new manager will now step in as the sponsor of your existing project. She asks for a briefing on the timeline and owners of outcomes yielded by the project that will provide value to the department. What document will you likely reference during the briefing?

    A. Product backlog

    B. Benefits management plan

    C. Project management plan

    D. Burndown chart

56. Using the following three-point estimates, calculate the expected value using the triangular distribution formula: Optimistic = 25, Pessimistic = 50, Most Likely = 35.

    A. 25

    B. 36

    C. 35

    D. 37

57. Alyssa is a project manager tasked with managing an infrastructure project that will consolidate five data centers into one. She updates a stakeholder engagement matrix that she created at the start of the project to document the communication needs of the project. What tool or technique is Alyssa using?

    A. Project management information system

    B. Interpersonal and team skills

    C. Expert judgment

    D. Data representation

58. Marysil recently accepted a new role as lead project manager within a well-established healthcare company. Over the past three months she has worked hard to introduce new concepts and styles into the environment. She has been met with some resistance by Rachel and Ron, two colleagues who prefer different styles of leadership. Rachel prefers to use a combination of transactional, transformational, and charismatic approaches. What type of leadership style does Rachel follow?

    A. Servant leadership

    B. Interactional

    C. Laissez-faire

    D. Charismatic

59. Which of the following stages of the Tuckman ladder addresses the stage at which the team is the most productive and effective?

    A. Forming

    B. Storming

    C. Norming

    D. Performing

60. Which of the following is a valid input that aids the project manager in managing the overall work of the project?

   A. Project documents

   B. Expert judgment

   C. Issue log

   D. Work performance data

61. Your project selection committee is meeting later this week and is considering initiating one of two projects. They've asked you to recommend the project that will benefit the organization the most. The information you've gathered shows the initial investment for Project 1 is $795,000. Monthly cash inflows for the first year are $44,000, and expected cash inflows beginning in year 2 are $156,000 per quarter. Project 2 has an initial investment of $845,000. Expected quarterly inflows for the first year are $180,000. Beginning in the second year, inflows are expected to be $136,000 per quarter. Which project should you recommend to the committee and why?

   A. Project 1, because it has a payback period of 18 months, which is shorter than Project 2's payback period

   B. Project 2, because it has a payback period of 15 months while Project 2 has a payback period of 18 months

   C. Project 1, because it has a lower initial investment than Project 2

   D. Project 2, because it has a payback period of 16 months while Project 1 has a payback period of 19 months

62. You are the project manager for the Heart of Texas casual clothing company. Your project involves installing a new human resources system, and you are using a hybrid approach to delivering project outcomes. You've identified the risks associated with this project and are ready for the next step. What is the next step?

   A. You should evaluate the risks and assign probabilities and impacts using Qualitative and/or Quantitative Risk Analysis.

   B. You should use the Delphi technique to confirm the risks you've detailed and identify others you may have missed.

   C. You should develop responses to the risks by performing the Develop Risk Response process.

   D. You should define the steps to take to respond to the risks and detail them in the risk response plan.

63. Your project has experienced some changes in performance, and some risks have occurred. EAC and BAC now differ as a result. Your project sponsor is asking for an estimate of the cost of the project at completion. Which of the following is true?

   A. BAC may no longer be reasonable given the changes in performance, so you should use EAC to forecast the cost at completion.

   B. EAC may no longer be reasonable given the changes in performance, so you should use BAC to forecast the cost at completion.

   C. BAC may no longer be reasonable given the changes in performance, so you should use ETC to forecast the cost at completion.

   D. EAC may no longer be reasonable given the changes in performance, so you should use ETC to forecast the cost at completion.

64. Mike is a seasoned project manager who has been tasked with mentoring Bernard, a junior project manager. During a mentoring session, Mike talks about the two types of knowledge. One type, he shares, can be codified using words, pictures, and numbers. What type of knowledge is Mike referring to?

   A. Tacit

   B. Known

   C. Unknown

   D. Explicit

65. In what order do servant leaders approach their work?

   A. Process, people, purpose

   B. People, process, purpose

   C. Purpose, people, process

   D. Process, purpose, people

66. What challenges can cross-cultural communication present to team members?

   A. Priorities often vary and differ.

   B. Team members tend to be globally disbursed, presenting timing issues.

   C. The meaning of the message is not always understood.

   D. The emotional state of team members fluctuates.

67. What model can a project manager use to classify stakeholders based on their power, urgency, and legitimacy?

   A. Stakeholder cube

   B. Stakeholder register

   C. Directions of influence

   D. Salience model

68. A project manager is in the process of holding a kickoff meeting to signal that execution of the project work is about to begin. She reviews the project baseline, communication cadence, and guidelines with the team, and she treats them to a pizza party to increase morale. Which of the following documents serves as the project baseline?

   A. Project management plan

   B. Approved project schedule

   C. Work plan

   D. Approved project budget

69. This methodology uses an iterative-based Agile approach. It is a single-team framework that is primarily used to manage product development. At the end of each iteration, the team facilitates a meeting to review what went well and ideas for improvement. Which methodology does this describe, and what technique is this question referring to? (Select two.)

   A. Sprint retrospective

   B. Scrum

    C. Sprint review

    D. Kanban

70. A project manager is responsible for a project that consists of Agile team members dispersed across four time zones. The team has experienced communication issues as a result. What can the project manager do to alleviate the communication challenges?

    A. Create a fishbowl window

    B. Set up remote pairing

    C. Assign work based on location

    D. Colocate the team

    E. A, B

    F. A, B, D

71. Marysil, an enterprise project manager for Cups on Fire, kicked off activities to develop the schedule. To date, she has generated the schedule management plan and led the team through a decomposition of work packages into activities. Now, she and the team are sequencing activities. She plans on displaying a visual using a network diagram during the next meeting. What network diagramming method is she most likely to use?

    A. Arrow diagramming method

    B. Activity on arrow

    C. Precedence diagramming method

    D. Activity online

72. You work within an organization that uses Agile practices to manage projects. What type of performance measurements are you likely to use when evaluating your project?

    A. Predictive and cost-efficiency measurements

    B. Value-based and empirical measurements

    C. Cost-efficiency measurements only

    D. Empirical measurements only

73. You are in the process of translating the quality management plan into executable quality activities that account for existing quality policies. What process are you in?

    A. Plan Quality Management

    B. Manage Quality

    C. Control Quality

    D. Validate Scope

74. Which of the following are components of the sender/receiver communication model? (Select three.)

    A. Push

    B. Encode

    C. Transmit

    D. Decode

75. What is the goal of a team charter?

A. Formalize the team so that resource assignments and engagement can be clearly understood

B. Create an environment where the team can be self-managed and self-directed

C. Create an environment in which team members can work to the best of their ability

D. Create a sense of team-belonging that fosters inclusive and collaborative behaviors

76. A project manager is in the process of building the project team and obtaining the materials and supplies the team will need to achieve the project's planned outcomes. In what activity are they engaged?

A. Developing resources

B. Managing resources

C. Acquiring resources

D. Estimating resource needs

77. You are the project manager for Changing Tides video games. Your project is a long-term project and will be completed in three phases over the next two years. You have gathered the inputs for the Estimate Activity Durations process and are ready to produce the activity duration estimates. Your sponsor would like a project estimate for all three phases by the end of the week. He understands that at this stage it will be a rough order of magnitude estimate and not entirely accurate. Which of the following tools and techniques will you use to produce this estimate?

A. Parametric estimating

B. Expert judgment

C. Analogous estimating

D. Three-point estimating

78. A small sample of your project's critical path is shown in the following table. Assuming each activity must finish before the next activity can begin, what is the late start and late finish date for activity 3?

Activity	Duration	Early Start	Early Finish
1	22	5/1	5/22
2	5	5/23	5/28
3	7	5/29	6/4
4	1	6/5	6/5

A. Late start is 5/30, and late finish is 6/5.

B. Late start is 5/29, and late finish is 6/4.

C. Late start is 5/31, and late finish is 6/6.

D. Late start is 6/5, and late finish is 6/11.

79. A small sample of your project's critical path is shown in the following table. Assuming each activity must finish before the next activity can begin, which of the following options is not correct?

Activity	Duration	Early Start	Early Finish
1	22	5/1	5/22
2	5	5/23	5/28
3	7	5/29	6/4
4	1		

   A. Activity 1-2-3-4 is the critical path.

   B. Late start and late finish are the next set of calculations to perform.

   C. To complete the chart and determine the remaining dates for activity 4, you have to perform a backward pass.

   D. After early start, early finish, late start, and late finish dates are established, you can calculate the float for each activity.

80. A small sample of your project's PERT calculations is shown here. Activity 2 is particularly important to the project, and your stakeholders are asking for a confidence level for this activity. You tell them there is a 95.44 percent chance of completing activity 2 within how many days?

Activity	Optimistic	Pessimistic	Likely Expected Value
1	10	14	12
2	20	30	23
3	3	3	3

   A. Between 18 and 28 days

   B. Between 21 and 25 days

   C. Between 13 and 33 days

   D. Between 23 and 28 days

81. The president of the company has asked you to lead a large new project that links to the company's number-one strategic priority. As a result, you will need to transition one of your other projects to another project manager. During a transitionary meeting, your colleague asks to see what training has been planned for the team. Where is this information captured?

   A. Training management plan

   B. Communications management plan

   C. Team charter

   D. Resource management plan

82. You are a project manager working within a division that recently experienced a reorganization. During a staff meeting, you learn that division leadership announced shifting technology to the cloud as the top strategic priority. You have been managing a project using an Agile approach, and you know this has a direct impact on your project. What are you likely to do next?

    A. Sit down with the sponsor to assess the impact and proceed with the change management process

    B. Assess the impact to the backlog and refine the backlog with the help of the team

    C. Cancel the project and submit a new project that will properly address the updated scope

    D. Meet with division leadership to obtain an exception against going to the cloud

83. Your organization is experiencing a shake-up at the top levels of management. Your project team has expressed concerns that their project might be canceled because of the changes going on at the top. Sure enough, your project team was correct in their suspicions. You've received notice that the project is canceled. The team has one remaining deliverable for the project that was scheduled for completion next month. Your next step is to document the work results to date. Which of the following describes the tools and techniques of the process this question describes?

    A. Information management systems, expert judgment, and meetings

    B. Seven basic quality tools, statistical sampling, inspection, and approved change requests review

    C. Inspection and decision-making techniques

    D. Variance analysis

84. A project manager is developing a high-level summary timeline of the schedule, based on the product road map, in collaboration with the team. This exercise will determine the number of sprints that are included within the release. Which tool or technique is the project manager and team using to develop the schedule?

    A. Agile release planning

    B. Sprint planning

    C. Schedule network analysis

    D. Release-driven development

85. According to Edward de Bono, what type of alternatives analysis can be used to determine a project's scope?

    A. Bottoms-up

    B. Expert judgment

    C. Lateral thinking

    D. Brain writing

86. A project manager became aware of a disagreement between two developers who have been paired together to write code. Which conflict-resolution technique should the project manager use to create a win-win situation?

A. Smoothing

B. Compromising

C. Directing

D. Collaborating

87. You are a project manager for SubZero Delights, a company that offers extraordinary experiences to travelers. You have been working hard at developing your own personal leadership skills and have recruited a mentor to help you. During a mentoring session, you ask your mentor to talk about the characteristics that good leaders exhibit. What characteristics are they likely to call out? (Select three.)

A. Leaders use referent power.

B. Leaders impart vision.

C. Leaders are concerned with strategic plans.

D. Leaders are concerned with satisfying stakeholder needs.

88. Match the examples provided to the corresponding categories of influence that affect projects.

Categories of Project Influence

Examples	Category
A. Organizational culture	1. Enterprise environmental factors
B. Employee capability	2. Organizational process assets
C. Organizational policies	
D. Lessons learned	
E. Marketplace conditions	

89. Calculate the to-complete performance index (TCPI) based on the current EAC, using the following values: BAC = 15,000, AC = 12,000, EV = 10,000, EAC = 17,000.

A. 0.50

B. 1.67

C. 1.0

D. Insufficient information provided

90. Which of the following best defines backlog refinement?

    A. An ordered list of user-centric requirements that a team maintains for a product

    B. The iterative process of increasing the level of detail in a plan as greater amounts of information and more accurate estimates become available

    C. The progressive elaboration of project requirements and/or the ongoing activity in which the team reviews, updates, and writes requirements to satisfy the need of the customer

    D. A meeting held by the team where the work that was accomplished or completed during the sprint is reviewed

91. Which of the following are common sources of conflict? (Select three.)

    A. Role definition

    B. Scarce resources

    C. Personal work styles

    D. Scheduling priorities

92. Your project sponsor approaches you to let you know that he is considering awarding a senior engineer on your project with a spot bonus of $1,000 for her work. While the engineer has delivered against commitments, she created a lot of friction with others in the process and was constantly violating the agreement documented within the team charter. What should you do?

    A. You notify the sponsor that the reward is appropriately linked to the performance.

    B. You notify the sponsor that the reward should be distributed among the team equally.

    C. You notify the sponsor that rewards are not an optimal way of motivating the team.

    D. You notify the sponsor that the reward is not in line with performance.

93. Paul meets with his sponsor to review and obtain feedback on the project's benefits management plan. He carefully reviews the list of benefits captured to date, who owns each benefit, and how they map to the company's strategic objectives. What feedback is the sponsor likely to provide Paul about the plan?

    A. The benefits management plan looks complete, with key components in place.

    B. The benefits management plan is lacking a system that will provide a feedback loop between him and Paul.

    C. The benefits management plan is lacking a system that will trace each benefit to organizational strategy.

    D. The benefits management plan is lacking a system that will ensure benefits are tracked.

94. You work for a company that writes billing software programs for the communication industry. Your customer is located in a country that limits the number of foreigners allowed into the country. You identify this risk in your risk management plan. The critical point during the project is installation and setup. You have assessed the risks and are using the Perform Qualitative Risk Analysis process. Which of the following tools and techniques will you use to determine the potential effect on the project objectives (such as time, cost, scope, or quality) and determine the likelihood of the risk occurring?

    A. Risk categorization

    B. Risk probability and impact assessment

C. Risk data quality assessment

D. Risk urgency assessment

95. Mike is a seasoned project manager who has been tasked with mentoring Bernard, a junior project manager. During a mentoring session, Mike stresses the importance of managing lines of communication and then asks Bernard how many stakeholders are engaged in his project. Bernard responds with 15. How many lines of communication must Bernard manage for his project?

A. 113

B. 105

C. 210

D. 225

96. Kristin has recently joined a growing startup company in the medical device industry. While she is considered an experienced project manager, the industry is new for her. To be effective, what should Kristin do?

A. Research the medical device industry

B. Assess the organization's culture

C. Review the portfolio of projects

D. Shadow her colleagues

97. You recently joined an organization as a project manager. Your first project assignment involves a project that has been active for six months. The prior project manager retired from the company after a 20-year tenure. During your first week on the job, you notice that team members are experiencing a multitude of conflicts with one another. In leaning on your experience, you know that conflicts typically come about as a result of what? (Select three.)

A. Resource availability

B. Personal work habits

C. Geographical issues

D. Scheduling issues

98. You are working on an Agile project that is most concerned about providing finished deliverables that the customer may use immediately. Which development life cycle are you most likely to use?

A. Incremental

B. Predictive

C. Agile

D. Iterative

99. A project manager managing a small project has a total of 45 active stakeholders. How many lines of communication exist?

A. 1,035

B. 968

C. 1,013

D. 990

100. A RAM or RACI chart is considered which of the following?

    A. A type of OBS chart

    B. A hierarchical chart

    C. A type of RBS chart

    D. A matrix-based chart

101. A project manager who follows a servant leader approach to managing the team is in the process of onboarding a new team member to the project. This new team member will help fill skill-level gaps that were found to exist within the current team. She provides the new team member with a copy of the project charter and commits to sending a copy of another document that addresses team values, ground rules, and working agreements among the team. What document will the project manager send the team member that addresses these items?

    A. The project charter

    B. The resource management plan

    C. The release backlog

    D. The team charter

102. Which of the following best defines explicit knowledge?

    A. Technical knowledge documented from past project experiences by the team

    B. Standardized knowledge defined and published by industry-recognized organizations

    C. Knowledge that can be captured and expressed using words, pictures, and numbers

    D. Knowledge that is difficult to capture or express, such as beliefs, experiences, and "know-how"

103. Which of the following statements are true? (Select three.)

    A. Estimate Activity Resources is a key step in developing the schedule and is a process belonging to the Project Schedule Management Knowledge Area.

    B. Plan Resource Management, Estimate Costs, and Control Procurements are all project management processes.

    C. Project Integration Management, Project Scope Management, and Project Schedule Management are examples of project management Knowledge Areas.

    D. There are a total of 49 project management processes.

104. In flow-based Agile, what questions are teams likely to pose during stand-ups? (Select two.)

    A. What do we need to finish as a team?

    B. What did I complete since the last stand-up?

    C. What am I planning to complete between now and the next stand-up?

    D. In anyone working on anything that is not on the board?

105. A project manager considers the skills and capabilities needed to accomplish planned outcomes of a project, including the type and quantities of material, equipment, and supplies. What activity is the project manager engaged in?

A. Developing the project team

B. Developing the schedule

C. Estimating resource needs

D. Managing the project team

106. A project manager recently received agreement to crash the schedule. He begins negotiating with the head of development to utilize their most senior Java developer. What project management activity is the project manager performing?

A. Controlling the schedule

B. Controlling resources

C. Controlling costs

D. Monitoring and controlling the project work

107. Manfrit recently took over a project after the project manager left the company. The project is in the middle of its fifth iteration. As Manfrit begins joining team meetings, he immediately notes that the team is unable to reach even a single outcome when attempting to do so. Team members would respectfully share their ideas until the time allotted for the meeting came to an end. Manfrit decides to review the team charter. What gaps within the charter is he likely to find?

A. Lack of project vision

B. Lack of team responsibilities

C. Lack of team values

D. Lack of decision-making criteria

108. Mike is a seasoned project manager who has been tasked with mentoring Bernard, a junior project manager. During a mentoring session, Mike talks about the importance of regularly monitoring enterprise environmental factors. Bernard expresses confusion and asks Mike to explain why he should be concerned with something that is out of his control. What is Mike most likely to respond as the *primary* reason?

A. Project managers should always be curious and up to speed with the business landscape.

B. Project managers may benefit from leveraging newly published resources.

C. Enterprise environmental factors may positively or negatively affect a project.

D. Enterprise environmental factors may result in the cancellation of a project.

109. Kaylee is a risk manager working in collaboration with Alyssa, a project manager, and both work for a top healthcare company. They are currently in the process of performing risk analysis. To determine the most likely date of project completion, based on known risks, they run a simulation using a risk management tool that will run through thousands of possible scenarios. What tool are they using?

A. Monte Carlo analysis

B. Decision-tree analysis

C. Sensitivity analysis

D. Influence diagrams

110. You are managing a project using the Crystal methodology. As is customary within your organization, you leverage a communications platform that allows the team to chat, upload and download files, and host meetings virtually. Using this platform, you upload a document and email an electronic link to the team to request that they review it within two business days. You know that some members of the team are not proactive about downloading key project documents, so you set up time with them to review the information. Which of the following statements is true regarding this scenario?

A. You are using a pull communication method of communicating with the team.

B. You have a combination of proactive and high maintenance team members.

C. You are using a combination of methods to communicate with the team.

D. You are using an interactive method of communicating with the team.

111. You are a project manager for SubZero Delights, a company that offers extraordinary experiences to travelers. Your latest project involves the development of a smart phone app that automatically picks up a customer's GPS coordinates to provide tailored resources and recommendations. You take time to consider the project complexity and decide to plot the degree of uncertainty against requirement uncertainty. What model are you using?

A. Release Model

B. Stacey Complexity Model

C. Shu-Ha-Ri Model

D. Agile Model

112. This motivational theory states that people will behave a certain way if they think there will be a good reward for doing so.

A. Hygiene Theory

B. Hierarchy of Needs

C. Expectancy Theory

D. Achievement Theory

113. You are working on a project that involves multiple vendors. One of the vendors has been difficult to work with and is not very cooperative. You have received the latest invoice from them for services and disagree with them about the charges they have listed for the change request that was submitted last month. When you called and spoke with your representative at the company, they refused to budge on the charges. You will likely need to use an alternative dispute resolution (ADR) to get to the bottom of this matter. Which tool and technique of the Control Procurements process does this question describe?

    A. Payment systems

    B. Claims administration

    C. Procurement performance reviews

    D. Contract change control system

114. To increase communication across ambiguous projects, a project manager using an Agile approach is likely to do what?

    A. Communicate daily

    B. Communicate digitally ad hoc

    C. Communicate frequently

    D. Communicate based on a plan

115. A project manager is facilitating a meeting to further define user stories for the upcoming iteration. Two team members involved, Bob and Jenny, are very vocal during the start of the meeting, with Jenny passionately noting that the second user story should be punted to the next iteration. She moves on to the next user story, ignoring Bob's opposing views on the topic. Bob accepts the decision hesitantly and remains quiet for the remainder of the meeting, accepting other decisions made by Jenny and the rest of the team. At the end of the meeting, the project manager notes to Bob that she will prioritize user story #2 at the top of the backlog, to be pulled into the iteration should capacity allow. Which of the following conflict-resolution technique did Bob use in this scenario?

    A. Smoothing

    B. Compromising

    C. Directing

    D. Collaborating

116. Which organizational management theorist developed Theory X and Theory Y?

    A. Robert Tannenbaum

    B. William Ouichi

    C. Douglas McGregor

    D. Victor Vroom

117. Alyssa is a project manager tasked with managing an infrastructure project that will consolidate five call centers into one. To date, she has completed and received sign-off of the project charter and identified her stakeholders. Currently, she is in the process of defining and documenting which processes and methodology she will use to manage the project. What process is she performing?

    A. Develop Project Charter

    B. Develop Project Management Plan

    C. Manage Project Knowledge

    D. Monitor and Control Project Work

118. You are a lead project manager for a company that develops and manufactures healthcare devices. Recently, your team went through major organizational changes, which required resource shifts within project teams. One of your projects experienced a 50 percent change in team member assignments. June, a team member who remained on the project, seeks you out to express concerns regarding one of her new colleagues, who she feels does not have the technical aptitude to complete work assigned to him this iteration. You trust her judgment. What should you do regarding the new team member?

    A. Release the team member immediately

    B. Nothing, since the assignment has been made

    C. Incorporate training and mentorship into the assignment

    D. Retain the team member but reassign the work

119. You are guiding your organization through the adoption of an Agile approach and are also teaching project managers about servant leadership. A tenured project manager approaches you and asks how this will change his role and approach to managing the team. How should you respond?

    A. The emphasis will now be on allowing the team to make their own decisions and set their own goals by taking a more hands-off approach.

    B. The emphasis will now be on fostering a collaborative environment and serving as an inspiration to the team that will be executing the work.

    C. The emphasis will now be on reducing the impact of change by stressing the collection of requirements early on within the project's life cycle.

    D. The emphasis will now be on coaching team members, distributing responsibility to the team, and fostering a collaborative environment.

120. You work within a PMO that is in the process of transitioning to an Agile way of working. The team has met with high resistance from leadership who are unaccustomed to adaptive approaches. What can the PMO leader do to encourage adoption?

    A. Forge forward and provide point-in-time training on the new methods as they are being used

    B. Train project managers on the various adaptive approaches to help spread the word

    C. Remain with a predictive approach until support from leadership increases

    D. Use a hybrid method that combines predictive and adaptive approaches

121. Marysil recently accepted a new role as lead project manager within a well-established healthcare company. Over the past three months she has worked hard to introduce new concepts and styles into the environment. She approaches every situation by considering purpose, people, and process—in that order. What type of leadership style does Marysil follow?

A. Servant leadership

B. Interactional

C. Laissez-faire

D. Charismatic

122. You are a lead project manager for a company that develops and manufactures healthcare devices. Recently, your team went through major organizational changes. You notice that your new manager closely monitors what time employees arrive and leave for work. You overhear her say that she is concerned that the team lacks ambition. What type of management style does your new manager exhibit?

A. Theory X

B. Theory Y

C. Theory Z

D. Theory XY

123. Your project sponsor has asked you to monitor the project results for conformity to standards. You will use the tools and techniques of the Control Quality process to help accomplish this. You know that these tools can be used with which of the following to help identify and resolve problems related to quality defects?

A. Expert judgment

B. Facilitation techniques

C. Plan-Do-Check-Act cycle

D. Alternatives generation

124. Your project has come about because of a social need. You're calculating performance measurements and know the following information: BAC = 2400, ETC = 400, PV = 2200, EV = 2100, and AC = 2000. What are the CPI and SPI?

A. CPI = 1.14 and SPI = .87

B. CPI = 1.05 and SPI =.95

C. CPI = .87 and SPI = 1.14

D. CPI = .95 and SPI = 1.05

125. You have recently transitioned leadership of a project to another project manager and have been mentoring him as he gets up to speed on the project. During a mentoring session, he shares that a senior engineer critical to the project has been disruptive during meetings and has blatantly been violating team ground rules. How should you advise your colleague?

A. Encourage your colleague to use their gut instincts to determine the right course of action.

B. Immediately escalate to the engineer's manager due to the behavior being disruptive.

C. Due to the criticality of the resource, it is more important that they have flexibility against the rules.

D. Address the ground rule violation directly with the engineer as a first step.

126. This methodology is a hybrid of two Agile approaches, where the work is organized in sprints and uses a board to display the work of the sprint and monitor work in progress.

   A. Scrumfall

   B. eXtreme Programming

   C. Dynamic Systems Development Method

   D. Scrumban

127. A project manager of a large manufacturing company is working on a new system that will reduce the bolt manufacturing process by 30 seconds, saving the company 2 percent in annual operating costs. This project will touch all departments and engage senior leadership. The project manager knows stakeholder engagement will be critical to success and spends time analyzing levels of anticipated engagement. She starts by considering the head of logistics, who has not commented on or expressed any reactions about the project. The executive was present at a recent briefing where she reviewed the charter. What level of engagement will the project manager document for this stakeholder?

   A. Resistant

   B. Unaware

   C. Supportive

   D. Neutral

128. A project team member approaches you to inform you that she must leave work early due to personal issues. You later discover that her spouse has experienced severe medical issues and that as a result of related expenses, they are losing their home and having difficulty with basic expenses such as food. After obtaining her permission, you rally the team and hold several fundraising events to help cover the expenses. Which of the following statements describes this situation?

   A. According to Maslow's Hierarchy of Needs, this team member is at the self-actualization level of the pyramid.

   B. According to Maslow's Hierarchy of Needs, this team member is at the self-esteem level of the pyramid.

   C. According to Maslow's Hierarchy of Needs, this team member is at the safety and security needs level of the pyramid.

   D. According to Maslow's Hierarchy of Needs, this team member is at the basic physical needs level of the pyramid.

129. You are a project manager for Community Trends, a nonprofit organization. Your project has come about because of a social need. You're calculating performance measurements, and you know the following information: BAC = 900, ETC = 65, PV = 500, EV = 475, and AC = 425. Which of the following statements is true?

   A. This project is ahead of schedule, and costs are higher than planned.

   B. This project is behind schedule, and costs are higher than planned.

   C. This project is behind schedule, but costs are lower than planned.

   D. This project is ahead of schedule, and costs are lower than planned.

130. Which of the following domains are part of the Five-Factor Model that identifies personality traits? (Select two.)

    A. Neuroticism

    B. Conscientiousness

    C. Intuition

    D. Sensing

131. Which of the following best describes enterprise environmental factors?

    A. Factors that affect teams at an enterprise level from within the organization

    B. Factors that are internal to the organization, such as internal policies and procedures

    C. Federal regulations that affect projects at an enterprise-wide level

    D. Factors both internal and external to the organization that can influence the project

132. The project team recently participated in a working session to determine the costs associated with individual activities. To produce a more accurate estimate, they broke each activity down further into smaller chunks. What estimating technique is the team using?

    A. Analogous estimating

    B. Parametric estimating

    C. Bottom-up estimating

    D. Three-point estimating

133. A project manager of a large manufacturing company is working on a new system that will reduce the bolt manufacturing process by 30 seconds, saving the company 2 percent in annual operating costs. This project will touch all departments and engage senior leadership. The project manager knows stakeholder engagement will be critical to success and sets up a brainstorming session with the sponsor to develop the initial list of stakeholders. She then engages those individuals to further capture other stakeholders that will need to be involved and collect any information available about them in order to conduct stakeholder analysis. Where will the project manager capture this information?

    A. Stakeholder register

    B. Stakeholder engagement plan

    C. Assumptions log

    D. Team charter

134. A stakeholder register documents which of the following? (Select three.)

    A. Stakeholder ground rules

    B. Stakeholder identification information

    C. Stakeholder assessment information

    D. Stakeholder classification

135. What should project managers consider when tailoring planning activities associated with resource management?

    A. Life-cycle approach used

    B. Diversity of team members

    C. Physical location of team members

    D. Team member biases

    E. A, B, C

    F. None of the above

136. You are a lead project manager for a company that develops and manufactures healthcare devices. Recently, your team went through major organizational changes, which required resource shifts within project teams. One of your projects experienced a 50 percent change in team member assignments. What can you do to help the team build a collaborative and cooperative working environment?

    A. Negotiate with other leaders

    B. Use your influencing skills

    C. Spotlight your best performers

    D. Facilitate team-building activities

137. You are using a set of defined minimum requirements and information about the sellers (including past performance, contract compliance, and quality ratings) to make a selection among vendor proposals. What two tools and techniques does this represent?

    A. Screening systems and seller rating systems, respectively

    B. Screening systems and internet search, respectively

    C. Seller rating systems and screening systems, respectively

    D. Internet search and screening systems, respectively

138. You are the project manager for a large software development project. Your project is being performed under contract, and the project has just been canceled. Which of the following processes should document the level of completeness of the project?

    A. Close Project or Phase

    B. Control Quality

    C. Validate Scope

    D. Perform Integrated Change Control

139. Forming successful Agile teams involves establishing which of the following underlying factors? (Select three.)

    A. Building a foundational trust

    B. Building an Agile mindset

    C. Building dedicated teams

    D. Building a safe working environment

140. You are a project manager for SubZero Delights, a company that offers extraordinary experiences to travelers. Your latest project involves the development of a smartphone app that automatically picks up a customer's GPS coordinates to provide tailored resources and recommendations. You are new to the company and are considering culture in determining how best to manage the project. What can you examine to evaluate culture?

   A. Organizational bias

   B. Project team preferences

   C. History of past projects

   D. How people behave

141. Manfrit and Frank are two project managers who have supported one another throughout their careers. During a casual lunch, Frank asks Manfrit for advice, noting that he has been struggling to get his team to embrace eXtreme Programming practices. He notes that, after undergoing a few training sessions, the team doesn't understand the terminology and finds it confusing. What advice should Manfrit provide in this situation?

   A. Push for colocated teams

   B. Demonstrate transparency

   C. Modify the terms so they feel more familiar

   D. Provide education and training

142. Kaylee is a risk manager working in collaboration with Alyssa, a project manager, and both work for a top healthcare company. They are currently in the process of performing risk analysis. Of the 20 risks identified, 5 are deemed to be low priority. Where will these risks be documented?

   A. A watch list

   B. The risk report

   C. The project management plan

   D. The risk management plan

143. Ronaldo has just joined the company as a project manager and is taking over an active project that is in the process of developing the schedule. The previous project manager did a good job of maintaining project management documents up-to-date. Which project management document can Ronaldo reference that will outline the methodology and tools the team is using to perform schedule network analysis?

   A. Cost management plan

   B. Activity list

   C. Schedule management plan

   D. Project schedule network diagram

144. A project manager is facilitating a meeting to further define user stories for the upcoming iteration. Two team members involved, Bob and Jenny, are very vocal during the start of the meeting, with Jenny passionately noting that the second user story should be punted to the next iteration. She moves on to the next user story, ignoring Bob's opposing views on the topic. Bob accepts the decision hesitantly and remains quiet for the remainder of the meeting, accepting other decisions made by Jenny and the rest of the team. At the end of the meeting, the project manager notes to Bob that she will prioritize user story #2 at the top of the backlog, to be pulled into the iteration should capacity allow. Which of the following conflict-resolution techniques did Jenny use in this scenario?

   A. Smoothing

   B. Compromising

   C. Directing

   D. Collaborating

145. Given the following information, are project costs ahead or behind what was planned for this period? EV = 95, PV = 85, AC = 100.

   A. Ahead, because the result of the variance formula is negative

   B. Behind, because the result of the variance formula is negative

   C. Ahead, because the result of the variance formula is positive

   D. Behind, because the result of the variance formula is positive

146. A business analyst has just facilitated a requirements-gathering session. The following week, the project manager begins the process of capturing and documenting the project's deliverables and creating a WBS. The business analyst and project manager are carrying out processes that belong to which of the following Knowledge Areas?

   A. Project Schedule Management

   B. Project Integration Management

   C. Project Requirements Management

   D. Project Scope Management

147. Which of the following statements about project governance frameworks are true? (Select three.)

   A. Project governance specifies operational, legal, and risk policies.

   B. Project governance guides project management activities in order to achieve intended goals.

   C. Project governance provides stakeholders with structure, processes, and decision-making models for the project.

   D. Project governance clarifies how changes to the project are addressed when beyond the authority of the project manager.

148. The president of the company has asked you to lead a large new project that links to the company's number-one strategic priority. As a result, you will need to transition one of your other projects to another project manager. During a transitionary meeting, your colleague asks to see the team's social contract so that they can become familiar with established ground rules. What document are they referring to?

   A. Resource management plan

   B. Project management plan

   C. Project charter

   D. Team charter

149. Your project team is struggling to complete the latest set of features, which requires advanced knowledge of facial recognition technology. In talking with a peer, they encourage you to consider expanding the team to include virtual team members. What benefits can this provide, which can alleviate some of the challenges you are facing?

   A. Costs are reduced.

   B. Less travel will be required.

   C. The pool of skilled resources widens.

   D. The team will be closer to customers and suppliers.

150. Which of the following is a valid input that a project manager can use to disseminate information to appropriate stakeholders?

   A. Communication technology

   B. Work performance reports

   C. Project management information system

   D. Project reporting

151. This tool and technique of the Develop Schedule process is used in conjunction with some of its other tools and techniques, including critical path method, to produce the project schedule using a predictive approach.

   A. Applying leads and lags

   B. Schedule network analysis

   C. Resource leveling

   D. Scheduling tool

152. There are various elements that make up project artifacts created by a project manager. Match the element described with the project artifact that documents it.

Project Artifacts and Elements

Elements Documented	Project Artifact
A. Roles and responsibilities	1. Resource management plan
B. Meeting guidelines	2. Team charter
C. Team agreements	
D. Training needed	
E. How team will be developed	

153. Marysil is an enterprise project manager for Cups on Fire. She is managing the implementation of an enterprise relationship management system using a hybrid of waterfall and Scrum. This is the most complex project the team has undertaken to date. For this reason, she puts careful attention to risk management activities. She recently learned that a risk had materialized and become an issue, with the team missing early warning signs that could have increased the response to the situation. The sponsor of the project asks Marysil to debrief him on the situation and to provide a summary of overall project risk. What document will Marysil review with the sponsor?

A. Risk register

B. Risk report

C. Risk management plan

D. Assumptions log

154. All of the following statements are true regarding configuration management except which one?

A. The configuration management system is a subset of the records management system.

B. Change control systems are a subset of the configuration management system.

C. Configuration control is managed through the configuration management system and is concerned with changes to the specifications of the deliverables.

D. Configuration control is managed through the configuration management system and is concerned with changes to the project management processes.

155. A project manager rallies the team together for one final meeting, which will wrap up with a celebration for the successful achievement of the project's final feature and completion of all transition activities. Post-meeting, the project manager sits down to summarize the project's journey, including its performance against planned business value and objectives. This summary document will then be handed over to the sponsor and archived with the remaining project artifacts for future reference. What is this summary document also known as?

A. Performance review

B. Project charter

  C. Lessons learned register

  D. Final report

156. Within an Agile project, the role of project manager may or may not be used. What other roles within an Agile team reflect responsiblities similar to those of a project manager?

  A. Team facilitator

  B. Scrum master

  C. Team coach

  D. Project team lead

  E. A, B, C, D

157. What questions should a team ask when developing an implementation strategy using an Agile mindset? (Select two.)

  A. How can the project team act in an Agile manner?

  B. How can the team avoid changes to maintain progress against the plan?

  C. How can the team finalize clear requirements early?

  D. What work can be avoided in order to focus on high-priority items?

158. Which of the following represent characteristics of a servant leader? (Select three.)

  A. Promote self-awareness

  B. Prefer to coach versus control

  C. Maintain a strong conviction

  D. Help others grow

159. Control charts measure the results of processes over time and depict common causes of variances. Common causes of variances are a result of all of the following except which one?

  A. Random variances

  B. Quantifiable variances

  C. Predictable variances

  D. Variances that are always present

160. You are a project manager working for Mail House King. Your company processes orders for several mail-order catalog companies. Your project is to install new mail-sorting equipment and software. You've had some problems and experienced some variances during the project. You expect these variances to continue throughout the life of the project and expect they will be similar to the variances you've seen so far. You know the following information: PV = 900, BAC = 1400, EV = 925, AC = 925. Which of the following is the correct ETC given the circumstances?

  A. 490

  B. 1,400

  C. 475

  D. 500

161. Which interpersonal and team skills can a project manager use to manage the project team? (Select three.)

   A. Conflict management

   B. Project management information system

   C. Emotional intelligence

   D. Influencing

162. Which of the following best describes a burndown chart?

   A. A chart that represents the work completed toward the release of a product

   B. A chart that tracks the remaining work to be completed versus the time remaining in a timebox

   C. A bar chart that represents schedule information where activities are listed on the vertical axis, with dates on the horizontal axis

   D. A chart that identifies the scheduled start or completion of major deliverables and key external interfaces

163. A project manager working within an Agile PMO is using a new approved contractor to fast-track the implementation of cloud-based solutions for her project. As part of overseeing the procurement activities for the project, she conducts a structured review of the work performed by the contractor. Which tool and technique does this question describe?

   A. Payment systems

   B. Claims administration system

   C. Contract change control system

   D. Inspection

164. All of the following are outputs of the Manage Project Knowledge process except for which one?

   A. Deliverables

   B. Lessons learned register

   C. Project management plan updates

   D. Organizational process asset updates

165. Manfrit and Frank are two project managers who have supported one another throughout their careers. Lately, Frank has sought Manfrit's advice on getting his team to adopt eXtreme Programming practices. During the latest conversation, Frank asks Manfrit how to get teams to overcome fear resulting from transparency of work. What advice should Manfrit provide in this situation?

   A. Push for colocated teams

   B. Demonstrate transparency

   C. Modify the terms so they feel more familiar

   D. Provide education and training

166. Which of the following best describes the purpose of the change log?

   A. It is used to document corrective action needed during a project.

   B. It is used to document changes that occur during a project.

   C. It is used to document preventive action needed during a project.

   D. It is used to document defect repairs that are needed during a project.

167. You are a lead project manager for a company that develops and manufactures healthcare devices. Recently, your team went through major organizational changes, which required resource shifts within project teams. One of your projects experienced a 50 percent change in team member assignments. Many of the team members do not know one another as a result. What phase of the team development model is your project team currently in?

   A. Norming

   B. Performing

   C. Forming

   D. Storming

168. You are a project manager for SubZero Delights, a company that offers extraordinary experiences to travelers. Your latest project involves the development of a smartphone app that automatically picks up a customer's GPS coordinates to provide tailored resources and recommendations. You chose a hybrid approach with a goal of delivering results faster and maximizing the speed at which the team can work. Which of the following technical practices can the team incorporate to accomplish this goal?

   A. Continuous integration

   B. Test at all levels

   C. Test-driven development

   D. Spikes

   E. All of the above

   F. None of the above

169. Marysil is an enterprise project manager for Cups on Fire. She is managing the implementation of an enterprise relationship management system using a hybrid of waterfall and Scrum. This is the most complex project the team has undertaken to date. For this reason, she puts careful attention to risk management activities. She recently learned that a risk had materialized and become an issue. Because of the nature of the issue, Marysil will need to follow the escalation process to inform the appropriate individuals. Where will she need to look in order to find the escalation processes?

   A. Project management plan

   B. Issue log

   C. Risk management plan

   D. Communications management plan

170. A stakeholder's influence is highest at what point of the project life cycle?

    A. Initiating stages

    B. Planning stages

    C. Executing stages

    D. Closing stages

171. Match the power type with its description.

Power types

Type	Description
A. Punishment	1. When a person being influenced believes the manager, or the person doing the influencing, is knowledgeable about the subject
B. Expert	2. When power comes about as a result of the influencer's position
C. Legitimate	3. When power is inferred to the influencer by their subordinates
D. Referent	4. When the employee is threatened with consequences if expectations are not met

172. What is the most commonly used method of performance measurement?

    A. Variance analysis

    B. Trend analysis

    C. Forecasting

    D. Earned value management

173. During a meeting with the team, you collaborate to prepare stories for the upcoming iteration, with the intention of providing enough information about the stories for the team to understand what the stories are and determine sizing. In what activity are you engaged?

    A. Planning for the upcoming sprint

    B. Refining the backlog

    C. Creating the backlog

    D. Developing the product road map

174. Which of the following are elements captured within the team charter? (Select two.)

    A. Roles and responsibilities

    B. Communication guidelines

    C. Decision-making criteria

    D. Process for acquiring team members

175. A predictive life cycle approach is characterized by which of the following? (Select two.)

    A. Scope, time, and cost are determined in the early phases of the life cycle.

    B. Change is constrained as much as possible.

    C. Scope is determined early in the project life cycle, but time and cost are routinely modified.

    D. Deliverables contain sufficient capability to be considered complete after one iteration.

176. Agile practices promote dedicated team members. When this is not the case, team members must multitask and experience productivity losses. On average, what range of productivity loss occurs?

    A. 0 percent to 10 percent

    B. 15 percent to 30 percent

    C. 50 percent to 75 percent

    D. 20 percent to 40 percent

177. Which of the following best describes the purpose of corrective action taken during the Executing process activities of the project?

    A. An intentional activity that ensures the future performance of the project work is aligned with the project management plan

    B. An intentional activity to modify a nonconforming product or product component

    C. An unintentional activity that ensures that the work of the project is aligned with the project management plan

    D. An intentional activity intended to bring the work of the project back into alignment with the project management plan

178. A project manager rallies the team together for one final meeting, which will wrap up with a celebration for the successful achievement of the project's final feature. During the meeting, the project manager captures feedback from the team about what went well and what could have been improved throughout the project's life. The project manager also discusses the achievement of planned benefits. In what project artifact will the project manager capture this information?

    A. Performance review

    B. Project charter

    C. Lessons learned register

    D. Final report

179. Your project team is struggling to complete the latest set of features, which requires advanced knowledge of facial recognition technology. After considering various options, you decide to create a war room. What are you hoping to accomplish?

    A. Pair team members together to collaborate on coding

    B. Enable team members to focus on their assigned deliverables

    C. Bring team members together physically for the entire project

    D. Bring team members virtually for the duration of the project

180. As a result of a face-to-face meeting you recently had, you have resolved an issue and have come away with an update to the issue log, change requests, project management plan updates, and project documents updates, and you have submitted a change request. You know all of the following are true regarding this except which one?

A. This describes the Manage Communications process.

B. The issue log acts like an action item log in this process.

C. Issues should be ranked and prioritized.

D. Responsible parties and due dates should be assigned to each issue.

181. You are a lead project manager for a company that develops and manufactures healthcare devices. Recently, your team went through major organizational changes, which required resource shifts within project teams. One of your projects experienced a 50 percent change in team member assignments. While the change posed challenges initially, the team has finally settled and are focused on the project. What phase of the team development model is your project team currently in?

A. Norming

B. Performing

C. Forming

D. Storming

182. Marysil is an enterprise project manager for Cups on Fire. She is managing the implementation of an enterprise relationship management system using a hybrid of waterfall and Scrum. In preparation for a meeting with the sponsor, Marysil plans to review how much work the team has and whether they will finish on time. Which of the following are useful point-in-time measurements that Marysil may use? (Select three.)

A. Release backlog

B. Burnup chart

C. Burndown chart

D. Lead time

183. You are managing a software development project with a team that is colocated. The project is managed through a set of iterations that begin with the creation of story cards. The focus of each iteration is to deliver business value, with programmers working together in pairs and as a group. Which of the following are true regarding this question? (Select two.)

A. You are using a technique called pair programming.

B. You are following the Feature Driven Development approach.

C. You are using eXtreme Programming to manage the project.

D. You are using an approach that is people-focused.

184. Match the theory with the name of the individual responsible for developing it.

Motivational Theories

Theory	Theorist
A. Theory of X and Y	1. David McClelland
B. Hygiene Theory	2. Victor Vroom
C. Achievement Theory	3. Douglas McGregor
D. Expectancy Theory	4. Frederick Herzberg
E. Maslow's Hierarchy of Needs	5. Abraham Maslow

185. Marysil is an enterprise project manager for Cups on Fire. She is managing the implementation of an enterprise relationship management system using a hybrid of waterfall and Scrum. This is the most complex project the team has undertaken to date. For this reason, she puts careful attention to risk management activities. She recently learned that a risk had materialized and become an issue, with the team missing early warning signs that could have increased the response to the situation. She decides to review information that had been captured about the risk to determine whether the risk triggers were noted correctly and to take learnings forward. What document will Marysil review to find the risk triggers that had been captured?

A. Risk register

B. Risk report

C. Risk management plan

D. Assumptions log

186. Adaptive life cycles are also known by what other name?

A. Hybrid life cycle

B. Predictive life cycle

C. Change-driven life cycle

D. Plan-driven life cycle

187. You are using Crystal Red to manage your project. At the start of the project, you negotiated with leadership to colocate the team together within a large team for the duration of the project. Your intent is to set up an environment where team members can overhear conversations as they occur within the room to politely eavesdrop and engage in conversations as needed. What is this communication method called?

A. Interactive communication

B. Push communication

C. Pull communication

D. Osmotic communication

188. You work for Writer's Block, a service that reviews and critiques manuscripts for aspiring writers. You were assigned to be the project manager for a new computer system that logs, tracks, and saves submitted manuscripts along with the editor's notes. You hired and worked with a vendor who wrote the system from scratch to your specifications. You are reviewing a report regarding certain aspects of the project's performance, and one of the measurements on the report calculates the difference between the budget at completion and the estimate at completion. Which of the following does this describe?

    A. TCPI

    B. VAC

    C. ETC

    D. EAC

189. A project manager looking to improve their emotional intelligence should focus on what? (Select two.)

    A. Inbound competencies

    B. Technical competencies

    C. Communication management competencies

    D. Outbound competencies

    E. A, D

190. You are a project manager working for a technology company that develops smart Bluetooth-enabled wearables for dogs. The product currently under development features a harness that gently vibrates when the dog gets beyond a specified range from the owner's smartphone. You are developing the application that controls the harness using an incremental approach and have decided to create a prototype to gain feedback from your top five customers. The prototype will contain only a subset of features. What technique is being used by the team?

    A. Inspection

    B. Minimum viable product

    C. Domain object modeling

    D. Incremental development

191. Which of the following describes an incremental life cycle? (Select three.)

    A. Optimized for speed of delivery

    B. Uses iterations to gather insight to rework deliverables

    C. Produces and builds on a subset of the overall solution

    D. Uses prototypes to encourage early feedback

192. Match the domains that make up the Five-Factor Model with their corresponding aspects.

Five-Factor Model Domains and Spectrums

Domains	Aspects of Domain Spectrum
A. Openness to experience	1. Outgoing vs. reserved
B. Conscientiousness	2. Efficient vs. careless
C. Extraversion	3. Inventive vs. easy-going
D. Agreeableness	4. Sensitive vs. confident
E. Neuroticism	5. Compassionate vs. detached

193. Marysil recently accepted a new role as lead project manager within a well-established healthcare company. Over the past three months she has worked hard to introduce new concepts and styles into the environment. She has been met with some resistance by Rachel and Ron, two colleagues who prefer different styles of leadership. Ron is a high-energy and enthusiastic leader who prefers to lead through inspiration and strong conviction. What type of leadership style does Ron follow?

   A. Servant leadership

   B. Interactional

   C. Laissez-faire

   D. Charismatic

194. Which of the following best describes the role of a team facilitator within an Agile team?

   A. The individual who guides and coaches the team, sometimes referred to as Scrum master, project manager, or team coach

   B. The individual responsible for guiding the direction of the product

   C. Individuals who possess the skills necessary to produce a working product

   D. The individual with decision-making authority who authorizes and releases team member assignments

195. Ron is a developer working on a release of a new smartphone application. He and his team are using Scrum to execute the work. Ron has just completed work on the user story he is tasked with for the current sprint and reviews the criteria to ensure that they are complete and ready for customer use. What are the criteria known as?

   A. Acceptance criteria

   B. Definition of done

   C. Value stream mapping

   D. Plan-Do-Check-Act

196. You are a project manager working for a technology company that develops smart Bluetooth-enabled wearables for dogs. The product currently under development features a harness that gently vibrates when the dog gets beyond a specified range from the owner's smartphone. You are developing the application that controls the harness using an incremental approach and have decided to create a prototype to gain feedback from your top five customers. The prototype will contain only a subset of features. What benefit does the team hope to gain by using this approach?

A. Spread out costs throughout the life of the product

B. Engage top customers to prioritize their requirements

C. Increase the speed of delivery and gain feedback early

D. Fail fast to reduce cost of development

197. All of the following statements are true regarding communications within an Agile work environment, except for which one?

A. Weekly stakeholder reviews should be held to encourage engagement among the team.

B. Communication should occur frequently and quickly when project environments are ambiguous.

C. Project artifacts should be posted in a transparent fashion.

D. Regular stakeholder reviews should be held to promote communication among stakeholders.

198. You are performing activities associated with change control. One of the activities you are involved in is documenting and storing the configuration management information needed to effectively manage product information and data associated with changes. Which of the following does this describe?

A. Configuration identification

B. Configuration verification and auditing

C. Configuration verification and documentation

D. Configuration status accounting

199. Within Agile, a "T" shaped person refers to what?

A. A generalist who can take on any work within the backlog, regardless of skills needed

B. An individual who is early in their career and requires coaching in tandem with an assignment

C. An individual who has deep specializations in one domain and rarely contributes outside of it

D. An individual who supplements their expertise in one area with less-developed skills in associated areas

200. Which of the following techniques can be used to control scope within a project using a predictive life cycle?

A. Requirements traceability matrix

B. Data analysis

C. Configuration management system

D. Project management software

Chapter

6

Full-Length Practice Exam 3

NOTE The process names, inputs, tools and techniques, outputs, and descriptions of the project management process groups and related materials and figures in this chapter are based on content from *A Guide to the Project Management Body of Knowledge (PMBOK® Guide) – Sixth Edition* (PMI®, 2017).

1. Using the following three-point estimates, calculate the expected value using the beta distribution formula: Optimistic = 25, Pessimistic = 50, Most Likely = 35.

   A. 25

   B. 36

   C. 35

   D. 37

2. Tom is a project manager working for a reputable editorial agency specializing in exam preparation. As part of his latest project, he uses an approach that enables the team to release partially completed work to customers in order to obtain early feedback. This then allows the team to use the feedback to modify the work. What type of project life cycle is Tom using?

   A. Incremental

   B. Predictive

   C. Agile

   D. Iterative

3. What assumption is made in the Expectancy Theory?

   A. Behavior is based on conscious choices.

   B. Behavior is based on unconscious choices.

   C. Behavior is based on cognitive bias.

   D. The two sets of factors operate independently from each other.

4. You are a contract project manager working for a customer who uses a predictive life-cycle approach and have entered into the activities definition phase of your project. You take the team through a decomposition activity to break down work packages into activities. Before concluding this phase, what else are you and the team likely to capture?

   A. The activity list

   B. The milestone list

   C. The network diagram

   D. The list of predecessors and successors

5. A project manager looking to increase cross-team collaboration and create a more cooperative working environment is likely to do what?

   A. Provide training opportunities

   B. Use a pull-based system of work assignment

   C. Hold team-building activities

   D. Support self-management

6. You've derived cost estimates and allocated them to the activities of your project. You know that these estimates will be used to measure cost variances and performance throughout the remaining life of the project. The cost baseline has been established and becomes the expected cost of the project. Which process did you perform to arrive at the cost baseline?

   A. Estimate Costs

   B. Cost Control

   C. Determine Budget

   D. Develop Costs

7. Immediately after a morning planning meeting, the project manager and the development lead hold an impromptu discussion about the schedule for a project they are working on. During their discussion they uncover that each thought a set of deliverables was going to be completed at different points in the schedule. In light of this new revelation, they agree to update the schedule and share the information with the rest of the team. What is the best type of communication to use when dealing with complex issues, such as this one?

   A. Informal written

   B. Formal written

   C. Informal verbal

   D. Formal verbal

8. A project manager leading a multiphase construction project is beginning to perform the risk management processes. Because of the project's complexity and the amount of money invested in the project, the project sponsor stressed the critical nature of managing risks. The project manager took this advice seriously and brought together a risk management team. Alongside the risk management team, the project manager worked on the development of the risk management plan. Which of the following is not likely to be covered within the risk management plan?

   A. When and how often to conduct risk management activities

   B. When and how often to communicate with stakeholders throughout the project

   C. The amount of funds set aside for risk management activities

   D. The approach used to carry out risk management

9. The project manager of an accounting firm has team members located across the globe for his latest high-tech project. The project will make use of cutting-edge technology that is not widely used yet. In this scenario, what is the key benefit to having a virtual team?

   A. It widens the potential resource pool.

   B. It reduces the cost of travel.

   C. It allows for multiple cultures to collaborate.

   D. The work continues around the clock.

10. In iteration-based Agile, what questions will the team pose during daily stand-ups? (Select three.)

    A. What did I complete since the last stand-up?

    B. What will I complete between now and the next stand-up?

    C. What do we need to finish as a team?

    D. What are my impediments?

11. What quality theorist believed that the quality standard should be zero defects?

    A. Edward Shewhart

    B. W. Edwards Deming

    C. Philip Crosby

    D. Joseph Juran

12. What are the two categories into which knowledge can be split? (Select two.)

    A. Explicit

    B. Known

    C. Tacit

    D. Unknown

13. You are using a hybrid life-cycle approach to manage your project and are creating the cost management plan. You have talked with your project sponsor and CFO and will document that you are rounding to the nearest thousand and will be using weeks to estimate resources. What two elements of the plan does this describe, respectively?

    A. Control thresholds and units of measure

    B. Units of measure and control thresholds

    C. Rules of performance and level of accuracy

    D. Level of accuracy and units of measure

14. You are the project manager for a project that will produce a mobile phone application that sends alerts when UV rays are at dangerous levels, alerting users to stay indoors. You are in the process of measuring schedule performance against the schedule baseline. Within a predictive life cycle, what process group are these activities associated with?

    A. Initiating

    B. Planning

    C. Executing

    D. Monitoring and Controlling

15. When evaluating whether to adopt a predictive, Agile, or hybrid approach, what three categories can an organization assess suitability against? (Select three.)

    A. Industry

    B. Culture

    C. Team

    D. Project

16. As the director of the PMO, you regularly meet with executives to facilitate the review of new project proposals as part of an enterprise project selection committee. During a meeting, the selection committee considers three proposals. You present a summary of the three proposals and break them down by initial investment, payback period, and net present value. Based on the information provided in Table 6.1, which project of the three should the selection committee choose?

TABLE 6.1   Project Selection

	Investment	Payback Period	IRR
Project Sunrise	$1,200,000	18 months	.5 percent
Project X	$50,000	24 months	3 percent
Project Revolution	$550,000	9 months	3 percent

   A. Project Sunrise

   B. Project X

   C. Project Revolution

   D. None

17. A project manager liked to hold meetings on a weekly basis with his team members. These meetings resembled brainstorming sessions, where ideas were generated regarding existing risks and project issues. The project manager never struck down any idea and, instead, attempted to foster an environment where creativity, innovation, and sharing of ideas were encouraged. What type of leadership style does this project manager use?

   A. Transactional

   B. Interactional

   C. Transformational

   D. Laissez-faire

18. Within a predictive life cycle, which of the following serves as the basis for estimating costs?

   A. Scope management plan

   B. WBS

   C. Resource management plan

   D. Cost baseline

19. Which of the following reflect characteristics of Agile teams? (Select two.)

   A. The team ranges in size from three to nine members.

   B. Team members come from a technical discipline.

   C. Each team member serves as an expert in one discipline.

   D. Team members are 100 percent dedicated to the team.

20. Which of the following describes the spectrum of the Conscientiousness domain included in the Big Five personality assessment?

A. Sensitive versus confident

B. Efficient versus careless

C. Inventive versus easygoing

D. Outgoing versus reserved

21. Nubs and Bits is a Seattle-based company that produces healthy snacks for dogs of all sizes. Its latest project involves creating a snack for large breeds that takes up to one hour to consume. The project manager, who has managed multiple projects for Nubs and Bits over the past five years, decides to build a prototype. What value do prototypes provide?

A. Allow for early feedback on the requirements

B. Provide customers with a preview of the product

C. Allow the marketing team to showcase the product

D. None. The project manager made a poor choice.

22. You are in the process of facilitating a working session with the project team to decompose the project deliverables into smaller chunks of work. What process are you carrying out?

A. Plan Scope Management

B. Collect Requirements

C. Define Scope

D. Create WBS

23. A team crowds around a board that contains cards categorized in the following way: to do, doing, and done. As team member capacity opens, they grab a card from the "to do" category and begin work. The team focuses on getting work done versus starting new work. What type of Agile approach is the team using?

A. XP

B. Kanban

C. Lean

D. Agile UP

24. Activity A has a probability of 10 percent and an impact of $4,000. What is the expected monetary value of Activity A?

A. $4,000

B. $4,400

C. $400

D. $3,600

25. Match the Agile approach with its description (Table 6.2).

TABLE 6.2   Agile Approaches

Approach	Description
A. Kanban	1. A pull-based concept where work progresses to the next step only when resources are available
B. Scrum	2. Focuses on delivering software that's ready when the customer needs it
C. Feature-driven development	3. Focuses on delivering usable, working software continually in a timely manner
D. eXtreme Programming (XP)	4. A family of methodologies designed to scale to the project needs
E. Crystal methods	5. A single-team process framework typically used to manage product development

26. You are in the Planning stage of the project and have just kicked off activities associated with the Determine Budget process. In addition to the cost baseline, what is a likely output of this activity?

   A.   Cost estimates

   B.   Project funding requirements

   C.   Basis of estimates

   D.   Cost management plan

27. Which of the following present project information in a hierarchical fashion, similar to a work breakdown structure? (Select three.)

   A.   OBS

   B.   BOM

   C.   RAM

   D.   RBS

28. Your organization is experiencing a shake-up at the top levels of management. Your project team has expressed concerns that their project might be canceled because of the changes going on at the top. Thankfully, the new management team has decided to continue with the project. Before the shake-up happened, you were in the Monitoring and Controlling process group, and your next step was to check for correct work results to make certain they comply with the standards set out in the quality management plan. One of the results you've inspected measures 70 miles per hour. The quality management plan outlined standards between 65 and 75 miles per hour. Which of the following does this describe?

   A. Statistical sampling

   B. Tolerable results

   C. Inspection

   D. Nonconformance

29. The stakeholder approaches the project manager to report that the schedule must be adjusted to finish one week earlier than originally planned. If a predictive approach is used to manage the project, what would be the preferred approach for the project manager to take in order to make this happen?

   A. Crash the schedule

   B. Fast-track the schedule

   C. Add duration buffers

   D. Level out resources

30. Alyssa is a project manager tasked with managing an infrastructure project that will consolidate five data centers into one. She has used a waterfall approach to carry out initial planning activities and is executing the work using an Agile-based approach. Recently, the sponsor has asked Alyssa to provide a forecasted date of project completion. To date, the team has managed to complete an average of 60 story points per iteration, and there are 420 remaining user story points left to complete. How many iterations will it take to complete the project work?

   A. 6 iterations

   B. 7 iterations

   C. 4 iterations

   D. Cannot be determined, based on the information provided

31. Servant leaders are practicing role models of Agile practices. How do servant leaders approach their work? (Select three.)

   A. They focus on purpose by working with the team to define the "why."

   B. They focus on people by working with the team to create an environment where all can succeed.

   C. They focus on process by looking for the results.

   D. They focus on outcomes by measuring progress against planned results.

32. Within predictive life cycles, this term is used for both costs and schedules to establish what you'll measure against later in the Executing and Monitoring and Controlling processes.

    A. Variance

    B. Expected value

    C. Baseline

    D. Estimates

33. A product owner is performing risk management activities for an upcoming release. She sits down with the team to perform a risk assessment exercise and uses a probability and impact matrix. Which of the following statements are true regarding the probability and impact matrix? (Select three.)

    A. It prioritizes risks according to their potential for meeting the project's objectives.

    B. It's defined in the risk management plan, which is an output of the Plan Risk Management process.

    C. It's used as a tool and technique in the Perform Qualitative Risk Analysis process.

    D. It's used as an input to the Perform Quantitative Risk Analysis process.

34. What is the difference between inspection and prevention, in regard to quality?

    A. Inspection focuses on the cause of errors found, while prevention focuses on resolving the errors.

    B. Prevention focuses on the cause of errors found, while inspection focuses on resolving the errors.

    C. Inspection keeps errors from reaching the customer, while prevention prevents errors from occurring.

    D. Prevention keeps errors from reaching the customer, while inspection prevents errors from occurring.

35. Alyssa is a project manager tasked with managing an infrastructure project that will consolidate five data centers into one. She has used a waterfall approach to carry out initial planning activities and is executing the work using an Agile-based approach. She shows the team how much work remains to be completed during their current iteration and the forecast of work to be completed for the remaining iterations based on existing velocity. What is Alyssa showing them?

    A. Schedule

    B. Burnup chart

    C. Milestone chart

    D. Burndown chart

36. Within Agile approaches, how are requirements documented?

    A. In the requirements log

    B. In the backlog

    C. In the team charter

    D. In the schedule

37. You are developing the cost baseline and the project budget. You know that all of the following are true regarding these two elements except for which one?

    A. The project budget includes management reserves.

    B. Work package estimates and contingency reserves are included in the cost baseline and project budget.

    C. The cost baseline includes the project budget.

    D. Activity cost estimates and contingency reserves are included in the cost baseline and project budget.

38. Using the values within the following table, identify the critical path.

Activity Name	Successor	Duration
A	B, C	5
B	D	2
C	D, E	4
D	F	4
E	F	6
F	None	6

    A. A-B-D-F

    B. A-C-D-F

    C. A-C-E-F

    D. A-B-E-F

39. Using the values within the following table, calculate the early finish of activity D.

Activity Name	Successor	Duration
A	B, C	5
B	D	2
C	D, E	4
D	F	4
E	F	6
F	None	6

    A. 10

    B. 12

    C. 13

    D. 15

40. Using the values within the following table, calculate the late start of activity C.

Activity Name	Successor	Duration
A	B, C	5
B	D	2
C	D, E	4
D	F	4
E	F	6
F	None	6

A. 6
B. 9
C. 4
D. 8

41. Using the values within the following table, calculate the total float of activity E.

Activity Name	Successor	Duration
A	B, C	5
B	D	2
C	D, E	4
D	F	4
E	F	6
F	None	6

A. 0
B. 2
C. 6
D. 1

42. What are three characteristics of an Agile PMO? (Select three.)
   A. Value-driven
   B. Invitation-oriented
   C. Solution-driven
   D. Multidisciplinary

43. Astral Bank is known for providing its customers with superior online services through its use of cutting-edge technology. The latest project includes the ability for customers to electronically sign for loans. Currently, the project is in its third week of executing the project work, and the project manager noticed that a key resource has been over-allocated. What technique is the project manager likely to use to resolve this issue?

A. Resource leveling

B. Monte Carlo technique

C. An adjustment of leads and lags

D. Critical chain method

44. What is the role of a servant leader?

A. To ensure the team delivers planned outcomes of the project

B. To charter the team and monitor adherence to agreements

C. To facilitate the Agile events, including daily stand-up

D. To facilitate the team's discovery and definition of Agile

45. Alyssa is a project manager tasked with managing an infrastructure project that will consolidate five data centers into one. She is using a waterfall approach to carry out initial planning activities and will execute the work using an Agile-based approach. Currently, she is facilitating the estimating process to calculate the duration of the project's activities. When she gets to the "run cable" activity, one team member tells her that in a past similar project, they ran a similar length of cable in 13 hours; another team member tells her that they can run 110 meters of cable per hour. The team will need to run a total of 1,320 meters of cable. Using the analogous estimating technique, how many hours will it take the team to run the cable?

A. 9

B. 13

C. 10

D. 12

46. You have been hired as a contract project manager for Grapevine Vineyards. You are carrying out activities relating to procurement planning. Grapevine wants you to head up a project to design a new visitor center, tasting room, and gift shop. They also want to double the number of fermenting tanks and increase the size of the warehouse (which requires extensive temperature and environmental controls). Grapevine would like to have the bar in the tasting room constructed out of specialty marble that is available from only two places in the world. Grapevine management estimates this project will take three years. You are concerned about the availability of the specialty marble and know that the following are true. (Select three.)

A. The project schedule can influence this process.

B. The Determine Budget process can be influenced by this process.

C. The make-or-buy analysis can be influenced by this process.

D. Your organization's business cycle might have an impact on this process.

47. Marysil is an enterprise project manager for Cups on Fire. To date, she has identified risks, analyzed them, and developed risk responses for her project. What activity is she likely to carry out next?

A. Develop a risk management strategy

B. Analyze the risks captured

C. Implement risk responses

D. Develop the initial risk register

48. You are the project manager for Kitchens Plus Inc. The latest project involves the development of an automatic dicer with unique industry features. The project uses a predictive life cycle, and you are analyzing schedule performance. Based on the information provided by the scheduling team, the current schedule performance index (SPI) is at 1.10, while the cost performance index (CPI) is at 0.80. What might be a good strategy for balancing out performance between the schedule and budget?

A. Crash the schedule by adding additional resources to critical activities

B. Fast-track the longest activities that fall on the critical path

C. Level out resource usage to further spread out cost over time

D. Nothing, since the project is performing as planned

49. Which of the following are events used by Scrum teams? (Select three.)

A. Sprint planning

B. Weekly scrum

C. Sprint review

D. Sprint retrospective

50. Alyssa is a project manager tasked with managing an infrastructure project that will consolidate five data centers into one. She is using a waterfall approach to carry out initial planning activities and will execute the work using an Agile-based approach. Alyssa is currently facilitating the estimating process to calculate the duration of the project's activities. When she gets to the "run cable" activity, one team member tells her that in a past similar project, they ran a similar length of cable in 13 hours; another team member tells her that they can run 110 meters of cable per hour. The team will need to run a total of 1,320 meters of cable. Using the parametric estimating technique, how many hours will it take the team to run the cable?

A. 9

B. 13

C. 10

D. 12

51. This earned value management calculation is the projected or estimated cost performance that the remaining work of the project must achieve to meet the BAC or EAC.

A. EV

B. Forecast

C. TCPI

D. VAC

52. Igor is a software developer for a large IT consulting company. Mary, the team lead, has just informed him that the project manager has compressed the schedule by two weeks, and as a result, she is requiring the team to work weekends to accommodate the release. The team has a high degree of respect for the project manager, and they happily comply. Which of the following is a type of power that is based on the respect or admiration that others hold for an individual?

A. Formal

B. Reward

C. Referent

D. Expert

53. Which of the following statements are true? (Select three.)

A. The Precedence Diagramming Method (PDM) uses dummy activities.

B. The PDM displays activities on the node.

C. The Arrow Diagramming Method (ADM) uses only one type of logical relationship.

D. Both the PDM and the ADM use the finish-to-start dependency.

54. Which of the following are examples of project life cycles? (Select two.)

A. Predictive

B. Scrum

C. Kanban

D. Adaptive

55. The project charter has just been approved. What comes next?

A. Develop the project management plan

B. Develop the project scope statement

C. Develop the project backlog

D. Perform stakeholder analysis

56. A project with a CPI of 1.12 and an SPI of 0.90 is performing:

A. Under budget and ahead of schedule

B. Over budget and behind schedule

C. Under budget and behind schedule

D. Over budget and ahead of schedule

57. The company's quality research team has been assigned to review the project materials. This team is not part of the group that developed the material. This is an example of what type of review?

A. Design of experiments

B. Independent peer review

C. Quality audits

D. Defect repair review

58. Tom is a project manager working for a reputable editorial agency specializing in exam preparation. He and his team use Agile approaches to manage projects. Because of the company's growth, three new project managers have been hired, and Tom has stepped up to mentor the new hires. One of the new project managers is struggling with her project and has asked Tom for help. She notes that her team is not working effectively together, frequently missing team meetings and having difficulty in reaching agreements. What can Tom suggest to turn the team around?

    A. Charter the team

    B. Shift to a waterfall approach

    C. Discipline the team

    D. Facilitate team-building activities

59. You are the project manager for a project that will produce a mobile phone application that sends alerts when UV rays are at dangerous levels, alerting users to stay indoors. Your team has recently adopted Agile, and you have modeled your approach on that of a servant leader. Which of the following characteristics are you likely to follow?

    A. Listening

    B. Coaching

    C. Controlling

    D. Promoting self-awareness

    E. A, C, D

    F. A, B, D

60. This quality management and control tool consists of two-dimensional diagrams (L-Type, T-Type, and X-Type) and three-dimensional diagrams such as C-Type. Which tool within this tool and technique does this question describe?

    A. Prioritization matrices

    B. Tree diagrams

    C. Matrix diagrams

    D. PDPC

61. Jon, a senior research technician, has been with the company for one year and is considered to be the top performer of his group. Because of his exceptional performance, the company has decided to promote him to the role of project manager of his department. This is an example of:

    A. Fringe benefits

    B. Perquisites

    C. Halo effect

    D. Performance bonus

62. A project management team is in the process of acquiring the necessary resources to complete the project activities, as specified within the human resource management plan. After considering those resources that had been promised as part of the customer contract, they discover that a key resource was not included within the initial agreement and was already committed to two other projects. To work through the best scenario, what technique can the team use?

   A. Virtual teams

   B. Pre-assignment

   C. Acquisition

   D. Negotiation

63. To prevent the problem from happening again, the project manager has instructed the quality team to focus on the top 20 percent of causes that resulted in the identified defect. This is an example of:

   A. Specification limits

   B. 80/20 rule

   C. Assignable cause

   D. Trend analysis

64. Which of the following best describes an incremental life cycle?

   A. Provides finished deliverables that the customer can immediately use

   B. Reduces uncertainty and complexity so that the team can complete the work in sequence

   C. Allows for early feedback on partially completed or unfinished work

   D. Obtains early feedback and iterates over the product to create finished deliverables

65. The project manager of a pharmaceutical company sent an email to one of his project team members apologizing for ending their recent conversation abruptly. What type of communication did the project manager use?

   A. Formal written

   B. Informal written

   C. Written

   D. Informal electronic

66. Which of the following statements are true? (Select three.)

   A. Risk management is a proactive practice within project management.

   B. Risks are prioritized during qualitative risk analysis.

   C. Watch lists contain near-term risks that must be monitored carefully.

   D. Risk symptoms are considered when evaluating if a risk is a near-term risk.

67. Cloud Divine is a startup company that provides SaaS using cloud computing. The first major project launched by the company involved a high degree of ambiguity and experienced issues, including a large number of changes to the project deliverables, nearly resulting in a failed project. All projects within the company are managed using a predictive life-cycle approach. What is the most likely cause for the high degree of issues experienced in the project? (Select two.)

    A. The project manager is not PMI certified.

    B. A poorly written scope

    C. Informal change control procedures

    D. The lack of a configuration management system

    E. The wrong project life-cycle approach was chosen.

68. A project manager of Cyber Channels Inc. is in the process of assigning resources to her current project. At the end of the day, she receives an angry call from the director of engineering, who is upset that his senior systems administrator was assigned to the project without his consent. At this stage, what should the project manager do to keep this resource?

    A. Negotiate with the director for the resource

    B. Agree by phone but keep the resource

    C. Get the project sponsor involved

    D. Call the CEO, who is a personal friend

69. During the execution phase of a biotech project, a new issue has surfaced. What is one of the first things that the project manager should do?

    A. Contact the stakeholders to report the issue

    B. Note the issue within an issue log

    C. Notify the team of the issue in the next status meeting

    D. Attempt to resolve the issue immediately

70. When should Agile teams hold retrospectives?

    A. At the start of the project

    B. When the team feels stuck

    C. When a major milestone is reached

    D. At the conclusion of an iteration or increment

    E. B, C, D

    F. A, C, D

71. Around 2:37 p.m., Bruce Bethor, the project manager for Happy Holiday Cruise Ships, Inc., walks around the office to interact with each member of his team. The majority of his team members enjoy this type of informal interaction because it gives them an opportunity to bring up issues they may have forgotten to mention during the morning meetings or those issues that were recently uncovered during the day. Which of the following techniques does Bruce use to stay in touch with the work and attitudes of his project team members?

A. 360-degree feedback

B. Observation and conversation

C. Issue log

D. Team-building activities

72. A project manager is working through potential options using a decision tree. Scenario A has a failure impact of –$5,000 with a probability of 25 percent, and no impact if successful; and scenario B has a failure impact of –$3,500 with a probability of 65 percent, and no impact if successful. Which scenario should the project manager choose?

A. Scenario A

B. Scenario B

C. Neither scenario

D. Insufficient information provided

73. You are the project manager for a project that will produce a mobile phone application that sends alerts when UV rays are at dangerous levels, alerting users to stay indoors. During a team meeting, you stress the importance of documenting both explicit and tacit knowledge. What does tacit knowledge refer to?

A. Technical knowledge documented from past project experiences by the team

B. Standardized knowledge defined and published by industry-recognized organizations

C. Knowledge that can be captured and expressed using words, pictures, and numbers

D. Knowledge that is difficult to capture or express, such as beliefs, experiences, and "know-how"

74. A project manager plots the degree of certainty and complexity of a project along x- and y-axes to determine what type of project management approach would suit the project best. The exercise reveals that the project falls within the "complex" quadrant due to moderately uncertain requirements and highly uncertain technical challenges. Based on this information, what type of approach should the project manager use to manage the project?

A. Predictive approach

B. Linear approach

C. Hybrid approach

D. Adaptive approach

75. Nicolas is the sponsor of a project that will replace all equipment that has already surpassed its end of lifetime span. He decides to assign this project to Carina, his top-performing project manager. Carina's first task will be to write the project charter. Who will be responsible for signing the project charter document, thereby approving the project?

A. Carina

B. Nicolas

C. Project management team

D. Both Carina and Nicolas

76. Making small, incremental improvements within a product or process is known as:

A. Halo effect

B. Kaizen

C. Kanban

D. Muda

77. You are a senior project manager working at a manufacturing plant that produces components used by the aviation industry. You are using a predictive life-cycle approach and are in the process of implementing approved changes. What key information will you need to successfully complete the associated activities?

A. Lessons learned register

B. Change requests

C. Approved change requests

D. Project schedule

78. Alyssa is a project manager tasked with managing an infrastructure project that will consolidate five data centers into one. She has used a waterfall approach to carry out initial planning activities and is executing the work using an Agile-based approach. This hybrid approach is new to her and the team. After completing their second iteration, Alyssa gets the team together to brainstorm how they can continue to improve the process. One team member with experience using Agile approaches recommends getting together at the conclusion of each iteration to talk about what went well, what could be improved, and what they will commit to change during the next iteration. What is the team member recommending?

A. Lessons learned

B. Retrospectives

C. Iteration planning

D. Backlog refinement

79. Which of the following does a project manager use to build trust with stakeholders and overcome resistance to change?

   A. Conflict management techniques

   B. Communication methods

   C. General management skills

   D. Interpersonal skills

80. Team charters are also known by what other name?

   A. Project charter

   B. Team agreement

   C. Ground rules

   D. Social contract

81. One of your subproject managers, a recent graduate with limited experience in managing projects, prepared a procurement SOW. When you were researching independent estimates, you discovered that your vendor's proposals are way off of your expectations. You review the SOW and find that it was not detailed enough for the vendor to come up with an accurate estimate. Of the following options, which area of the *PMI Code of Ethics and Professional Conduct* does this question relate to, and which process does the independent estimates tool and technique belong to?

   A. Contribute to the project management knowledge base and Plan Procurement Management

   B. Ensure personal integrity and professionalism and Control Procurements

   C. Promote interaction among team members and other stakeholders and Plan Procurement Management

   D. Truthful reporting and Control Procurements

82. A project manager meets with a key set of experts within her project team. They express concerns over recent cost estimates produced, insisting that they have not sufficiently considered alternatives. It is still early in the project life cycle. Which of the following is a valid tool or technique that can aid the project manager in addressing the team's concerns?

   A. Analogous estimating

   B. Expert judgment

   C. Decision-making

   D. Data analysis

83. If earned value = 1,700, planned value = 2,000, and actual costs = 1,950, what is the CPI?

   A. 0.87

   B. 1.15

   C. 0.85

   D. 1.18

84. Ronald Pierce is a high-end furniture store chain. The company is in the process of developing a new renaissance style edition for release in six months. The project manager leading the development of the new edition is currently developing risk responses, alongside the risk management team. In response to one of the threats, insurance was purchased to cover any potential losses, should the risk emerge. What type of response did the team utilize?

   A. Mitigate

   B. Avoid

   C. Transfer

   D. Exploit

85. During quantitative risk analysis, a project manager held a planning meeting with key stakeholders to share the results of the latest analysis conducted. What-if scenarios were performed on several important risks and then displayed using a tornado diagram. This is an example of:

   A. Expected monetary value analysis

   B. Decision tree analysis

   C. Sensitivity analysis

   D. Data validation analysis

86. Match the conflict resolution technique with its description (Table 6.3).

TABLE 6.3   Types of Conflict Resolution Techniques

Type	Description
A. Avoid	1. To push one's viewpoint at the expense of others. This is considered a win-lose situation.
B. Reconcile	2. To search for a temporary solution that satisfies all parties. This is considered a lose-lose situation.
C. Direct	3. To incorporate multiple viewpoints and lead to consensus and commitment. This is considered a win-win situation.
D. Problem Solve	4. To emphasize agreement and concede one's position to maintain harmony or relationships. This is considered a win-lose situation.
E. Accommodate	5. To retreat from the conflict situation. This is considered a lose-lose situation.

87. Kishore is in Las Vegas and works remotely from his home. Bryan is also remote and works from home as well. Their project manager resides on the same campus as four other team members, although they are in different buildings. Every morning at 9 a.m. the four team members meet in the project manager's office, and Kishore and Bryan call in using a phone bridge to take part in the same morning meeting. All team members connect to discuss a shared goal: successfully completing the project. A group of individuals with a shared goal who fulfill their roles with little or no time meeting face to face is best described as:

A. Colocation

B. Stakeholders

C. Virtual teams

D. Project team

88. Martha has just been told that she will be assigned as the project manager for the new office expansion project. After the project charter is created and approved, she begins the process of performing stakeholder analysis. She decides to group stakeholders by their level of authority and level of concern. What type of classification model has she chosen to use?

A. Power/Influence Grid

B. Power/Interest Grid

C. Influence/Impact Grid

D. Salience Model

89. Kaylee is a senior project manager for a fitness company that is developing a new franchise model. She has just finished overseeing the implementation of several planned risk responses. What activity is she likely to perform next?

A. Risk audit

B. Trend analysis

C. Technical performance analysis

D. Sensitivity analysis

90. Two project team members have been involved in a dispute that has escalated to the point of involving the project manager. What is the primary source of most disputes among team members?

A. Scarce resources

B. Technology used

C. Budget

D. Schedule priorities

91. A project is considered complete when:

    A. The lessons learned have been archived

    B. Project team has been released

    C. All payments for the project have been received

    D. Formal documented acceptance has been received by the customer

92. The Agile Manifesto is made up of four values and twelve principles. Which of the following is an example of an Agile value?

    A. Individuals and interactions over processes and tools

    B. Working software over comprehensive documentation

    C. Customer collaboration over contract negotiation

    D. Following a plan over rework and change

    E. A, B, C

    F. A, B, C, D

93. Which of the following is addressed within the resource management plan? (Select three.)

    A. Qualified sellers

    B. Recognition and rewards

    C. Compliance

    D. Safety

94. The project manager of an accounting software upgrade project was approached by the vice president of marketing regarding the schedule milestone update report. The VP was concerned because the report was not being sent out weekly as scheduled. The project manager understood that this report was scheduled for biweekly distribution. What or whom can the project manager consult to clarify the report distribution frequency?

    A. The project team member responsible for distributing the report

    B. The communications management plan

    C. The risk management plan

    D. The project management plan

95. A project manager was holding a one-on-one meeting with the scheduler located across the globe. The meeting was difficult to manage, due to sporadic static. The static can best be described as:

    A. Noise

    B. Medium

    C. Obstacle

    D. Interference

96. Alfred has just been assigned as the project manager for the Realtor Dual Co. project, which has just kicked off its second phase. As part of getting up to speed on the project, Alfred investigates the procurement activities that will be required to carry out this phase of the project. He discovers that a key deliverable has been flagged as requiring external resources and begins working immediately to procure those resources. Where can Alfred look to review the company's existing procurement policies, procedures, and guidelines?

   A. Enterprise environmental factors

   B. Organizational process assets

   C. Procurement documents

   D. Contract documentation

97. A project manager using probability distributions to display data is most likely to use which of the following:

   A. Uniform distributions

   B. Normal distributions

   C. Beta distributions

   D. Lognormal distributions

98. What type of contract poses the greatest risk to the buyer?

   A. Fixed price

   B. Lump sum

   C. Cost plus

   D. Time and materials

99. Using templates is beneficial to the project manager in which way?

   A. It allows more time available to spend with the project team.

   B. It lessens the repercussions of procrastination.

   C. It removes the need of using the project team to create the list of activities.

   D. It allows for greater efficiency and consistency of results.

100. A project manager plots the degree of certainty and complexity of a project along x- and y-axes to determine what type of project management approach would suit the project best. The exercise reveals that the project falls within the "complex" quadrant due to moderately uncertain requirements and highly uncertain technical challenges. What model is the project manager using?

   A. Tornado Diagram

   B. Probability and Impact Matrix

   C. Stacey Complexity Model

   D. Chaos Model

101. Kishore is in Las Vegas and works remotely from his home. Bryan is also remote and works from home as well. Carolyn, the project manager, resides on the same campus as four other team members, although they are in different buildings. To help the team feel connected, Carolyn opens a video conferencing link every workday beginning at 8 a.m. and closing it at 5 p.m. Each team member joins the stream and leaves the video open so that they feel as though they are in a virtual open workspace. What is this an example of?

- **A.** Remote pairing
- **B.** Web conference
- **C.** Virtual desktop
- **D.** Fishbowl window

102. A project team member called the project manager to notify him that there seemed to be confusion about the resources needed to complete her activity. The project manager, who was running late for a meeting, told the team member not to worry about it and ended the conversation by telling her to have a good day and that they would touch base in the coming weeks. The project team member was left wondering whether the project manager understood the severity of the situation, since without the resources, her activity could not proceed, and the deadline would be missed. In this scenario, what was the communication role of the project manager?

- **A.** Sender
- **B.** Encoder
- **C.** Receiver
- **D.** Decoder

103. Sally, a member of the project management team, walks into a room where two project team members are seen arguing over the schedule. One team member feels that an additional resource is needed to meet an upcoming deadline, while another feels that the risk is not as high and that the schedule should be left alone. Sally takes a moment to review the schedule and instructs the team members to leave it. What type of resolution technique did Sally use?

- **A.** Collaborating
- **B.** Smoothing
- **C.** Withdrawing
- **D.** Forcing

104. Which of the following best describes a RACI chart?

- **A.** A chart arranged by company departments, units, or teams
- **B.** A chart that displays categories by types of resources
- **C.** A chart that appears similar to a job description
- **D.** A type of RAM that stands for Responsible, Accountable, Consult, and Inform

105. First Strike Engineering Co. has won a contract to produce 1,000,000 night-time vision goggles for the military. However, part of the requirement is that they must ensure the product accuracy is within Six Sigma. This prevents a problem for First Strike Engineering Co. because they are not accustomed to delivering products within a Six Sigma level of accuracy, and as a result, the cost of quality to achieve that level of accuracy will decrease their profit margin by 67 percent. Cost of quality, which is a factor in this scenario, can best be defined as:

   A. The prevention of rework

   B. The cost of conformance to requirements

   C. The investment made toward customer service

   D. Providing customers with extras

106. Which of the following describes a resource that has been committed to a project as part of a contract or within the project charter?

   A. Committed

   B. Pre-assignment

   C. Negotiated

   D. Asset

107. Ricardo was late to the Monday morning project meeting and had to dial into the phone bridge to join the meeting. Unfortunately, he was 20 minutes late and the majority of the topics that were of interest to him had already been discussed. He sent an email to the meeting chairperson and asked if the notes for the meeting would be distributed by email or placed on the team wiki site because he was unable to attend the full meeting. Meetings, email, web publishing, and telephone, when used for sharing information, are all examples of:

   A. Communication tools

   B. Lessons learned

   C. Information gathering and retrieval systems

   D. Information management systems

108. While projects contain varying levels of ambiguity, complexity, and size, most projects encompass the following generic phase(s):

   A. Organize and prepare

   B. Start the project

   C. Close the project

   D. Carry out the work

   E. A, B

   F. A, B, C, D

109. The project was going well until you recently discovered that the site of the offshore development team has just conducted an emergency evacuation due to a political rally that has become violent. This comes as a shock to the local project team. How could this have been avoided?

    A. By being aware of the project environment

    B. By not working with an offshore team

    C. Creating policies that require employees to continue working during political rallies

    D. The situation could not have been avoided.

110. Giving customers extras, such as adding in functionality or increasing performance not included in the project scope, is known as:

    A. Voice of the customer (VOC)

    B. Halo effect

    C. Customer service

    D. Gold plating

111. After conducting a lessons learned session at the end of each project phase, the project manager is responsible for collecting feedback from the team and creating a process improvement plan. The process improvement plan contains all of the following except for which one?

    A. Process boundaries

    B. Process configuration

    C. Failure rate

    D. Targets for improved performance

112. The 100 percent rule signifies that:

    A. 100 percent of the deliverables are included within the WBS

    B. 100 percent of the scope baseline represents the project scope statement

    C. 100 percent of activities are included within the activity list

    D. 100 percent of the scope is represented within the WBS

113. Which of the following statements best describes mitigation of a risk?

    A. To transfer a risk to a third party

    B. To remove the possibility of a risk occurring

    C. To increase the probability and/or impact of a risk

    D. To reduce the probability and/or impact of a risk

114. The net quantifiable benefit derived from a business endeavor is described by what?

    A. Net present value

    B. Business case

    C. Benefits management

    D. Business value

115. Rosco Enterprises is currently working on a large commercial fencing project that will construct a custom-built fence around a 10,000-square-foot property. To deliver by the committed date, the company will need to hire a subcontractor to produce the custom maple wood post endcaps. So far, the procurement statement of work has been clearly outlined, as well as the delivery date for the end caps. Based on the information provided, what type of contract will Rosco Enterprises likely use for the work carried out by the subcontractor?

   A. Fixed price

   B. Cost reimbursable

   C. Cost plus

   D. Time and materials

116. As a proactive approach to dealing with a recent issue, the project team has been asked to determine all the possible causes of the issue. Which of the following tools would be the best choice for the project team to use?

   A. Histogram

   B. Scatter diagram

   C. Cause-and-effect diagram

   D. Control chart

117. Richard, the project manager, has a difficult time with Rob, who is the department manager of Information Systems, when it comes to dealing with risk. Rob does everything possible to avoid risk, even if it means negatively impacting the project. What type of risk attitude does Rob have?

   A. Risk averse

   B. Risk tolerant

   C. Risk neutral

   D. Risk seeking

118. Jane, who is the project manager, has a question about the Research activity's progress and is interested in knowing why it appears to have fallen behind. According to the RACI chart provided, who is to perform the work of this activity?

Activity	Todd	Alfred	Anne	Henry
Define	A	R	C	I
Research	I	R	A	I
Compile	A	I	R	I

   A. Todd

   B. Alfred

   C. Anne

   D. Henry

119. At the end of each quarter, the PMO of the Big Bang Software Development Company performs a review that focuses on measuring the project team's effectiveness. This type of activity can best be described as:

A. Colocation

B. Team-building activities

C. Team performance assessments

D. Project performance appraisals

120. Tom is a project manager working for a reputable editorial agency specializing in exam preparation. He and his team use Agile approaches to manage projects. As part of kicking off his latest project, Tom drafts a team charter. What will he capture in this document?

A. Ground rules

B. Team values

C. Working agreements

D. Group norms

E. A, C, D

F. A, B, C, D

121. Tony is the CEO of a new startup company called Power Cloud Stock Trading Online. In his excitement to make the company public, he has launched a project that will potentially increase the revenue of the business by 496 percent. Grant, who is the project manager of this project, performs an analysis of the stakeholders identified to date, using an influence/impact grid. He assesses Tony as having a high level of influence and a high level of impact. What type of strategy is Grant likely to choose in managing Tony's expectations throughout the project?

A. Monitor

B. Keep informed

C. Manage closely

D. Keep satisfied

122. A company is currently rolling out a time management software that will be developed in five different language versions to be marketed globally. The rollout of the product will be developed, released, and marketed within three months of each other. This can best be described as a:

A. Project

B. Portfolio

C. Program

D. Backlog

123. Which of the following is considered a cost of quality?

    A. Quality staff

    B. Time spent on quality activities

    C. Rework

    D. Quality tools

    E. A, B, C

    F. A, B, D

124. You are a project manager working as a consultant for a company that is in startup mode. One of your responsibilities for this week is to create an organizational chart. What format can you use to display an organizational chart? (Select three.)

    A. Hierarchical type

    B. Matrix-based

    C. Run chart

    D. Text-oriented

125. Hal has been assigned as part of the research team on a project that involves working with the latest lab software. You've noticed Hal working longer hours than the rest of the research team. When you approach him about this, he shares that he hasn't quite grasped how to utilize the new program and has been wrestling with it for some time. As the project manager, what should you do?

    A. Provide a sounding board for Hal so that he can channel the frustration within a controlled conversation

    B. Look into providing training for Hal and others in the research team that may be in need of it as well

    C. Replace Hal, since he is clearly not qualified for the role

    D. Commend Hal on his hard work and dedication in staying longer hours to learn the program

126. Every Friday the development teams at Blazing Broadband Internet Solutions are treated to a free massage and a catered lunch. The CEO authorized this extra activity as a means of retaining top performers at the company and to give the human resources department extra leverage in attracting new employees with an added benefit. Benefits provided to employees who are doing a great job are known as:

    A. Fringe benefits

    B. Perquisites

    C. Halo effect

    D. Performance bonus

127. If activity A has a duration of 10 days and activity B has a duration of 7 days with a 2-day lag, what is the overall duration of both activities combined, given a start-to-start relationship with an assumption that both activities will begin as soon as possible?

    A. 9

    B. 10

C. 17

D. 7

128. The project manager had received two complaints that three project team members were arguing over the interpretation of schedule analysis results conducted the previous day. The project manager had waited to see whether they would work it out among themselves, but another two complaints were made that the situation was affecting the work of others. What should the project manager do?

A. Give the disputing team members more time to work it out among themselves

B. Issue corrective action to the team members negatively affecting the work of others

C. Adjust from a predictive to an adaptive life cycle approach

D. Collaborate to resolve the dispute

129. Match the leadership style with its description (Table 6.4).

TABLE 6.4 Leadership Styles

Type	Description
A. Servant Leader	1. Focuses on management by exception; rewards based on goals, feedback, and accomplishments
B. Transactional	2. Uses a combination of transactional, transformational, and charismatic
C. Charismatic	3. Enthusiastic, high-energy, and able to inspire others
D. Interactional	4. Allows the team to make their own decisions and establish their own goals
E. Laissez-faire	5. Puts others first and demonstrates commitment to serve

130. You are currently assigned to work on a project involving the release of a new pharmaceutical drug. The vice president (VP) of strategic partnerships, who to date has not been a part of the project, asked to see the work performance data. This raises a red flag for the following reason:

A. The VP of strategic partnerships is not a part of the project and should therefore not have access to the report.

B. The VP may have heard of existing performance issues and is investigating.

C. All stakeholders of the project have not been identified to date.

D. There are no red flags raised for this project, and the project manager has nothing to worry about.

131. Which of the following is not a characteristic of a project?

   A. A temporary endeavor

   B. Meant to sustain the business

   C. Performed by people

   D. Is planned, executed, and controlled

132. A project team using an Incremental life cycle may opt to deliver what to a subset of customers?

   A. Minimum viable product

   B. Prototype

   C. Deliverable

   D. Feature

133. A project manager is currently working on a pharmaceutical project. The activities that will produce the deliverables of Phase 1 are currently being planned out in detail. All other work will be planned out at higher levels until additional product details are known through testing results. This strategy is known as:

   A. Rolling wave planning

   B. Progressive elaboration

   C. Scope creep

   D. Initiating

134. Upon returning from lunch, you discover that a quality audit will be taking place. Some of the team members are upset, since there is an approaching deadline, and have therefore requested that the audit be moved to the following day. As the project manager, what should you do?

   A. Request that the audit be rescheduled

   B. Allow the audit to take place

   C. Express your dissatisfaction along with the team and allow the audit only if your own manager requires it

   D. Allow the audit to take place, but do not offer assistance, since you and your team are too busy

135. Which of the following best defines target benefits?

   A. The quantitative business value to be gained by the implementation of the product, service, or result

   B. The intangible business value to be gained by the implementation of the product, service, or result

   C. The tangible business value to be gained by the implementation of the product, service, or result

   D. The tangible and intangible business value to be gained by the implementation of the product, service, or result

136. A project manager sits down with the project sponsor to review progress. The sponsor asks to see the short-term and long-term timeline for realizing benefits. What document can the project manager reference that contains this information?

A. Project schedule

B. Product backlog

C. Project management plan

D. Benefits management plan

137. Tom is a project manager working for a reputable editorial agency specializing in exam preparation. He and his team use Agile approaches to manage projects. Because of the company's growth, three new project managers have been hired, and Tom has stepped up to mentor the new hires. During a mentoring session, Tom advises that the team take advantage of the open workspace environment and use osmotic communication. What is osmotic communication?

A. Planned quiet periods

B. Ad hoc team meetings

C. A three-way dialogue

D. A polite form of eavesdropping

138. The project manager of a multiphased gaming project made a phone call to one of her virtual project team members abroad regarding an upcoming schedule activity that the team member was responsible for. The project manager notified the team member that due to an unplanned risk, a prototype would be built into the schedule, and it was important that her activity be completed according to the plan. The project manager noticed that the team member did not say much during the call, and she hoped that the team member understood. What did the project manager fail to do?

A. Request that the team member respond with a status report

B. Be more attuned to existing noise on the call

C. Request that the team member write down the request and confirm status through the use of a written medium

D. Request that the team member repeat the message back to ensure it was understood

139. Susan is the director of engineering for a software consulting company. She needs to hire seven people for a project that will be starting over the next month and has just filled out the roles and responsibilities of the positions and provided them to the human resources department. Which of the following is considered in the development of roles and responsibilities?

A. Technical

B. Political

C. Interpersonal

D. Background

E. A, B, C

F. A, B, C, D

140. Which of the following best describes procurement audits?

    A. Structured reviews that audit the project manager's adherence to company procurement policies

    B. Structured reviews that audit the seller's deliverables

    C. Structured reviews that audit the procurement management processes

    D. Structured reviews that audit the procurement closing procedures

141. Which of the following is not a type of leadership style?

    A. Laissez-faire

    B. Transactional

    C. Forcing

    D. Charismatic

142. Janet is the project manager for First Strike Engineering, a company that specializes in providing military devices for jet fighters. Her departmental projects usually require that all deliverables be within an accuracy of Six Sigma. Today, she received her first contract stating that the accuracy of the deliverable can be within One Sigma. What is the level of accuracy of One Sigma?

    A. 68.27 percent

    B. 95.46 percent

    C. 99.73 percent

    D. 99.99 percent

143. You work for Rory's, a golf equipment manufacturer. Your organization is installing some new manufacturing equipment, and you are managing the project. Your project sponsor has asked for an EAC and has told you that he wants you to consider ETC work performed at the present CPI. If EV = 145, PV = 162, AC = 138, and BAC = 200, what is EAC?

    A. 190

    B. 61

    C. 58

    D. 196

144. Alfred is holding a meeting with select members of the project team to help identify and generate requirements. This is an example of:

    A. Brainstorming

    B. Expert judgment

    C. Product analysis

    D. Alternatives analysis

145. A project manager has structured his Agile project in a less prescriptive way to be less disruptive to the team. He and the team focus on driving work through a continuous flow as a way of delivering value to the customer versus using iterations. This approach is associated with which Agile method?

A. Scrum

B. Feature-driven development

C. Crystal

D. Kanban method

146. Susan and David are both project managers for Blazing Broadband Internet Solutions, but they work in different divisions of the company, each having led numerous successful projects for the organization. They have been teamed together to find innovative solutions to problems on a new project, including ways of harmonizing the group of stakeholders in order to accomplish the project objectives. What skill set will Susan and David need to use to facilitate consensus on project objectives, influence stakeholders to support the project, and negotiate agreements?

A. Conflict management techniques

B. Communication methods

C. General management skills

D. Interpersonal skills

147. Tom is a project manager working for a reputable editorial agency specializing in exam preparation. He and his team use Agile approaches to manage projects. Because of the company's growth, three new project managers have been hired, and Tom has stepped up to mentor the new hires. Given their limited experience with Agile, he decides to walk them through the four values and twelve principles that define Agile in order to help them adopt an Agile mindset. What is Tom reviewing with the project managers?

A. Agile Charter

B. Agile Principles

C. Agile Guide

D. Agile Manifesto

148. Which of the following best defines internal rate of return (IRR)?

A. The value of future dollars received in today's dollars

B. The comparison of future cash flows of a project to today's dollars

C. The length of time it takes the company to recoup the initial costs of investing in a project

D. The discount rate when the present value of the cash inflows equals the original investment

149. With the first major milestone around the corner, the project manager has decided to move all the active project team members to a war room. This is an example of:

    A. A virtual team

    B. Ground rules

    C. Colocation

    D. Team building

150. Which of the following best describes virtual teams?

    A. Team members located outside of the primary physical office where the project takes place

    B. Colocating team members in order to increase the efficiency of the project overall

    C. Team members located within another branch of the organization

    D. Specialized resources who access meetings via web or other technology tools

151. A project manager of a retail chain of hardware stores is in the process of generating the project schedule. After the project manager issues the project assignments, a team member approaches him to say that he has a two-week planned vacation right in the middle of a critical activity. What did the project manager fail to do?

    A. Call the team member in advance to see if their vacation can be rescheduled

    B. Check the resource requirements for the affected activities

    C. Cancel the team member's scheduled vacation in advance

    D. Check the resource calendars for team member schedule conflicts

152. Al and Veronica have agreed to put an end to the bickering about the project by settling their personal differences on the Go Kart track. In fact, they have made it a team-building activity by giving their team members a half-day off so that they can join in the race. Team-building activities accomplish the following:

    A. Clarify what is considered acceptable behavior

    B. Provide isolated team members with a better social life

    C. Encourage individuality

    D. Build trust

153. A key stakeholder approaches the project manager for a list of significant events in the project that can be used to benchmark the project's progress. What document will the project manager provide the key stakeholder with?

    A. Schedule management plan

    B. Schedule baseline

    C. Project schedule

    D. Milestone list

154. Tim works for a project management consulting firm that has just assisted a client in implementing a new process improvement plan. The executives of the company are pleased with the outcome of the project but are unsure how they will be able to maintain this new level of productivity. In response, Tim suggests that they use Kaizen events based around the Kaizen Theory. The Kaizen Theory is also known as:

A. Kanban

B. Continuous improvement

C. Prevention

D. Zero defects

155. A good project manager understands that:

A. Change is inevitable.

B. A well-constructed schedule requires no changes.

C. The baseline is fixed.

D. Each project is unique (or like no other).

156. Sue, the project manager of a pet facility build-out project, plans on attending an upcoming *Pets for the Environment* expo to mingle with other pet facilities and see the latest gadgets and technology used by the industry. This is an example of:

A. Pre-assignment

B. Research

C. Vacation

D. Networking

157. A small project team is in the process of performing a feasibility study on the potential build-out of an offshore data center. Several team members have expressed excitement about the project, since early indications from the study show that this may be a cost-effective solution that can save the organization millions of dollars in annual expenses. The Operations team, however, has expressed strong concerns about the impact to the team's morale if this project were to proceed forward. Where would the project manager document the various strategies for engaging with stakeholders, based on their needs and reactions to the project?

A. Stakeholder register

B. Stakeholder engagement plan

C. Stakeholder management strategy

D. Project management plan

158. Crystal is a family of methodologies intended to support a wide range of projects, depending on project size and criticality. Match the Crystal Method used when basing the selection solely on the range of stakeholders involved (Table 6.5).

TABLE 6.5   Crystal Methods

Crystal Method Name	Number of Stakeholders Involved
A. Crystal Clear	1. 20 to 40 people
B. Crystal Yellow	2. 5 to 100 people
C. Crystal Orange	3. 6 to 20 people
D. Crystal Red	4. 1 to 4 people

159. Al is a lead testing manager, and Veronica is a development manager; both work for Power Cloud Stock Trading Online. They are requesting a meeting with the project manager because every milestone that has been set for the project seems to experience a conflict. The top three reasons for conflict are:

A. Technical beliefs, resources, scheduling priorities

B. Personality, scheduling priorities, cost priorities

C. Personality, varying priorities, resources

D. Scheduling priorities, scarce resources, personal work styles

160. Which contract type poses a higher risk for the buyer?

A. Fixed price

B. Cost-reimbursable

C. Time and material

D. Cost-plus-fixed-fee

161. To expedite the scheduling process, a project manager alters an existing schedule management plan from a previous project for use on the current project. In this case, the schedule management plan represents:

A. A lazy project manager

B. A best practice

C. An enterprise environmental factor

D. An organizational process asset

162. The lowest level of the work WBS is the:

    A. Work package

    B. Activity list

    C. Planning package

    D. Control account

163. Alfred is holding a status meeting with several members of the project team to generate engagement among the team and to exchange information on the progress of various planned activities. At the conclusion of the meeting, Alfred distributes meeting minutes to attendees and archives the documentation to the project's central repository. What is this central repository used to capture, store, and distribute information to stakeholders called?

    A. Project management software

    B. SharePoint site

    C. Record management system

    D. Information management system

164. Stakeholder influence is highest within a project during which phase?

    A. Initial phase

    B. Intermediate phase

    C. Final phase

    D. All phases

165. Ron meets with Bob, the assigned project manager, to ask when the other project team members will be assigned to the project he is scheduled for. Since team assignments have not been issued yet, how does Ron know he will be assigned to the project?

    A. Bob is a friend of Ron's and mentioned the assignment early on.

    B. Ron must have heard about the assignment in passing.

    C. Ron was pre-assigned and listed in the project charter.

    D. Ron must have looked in Bob's files and should be reported.

166. There are 24 stakeholders within a project. How many communication channels exist?

    A. 276

    B. 288

    C. 552

    D. 24

167. An uncertain event or condition that, if it occurs, has a positive or negative effect on a project's objectives is known as:

    A. Workaround

    B. Issue

    C. Risk

    D. Trigger

168. A senior project manager is working on a project that will allow two servers across the globe to communicate with one another using web-based technology. Part of the project includes working with technology that is outdated, resulting in the need for a vendor with specific expertise. Because the vendor was in high demand, they included a requirement within the awarded contract that the parts provided by the buyer must be available before the start of the vendor's work. This is an example of which type of dependency?

A. External

B. Discretionary

C. Mandatory

D. Preferential

169. What is the highest level a person can reach, according to Maslow's Hierarchy of Needs?

A. Belonging

B. Self-actualization

C. Safety

D. Esteem

170. The duration of a milestone is:

A. The duration equal to half the length of the project

B. The duration equal to the length of the project

C. Zero

D. Typically one

171. Bob has been assigned as the project manager for a new supplement that his company, which is in the fitness and wellness industry, will be releasing in the next quarter. To prepare for the project, Bob has decided to attend an upcoming fitness expo, which will be attended by many colleagues in the industry. This is an example of:

A. Spying on the competition

B. Research

C. A leisure activity

D. Networking

172. One of your colleagues is experiencing trouble managing his project, which is already showing signs of poor performance. He feels that the project is too complex and has asked for your advice. Where should you direct him?

A. Offer to help him manage the project, even though you are currently at max capacity

B. Direct him to his functional manager, since it is his manager's job to provide him with training

C. Direct him to the PMO

D. Explain that he must take responsibility for his own project, since you are dealing with your own project issues

173. As the project manager, you've noticed that several project team members appear tense and withdrawn. It's unclear whether this is stemming from the recent issues that have emerged from within the project. How can you best discover what the attitudes of the project team members are toward the project?

A. Use observation and conversation

B. Perform a project performance appraisal

C. Institute ground rules

D. Perform conflict management

174. You will be participating in a weekly project team status meeting, along with 10 other team members. The meeting will take place by conference call, with only two of the participants located in the same office. What is this an example of?

A. Negotiation

B. Virtual team

C. Colocation

D. Project staff assignments

175. A risk manager of a software company is performing quantitative risk analysis. While numerically analyzing risks, she decided to utilize external subject-matter experts. What can the risk manager gain through this technique?

A. Assess the likelihood that all risks have been identified

B. Gain unbiased feedback on the evaluated risks

C. Better evaluate the results of modeling and simulation techniques

D. Validate the data and techniques used within the process

176. After Bruce, the project manager for the Happy Holiday Cruise Ships, Inc., makes his rounds through the office, he usually compiles the notes he's collected from talking to his team into a quick performance report and shares it on their team wiki site. Performance reports are an example of what type of communication?

A. Informal written

B. Formal written

C. Informal verbal

D. Formal verbal

177. The human resources associate at the Uptime Software Development Corporation is finding it difficult to attract new recruits due to the competitive nature of finding software developers. In response, she has suggested to her manager that the company increase the standard benefits package. Standard benefits provided to all employees is known as:

A. Fringe benefits

B. Perquisites

C. Halo effect

D. Performance bonus

178. Who developed the 14 Steps to Quality Management?

    A. Edward Shewhart

    B. W. Edwards Deming

    C. Philip Crosby

    D. Joseph Juran

179. Match the project life cycle with its corresponding goal.

TABLE 6.6 Project Life Cycles

Type	Description
A. Predictive	1. Correctness of solution
B. Iterative	2. Customer value via frequent deliveries and feedback
C. Incremental	3. Speed
D. Agile	4. Manage cost

180. Rita is a product owner responsible for the company's line of smart digital music devices. During a strategy session, she speaks with the division president regarding a new product idea. Based on the recent analysis and voice of the customer data obtained, they decide to move forward with the development of a minimum viable product (MVP). Which of the following best defines MVP?

    A. A product that contain a subset of features released to early customers as a way of obtaining feedback for future product development

    B. A product that contains partially completed features released to early customers as a way of obtaining feedback for future product development

    C. A product that contains a robust set of features released to early customers as a way of obtaining feedback for future product development

    D. A product that contains partially completed features released to customers as a way of obtaining feedback for enhancements

181. Joy is the technical lead of the testing department at Bing Bonk software. After she brings an issue to the attention of the CEO of the company, the CEO instructs Joy to tell the project manager to increase the duration of the testing phase by two weeks as a means of guaranteeing their upcoming release has no defects. Which of the following types of power is based on the respect that others have for someone else?

    A. Expert

    B. Referent

    C. Formal

    D. Coercive

182. Al is a lead testing manager, and Veronica is a development manager; both work for Power Cloud Stock Trading Online in the same team. They are requesting a meeting with the project manager because every milestone that has been set for the project seems to have a conflict, resulting from conflict between two specific team members. Who is responsible for resolving conflict between the two project team members?

A. The project manager

B. The project sponsor

C. The two project team members

D. The functional manager

183. 360-degree feedback is an example of:

A. Team performance assessment

B. Observation and conversation

C. Project performance appraisal

D. Conflict management

184. Thomas is the project manager for a software consulting company. The project he is working on has encountered numerous overruns due to regulatory compliance obstacles. A new bill passed by the government may even make it impossible for the deliverable to be distributed. He suggests to the CEO that it may be in the company's best interest to end the project and write off the costs they have incurred thus far. What type of cost refers to money already spent?

A. Sunk cost

B. Opportunity cost

C. Direct costs

D. Fixed costs

185. The project management team spent several days negotiating with a functional manager and another project manager to utilize the senior developer of the company as part of their project. This was the final resource needed to meet the resource requirements of the project. In what activity is the project management team engaged?

A. Acquiring the project team needed to perform the work

B. Estimating what resources are needed to perform the work

C. Estimating how long the work will take

D. Determining resource requirements

186. Frank's team is working on a gaming software product for a long-term customer. It was unanimously thought by Frank's team that the product needed the addition of a scoreboard on the screen as an enhancement. With the intention of increasing the quality of the product, a scoreboard was added. What has Frank's team done?

A. Prevented rework

B. Quality enhancement

C. Performed gold plating

D. Followed concept of "fitness for use"

187. Joseph Juran is known for the following:

    A. Zero defects

    B. Fitness for use

    C. 14 Steps to Total Quality Management

    D. Plan-Do-Check-Act cycle

188. A project manager of a construction company uncovered a risk that, if it were to occur, could shorten the length of the project by two months. This would mean a savings of $75,000 for the company. All of the stakeholders agreed that anything within reason should be done to make sure that this risk happens. What risk response strategy is the project manager most likely to use?

    A. Exploit

    B. Share

    C. Enhance

    D. Accept

189. Quality metrics can best be described as:

    A. Identifies what to measure within the project and what measurements are considered acceptable

    B. A tool to ensure that quality-related steps are performed

    C. Ensures that the concepts, designs, and tests selected at the beginning of the project are correct

    D. Detailed steps for determining waste and non-value-added activities within the processes

190. Which of the following does not represent a type of organizational structure?

    A. Project-oriented

    B. Functional matrix

    C. Strong matrix

    D. Balanced matrix

191. Empathy, influence, and creativity are all forms of:

    A. Communication skills

    B. Management skills

    C. Leadership skills

    D. Interpersonal skills

192. During the most recent team meeting, Nick left dissatisfied after not having had an opportunity to express his concerns over the schedule. When broaching the subject, he was cut off repeatedly by John, who felt that the focus of the meeting should be the recent server crash. What went wrong?

    A. Nick did not have the correct priorities since the server crash was the most pressing issue at hand.

    B. The project manager had not set clear ground rules.

C. John should be disciplined for repeatedly cutting Nick off, which was not a display of team cohesiveness.

D. Nick should have been advised to submit his concern through documentation.

193. The project team has had to re-architect a product that did not meet project standards. This has resulted in a one-week schedule delay, in addition to the cost of rework. This is an example of:

A. Poorly trained resources

B. Lack of specifications

C. Poor quality

D. Poorly structured scope

194. Janet is a project manager for the consulting division of the Java Architects. She has just been informed that the proposal she provided for a prospective client last week has gained approval from the company's governance board, and a project charter has been approved. What activity is most likely to be carried out next?

A. Facilitation of iteration planning

B. Creation of the project's backlog

C. Identification of stakeholders

D. Development of the project charter

195. Benchmarking refers to:

A. Determining where the project team should be through a status meeting

B. The investment made towards preventing non-conformance to requirements

C. Comparing actual or planned project practices to other projects as a way of generating ideas for improvement

D. Identifying the factors that may influence variables of a product or process being developed

196. A project team member called the project manager to notify him that there seemed to be confusion about the resources needed to complete her activity. The project manager, who was running late for a meeting, told the team member not to worry about it and ended the conversation by telling her to have a good day and that they would touch base in the coming weeks. The project team member was left wondering whether the project manager understood the severity of the situation, since without the resources, her activity could not proceed, and the deadline would be missed. What did the project team member fail to do during the conversation?

A. Ask the project manager whether it was a good time to talk

B. Confirm that the project manager understood the message correctly

C. Schedule a follow up conversation

D. Increase the pitch of her voice so that the project manager understood the severity of the situation

197. A project manager received feedback from team members that a certain team member was not up to speed on the project's technology, and it was impacting the progress of the work. The project manager then realized his error, since the team member was brought on board after the initial project training had occurred. Where can the project manager look to view the training needs and training plans for the team?

A. Project schedule

B. Schedule management plan

C. Project management plan

D. Resource management plan

198. Eric is a manager for a project that has teams located in two buildings on their corporate campus. As part of being a good project manager he knows that in order to keep the team functioning well, he has to spend time with them equally. Which of the following is used to stay in touch with the work and attitudes of project team members?

A. 360-degree feedback

B. Observation and conversation

C. Issue log

D. Team-building activities

199. You are the project manager of a software organization leading a project to develop a new reservation system. A new scheduling risk has been identified and determined to be critical to the project. As a result, you need to meet with project stakeholders to discuss the situation. What is the best method for dealing with stakeholders?

A. Call each stakeholder individually to get feedback

B. Schedule one-on-one meetings with all of the stakeholders

C. Schedule a phone conference with all of the stakeholders

D. Schedule an in-person meeting with all of the stakeholders

200. Which of the following techniques uses a weighted average?

A. Reserve analysis

B. What-if scenario analysis

C. Parametric estimating

D. PERT analysis

Appendix

Answers and Explanations

Chapter 1: People (Domain 1.0)

1. B. Carina is in the process of identifying stakeholders and analyzing their level of influence. Although the project has been active for three months, it is customary to perform this activity iteratively, especially at the start of a phase.

2. D. According to the *Agile Practice Guide*, servant leadership is the practice of leading through service to the team by focusing on developing team members and understanding and addressing their needs to generate the greatest possible performance.

3. D. Problem-solving involves asking questions to separate the causes of the problem from the symptoms. Decision-making involves considering alternative solutions to the problem. Choices are made from among the alternatives. Timing is important in decision-making, because good decisions made too soon or too late can turn into inferior solutions.

4. A. The PMI Talent Triangle® consists of the following three categories of skill set: technical project management, leadership, and strategic and business management. With the project being over budget and behind schedule, Nancy is most likely lacking in formal project management training and knowledge.

5. C. Negotiation is working with others to come to an agreement. Arbitration and mediation are two forms of negotiation.

6. A, C, D. Project teams may experience many pain points when a project contains a high degree of uncertainty, change, and complexity. Agile approaches directly address these pain points by performing activities such as creating clear team charters (i.e., vision, mission), among other activities. Examples of pain points include unclear purpose, unclear requirements, technical debt, and high defects.

7. B. This describes the use of interpersonal and team skills, which is a common skill set used when acquiring resources. This often encompasses negotiation with other project managers and/or managers.

8. A. When you hold the PMP certification, one of the responsibilities is to report violations of the PMP code of conduct. In some cases, we make poor judgments that can be corrected. To maintain the integrity of the profession, everyone who holds the PMP certification must adhere to the code of conduct that makes all of us accountable to each other.

9. D. Iterative life cycles use successive prototypes or proofs of concept to improve the product or result. Activities are repeated in cycles to produce new information and team insights.

10. B. Knowledge can be split into explicit or tacit knowledge. Tacit knowledge refers to knowledge that is difficult to express, such as insights, experience, beliefs, and know-how.

11. D. This question describes the collaborate/problem-solve style of conflict resolution. This style allows for discussion of multiple viewpoints and the examination of all perspectives on the issue.

12. A. Withdrawal happens when one of the parties leaves and/or refuses to discuss the conflict. This is a lose-lose conflict-resolution technique and does not typically result in a resolution.

13. C, D. The team charter is used to establish the team, clarify expectations, and create team norms. It typically highlights team values, agreements, and how the team will operate together throughout the project's life. It may also define team ground rules and other expected behaviors.

14. C. This question describes activities associated with monitoring the engagement levels of stakeholders. The tools and techniques used to perform these activities include data analysis, decision-making, data representation, communication skills, interpersonal and team skills, and meetings. Ground rules are used to manage stakeholder engagement.

15. C. Respect involves behaving in a professional manner. While project managers are not responsible for the actions of others, they are responsible for their own actions and reactions. Part of acting professionally involves controlling one's self and reactions in questionable situations, as David did in this scenario.

16. C. You know that your friend has reported the status untruthfully, and you are obligated to ensure that the truth is reported at all times. Giving your friend an opportunity to correct their behavior is appropriate; should the person not be truthful, it is your responsibility to report status based on accurate information provided.

17. A. Legitimate, or formal, power comes as a result of the influencer's position.

18. B. General management skills are likely to affect project outcomes. Estimating Costs is part of the Planning process group, and Control Costs is part of the Monitoring and Controlling process group. PMI requires either a degree or a certain number of years of experience in project management to sit for the exam, along with other requirements.

19. B. In a highly adaptive life cycle, changes are welcome. Feedback is continuously obtained from stakeholders.

20. C. Roles and responsibilities, training needs, and recognition and rewards are all elements documented in the resource management plan. Other elements covered in the plan are the list of methods for identifying resources, acquiring resources, project organizational charts, project team resource management, team development, and resource control.

21. D. Working in a foreign country can bring about an experience called *culture shock*. When you've spent years acting in certain ways and expecting normal, everyday events to follow a specific course of action, you might find yourself disoriented when things don't go as you expected. In this scenario, the project manager was attempting to prevent culture shock.

22. A. Directing, also referred to as forcing, is a conflict-resolution technique where one's viewpoint is pushed at the expense of others. This is typically a win-lose solution.

23. D. Diversity training is the best way to ensure that team members will learn to recognize and deal with cultural differences among the members because clashes could impede the project's progress. Team-building exercises are not a bad idea, but this question is specifically asking about cultural differences, which are best handled with diversity training.

24. D. The team is currently in the storming phase of Tuckman's team development model. In this phase, the team members begin to address the project work and are not yet collaborative or open with each other.

25. B. Theory Z was developed by Dr. William Ouchi. This theory is concerned with increasing employee loyalty to their organizations. This theory results in increased productivity, puts an emphasis on the well-being of the employees both at work and outside of work, encourages steady employment, and leads to high employee satisfaction and morale.

26. A, B, C. Influencing entails the ability to get things done using power and politics. Power is the ability to get people to do things they wouldn't ordinarily do, and it's the ability to change minds and influence outcomes. Politics involve getting groups of people with diverse interests to cooperate creatively, even in the midst of conflict and disorder.

27. A-4, B-3, C-1, D-5, E-2. There are various types of leadership styles. The *PMBOK® Guide* highlights the following six: laissez-faire, transactional, servant leader, transformational, charismatic, and interactional. Interactional, which is not an option listed in the question, refers to a combination of transactional, transformational, and charismatic.

28. A, D. Servant leadership enables the team to be successful by playing a supportive role, allowing the team to be self-organized and self-managed. A servant leader has several responsibilities intended to empower the team; two examples include providing greater team accountability and supporting the team through mentorship and encouragement.

29. C. As the project progresses, you should use different techniques to perform these processes, including using different techniques to motivate, lead, and coach. The techniques you'll use will depend on the makeup of the project team and the stakeholders involved in that stage. The processes in this Knowledge Area concern human and material resources, and they consist of Plan Resource Management, Acquire Resources, Develop Team, Manage Team, and Control Resources.

30. B. Based on the little information provided in the scenario, you can conclude that Antwon is the project sponsor through his title. A project sponsor is typically an executive in the organization with authority to assign resources and enforce decisions regarding the project. As a marketing associate, Lewis is least likely to be the sponsor, although it is possible that he may play an important role within the project.

31. A. Colocation is also known as a tight matrix. These terms refer to placing many or all of the project team members physically together in the same place.

32. D. You must consider the characteristics of potential project team members, whether they're from inside or outside the organization. This question describes the enterprise environmental factors that should be considered as an input to Acquire Resources.

33. B. There are several methods and tools that a project manager can use to develop the project team, including colocation, virtual teams, communication technology, interpersonal and team skills (conflict management, influencing, motivation, negotiation, team building), recognition and rewards, training, individual and team assessments, and meetings. Emotional intelligence is used to manage versus develop teams.

34. A. The Achievement Theory is attributed to David McClelland and says people are motivated by the need for power, achievement, and affiliation. Vroom introduced the Expectancy Theory, Herzberg introduced the Hygiene Theory, and McGregor is known for Theory X and Theory Y.

35. A. According to the *Agile Practice Guide*, the servant leadership approach contains the following characteristics: promoting self-awareness; listening; serving those on the team; helping people grow; coaching versus controlling; promoting safety, respect, and trust; and promoting the energy and intelligence of others.

36. B. The Contingency Theory proposes that people are motivated to achieve levels of competency and will continue to be motivated even after the competency is reached. The area of the role delineation study this question refers to is contributing to the project management knowledge base.

37. A. This question describes a manager, not a leader. The Responsibility domain covers the concept of confidential information.

38. D. Resource calendars are an output of the Acquire Resources process and include the availability, skills, and abilities of resources.

39. C. In the performing phase, the team members reach the point where they are performing as a well-organized unit; they are interdependent, and they work well through the issues. Other options describe the forming, storming, and norming phases.

40. B. Within a project environment, conflict is inevitable. The key is how conflict is dealt with and managed.

41. C. As part of upholding the value of responsibility and ensuring integrity, project managers are required to follow all applicable laws and regulations that apply to the industry, organization, or project. Bypassing customs is an example of violating a country's laws.

42. D. This question describes the enterprise environmental factors input of the Acquire Resources process and refers to the Responsibility section of the *PMI Code of Ethics and Professional Conduct*. Responsibility is concerned with making decisions that are for the good of the organization.

43. A, B, C. Good leaders use referent power, which is inferred to them by their subordinates. They are visionaries and are concerned with the big picture, or strategic direction and plans. A project manager's primary goal is to satisfy stakeholder needs.

44. A. You are in the Executing processes, so therefore you are in the Manage Stakeholder Engagement process. This question describes the interpersonal and team skills tool and technique for this process.

45. B, C, D. Recognition and rewards are often used when developing the team. Rewards should be in proportion to the achievement and linked to the performance. If you reward the same team members over and over again, it could be a morale killer for other team members.

46. C. The Expectancy Theory proposes that the expectation of a positive outcome drives motivation. Motivation may drive negative behaviors as well as positive ones. The Responsibility domain covers several elements including the following: ensuring integrity, accepting assignments, laws and regulations compliance, and confidential information. Accepting assignments concerns being honest about your qualifications, and fudging your experience is dishonest.

47. C. Sometimes you might find yourself working with teams of people from different countries or cultures. Some team members might be from one country and some from another. The best way to ensure that cultural or ethical differences do not hinder your project is to provide training for all team members.

48. B, C, D. Virtual teams may not work in the same location, but they all share the goals of the project and have a role to fulfill.

49. C. The question describes activities associated with developing the team, and that's also where sensitivity to the stages of team development are critical.

50. B. According to the *Agile Practice Guide*, there are three common roles used in Agile projects: cross-functional team member, product owner, and team facilitator. Many Agile frameworks and approaches do not address the role of project manager.

51. B. This question describes the Acquire Resources process because it states you will be hiring virtual team members from across the globe. Virtual teams are a tool and technique of this process. Because of the diversity of the team, you should pay particular attention to cultural awareness and perhaps provide diversity training.

52. A, D. Rewards and recognition systems are formal ways of promoting desirable behavior.

53. D. Measuring customer satisfaction is just one of the many activities that occur during administrative closure of a project. While some projects check in and measure satisfaction at key points throughout the project's life cycle, it should occur during project closure at a minimum.

54. D. As a project manager, it is important for you to establish relationships with the stakeholders. Project Stakeholder Management is concerned with identifying all of the stakeholders on the project and assessing their needs, expectations, and involvement on the project.

55. B, C, D. Structured interviews, ability tests, and attitudinal surveys are examples of individual and team assessments that can provide the project manager with insights into team member strengths and weaknesses. This enables them to be organized based on their strengths. Training is not an example of an assessment.

56. B-4, A-2, D-1, C-3. Compromise, also known as reconcile, involves resolving conflict by seeking to appease all parties involved (lose-lose outcome); collaborate is a win-win conflict-resolution technique that seeks to resolve the problem through open dialogue and varying perspectives; force, also known as direct, is a win-lose conflict-resolution technique where one person is able to get their way; and avoid, also known as withdraw, is a conflict-resolution technique where participants retreat from the situation in hopes that others will resolve the conflict.

57. B. A servant leader encourages the distribution of responsibility across the team; they support the team through coaching, removing blockers, helping to develop their skills, and fostering collaboration.

58. A. A stakeholder assessment matrix allows you to compare planned engagement levels against actual engagement levels. This can be used in conjunction with the multicriteria decision analysis technique, where predefined criteria that are prioritized and weighted can be used to assess engagement levels.

59. D. Leticia is performing activities associated with the Monitor Stakeholder Engagement process. Specifically, she is using the multicriteria decision analysis tool, which is a subset of the decision-making tool and technique of the process.

60. A. Knowledge can be split into explicit or tacit knowledge. Explicit knowledge refers to knowledge that can be codified using pictures, numbers, or words.

61. A. Team performance assessments are a result of developing the project team. This activity typically involves determining and documenting a team's effectiveness.

62. A. As the project progresses, project costs begin to taper off. The project is currently in the closing stage, and risk of overspending should be minimal at this point.

63. A, C, D. You are carrying out activities associated with the Manage Team process. The following information will provide useful insight into team member performance: resource management plan, issue log, lessons learned register, project team assignments, team charter, team performance assessments, work performance reports, enterprise environmental factors, and organizational process assets. A project management information system is a tool versus information that would be used to assess performance.

64. A. Rianna is currently performing the Manage Team process, which includes managing conflict. This process is concerned with tracking team member performance, providing feedback, resolving issues, and managing team changes to optimize project performance.

65. A, C. According to the *PMBOK® Guide*, virtual teams can be defined as groups of people with a shared goal who fulfill their roles with little or no time spent meeting face to face. Oftentimes, team members are dispersed across various locations.

66. C. You should always maintain respect and professional demeanor when interacting with others. You can't control their actions, but you can control your own. This question refers to the Conduct Procurements process. Procurement negotiation is a tool and technique of this process.

67. A. Collaborate is also called problem-solving and should be the technique most commonly used by project managers.

68. D. As part of closing out a project, ongoing activities (such as support and maintenance) are transitioned to the appropriate teams. When this does not occur, project resources cannot be fully released from these activities.

69. C. Conflict-resolution techniques include the following: withdraw/avoid, smooth/ accommodate, compromise/reconcile, force/direct, collaborate/problem-solve.

70. A. Smoothing, also known as accommodating, emphasizes areas of agreement rather than areas of difference.

71. D. The best answer to this question is Theory Y. Theory Y managers believe people are interested in performing at their best, given the right motivation and proper expectation. They support their teams, are concerned about team members, and are good listeners.

72. A. The Manage Team process has two tools and techniques: interpersonal and team skills and project management information system.

73. A-2, B-1, C-3. The *PMBOK® Guide* highlights three decision-making techniques: voting, autocratic, and multicriteria decision analysis.

74. D. Theory Y managers believe that people will give you their best if they know what's expected of them and they have the proper motivation.

75. A. The procurement manager's behavior can be viewed as a conflict of interest. A conflict of interest is when you put your personal interests above the interests of the project or when you use your influence to cause others to make decisions in your favor without regard for the project outcome. In other words, your personal interests take precedence over your professional obligations, and you make decisions that allow you to personally benefit regardless of the outcome of the project.

76. C. Extinction is the best type of project ending, meaning that the project came to an end because it was completed and accepted by the stakeholders.

77. B. Kaylee and Alyssa used the collaborate technique, also referred to as problem-solving. This technique involves getting multiple viewpoints from differing perspectives and reaching consensus and commitment after having an open dialogue. It is considered a win-win conflict-resolution technique.

78. B. The best response is transformational and legitimate. This leader is focusing on collaborating and influencing. She listens to your responses and then offers suggestions of her own. The situational style of leadership could have been a correct response to this question, but it wasn't an option. Her power of leadership is legitimate because of the position she holds.

79. C. While a case can be made that all of the options presented are valid answers, incorrectly reporting credentials is an example of an ethics violation. As a credential holder, it is your responsibility to report violations of the PMP code of conduct.

80. A. Trudy and Roy are using the stakeholder engagement assessment matrix tool, which is part of the data representation tool and technique of the Plan Stakeholder Engagement process. This matrix classifies stakeholders in five ways: unaware, resistant, neutral, supportive, or leading.

81. B. Resource leveling is used when resources are overallocated, available only at certain times, or assigned to more than one activity at a time. This is part of resource optimization techniques and a tool and technique of the Develop Schedule process.

82. B. Honesty involves not only information regarding your own background and experience but information regarding the project circumstances as well. This includes being up front and truthful about the project's status and information.

83. B. The project manager is responsible for understanding the interests of stakeholders and getting in front of any potential conflict that may arise as a result of their personal interests.

84. D. The question describes a daily stand-up, referred to as a Daily Scrum meeting. These meetings are typically held at the same time and place every day and are time-boxed to typically no more than 15 minutes. The purpose is to keep the team informed and alert the Scrum master of any obstacles in the way of completing tasks.

85. A. Stakeholders often have conflicting interests, which can generate conflict. It is the project manager's responsibility to understand these conflicts and try to resolve them.

86. A, B, C. A servant leader facilitates team success by helping the team be collaborative and deliver value more quickly. They do this by listening; promoting self-awareness, respect, and trust; and adopting the mindset that they are there to serve the team.

87. A. The *PMBOK® Guide – Sixth Edition* defines a stakeholder as "an individual, group, or organization that may affect, be affected by, or perceive itself to be affected by a decision, activity, or outcome of a project."

88. B. Teams that are resistant to change respond better to a gradual transition where components of both predictive and adaptive delivery models are used. This is referred to as a hybrid approach.

89. C. Joe is correct. The project manager is responsible for managing and performing activities relating to project integration management activities.

90. B. Fairness includes avoiding favoritism and discrimination against others, avoiding and reporting conflict-of-interest situations, and maintaining impartiality in a decision-making process.

91. C. Working in a foreign country can bring about an experience called *culture shock*. When you've spent years acting certain ways and expecting normal, everyday events to follow a specific course of action, you might find yourself disoriented when things don't go as you expected.

92. B. The Tuckman ladder, also referred to as stages of team development, consists of five stages that teams may go through: forming, storming, norming, performing, and adjourning. In the adjourning stage, teams complete the work and are released.

93. C. In iterative and incremental project life cycles, feedback helps to better plan the next iteration of the project. In Agile projects, incremental delivery exposes requirements that are hidden or misunderstood.

94. C. The producer is the project sponsor because the question states that he is the final decision-maker for all questions that arise on the project. He also created the budget, implying he has the authority to spend money on the project.

95. B. Sue is referring to leadership skills, which is one of the categories of skill set that make up the PMI Talent Triangle®. The *PMBOK® Guide – Sixth Edition* describes leadership as the knowledge, skills, and behaviors needed to guide, motivate, and direct a team to help an organization achieve its business goals.

96. B, D. Agile teams focus on measuring value and what the team delivers versus what the team predicted it would deliver. Measurements tend to be empirical and value-based in nature.

97. D. When managing project teams, many conflicts come about as a result of scheduling issues, availability of resources, or personal work habits.

98. D. Maslow's Hierarchy of Needs notes that there are five sets of needs that must be met in the following hierarchical order: basic physical needs, safety and security needs, social needs, self-esteem needs, and self-actualization. The idea is that these needs must be met before the person can move to the next level of needs in the hierarchy.

99. A. A role delineation study (RDS) can be best described as a job analysis. PMI conducts a role delineation study every five to seven years for every discipline it credentials. An RDS is conducted by bringing together volunteers to discuss the specific roles associated with each certification to identify the tasks and responsibilities that the roles will be expected to perform.

100. B. You have just completed activities associated with building the project team. Activities associated with developing the team are likely to follow.

101. A, B, D. The team charter, also referred to as a team's social contract, typically addresses how the team will work together and interact. Examples provided by the *Agile Practice Guide* include team values, working agreements, ground rules, and group norms. Team assignments are not typically included within this social contract.

102. C. As part of our responsibility as project management practitioners, we should report unethical or illegal conduct to appropriate individuals or management. Ensuring that confidentiality, regulations, and legal requirements are followed is part of upholding the responsibility value.

103. C. The project manager is utilizing strategic and business management skills, which is one of three categories of skill set that make up the PMI Talent Triangle®. The other two are technical project management and leadership.

104. C. The product owner speaks on behalf of the business unit, customer, or end user, and is therefore considered to be the voice of the customer. The product owner represents the stakeholders and is the liaison between stakeholders, the Scrum master, and the development team.

105. D. Cheryl and the project manager are engaged in capturing lessons learned in engaging with this particular vendor and also in activities associated with managing the vendor's performance; this includes discussing what went well and what could have been done differently, which will benefit future projects.

106. B. The Hygiene Theory states that hygiene and motivators are the two factors that contribute to motivators. Hygiene factors deal with work environment issues. Motivators deal with the substance of the work itself and the satisfaction one derives from performing the functions of the job.

107. D. While the project sponsor is typically accountable for the project, it is the project manager who assumes responsibility for the overall success of the project.

108. A. Meetings are one of the four sets of tools and techniques used to develop the project management plan. Other tools and techniques include leveraging expert judgment, utilizing data gathering techniques (brainstorming, checklists, focus groups, interviews), and interpersonal and team skills (conflict management, facilitation, meeting management).

109. D-3, A-4, B-2, C-1. Agile teams need a clear project vision and purpose, which are provided through a project charter. Agile project charters address the reasoning for the project, as well as team norms and how the team will collaborate.

110. A. There are three categories of skill sets that make up the PMI Talent Triangle®: business management and strategic skills, technical project management skills, and leadership skills. Business management and strategic skills encompass a project manager being able to describe the business needs of the project and how they align with the organization's goals.

111. D. Responsibility includes accepting assignments that you are qualified to take on. You should always honestly report your qualifications, your experience, and your past performance of services to potential employers, customers, PMI, and others.

112. D. Upholding confidentiality agreements is part of the responsibility value. Protecting proprietary or confidential information that has been entrusted to you is part of a project manager's responsibility.

113. C. Fairness includes avoiding favoritism and discrimination against others, avoiding and reporting conflict-of-interest situations, and maintaining impartiality in a decision-making process. In this case, scope creep should be brought to the project team's attention and treated as an unapproved change. This would need to go through the formal change control process.

114. B, C, D. The underlying success factors to forming effective agile teams are building a foundational trust and safe working environment, as well as an agile mindset.

115. C. The Contingency Theory is a combination of Theory Y and the Hygiene Theory. It states that people are motivated to achieve levels of competency even after competency is reached.

116. A. There are three categories of skill set that make up the PMI Talent Triangle®: business management and strategic skills, technical project management skills, and leadership skills.

117. D. Responsibility is the act of making decisions that are for the good of the organization rather than ourselves, admitting our mistakes, and being responsible for the decisions we make (or those we don't make) and the consequences that result, along with other actions. It represents one of four values that project management practitioners should uphold.

118. B. The salience model uses three elements in analyzing stakeholders: power, urgency, and legitimacy. This is a data representation technique of the Identify Stakeholders process.

119. A, C. According to the *Agile Practice Guide*, there are various ways for geographically distributed teams to come together via a virtual workspace. Two examples provided include fishbowl windows and remote pairing.

120. D. Activities such as team building, motivating, and recognition and rewards are a means of improving teamwork, motivating employees, reducing attrition, and improving overall project performance.

121. D. You could conduct a team celebration, thank your team members for their contributions, and guide them through a closure process.

122. A. This describes the adjourning stage of team development.

123. D. Obtaining feedback prevents the team from moving in the wrong direction. Early and continuous feedback allows for microcorrections to ensure stakeholder feedback is achieved and incremental value is delivered.

124. A. Ron is a Scrum master. In Agile project management, the Scrum master coordinates the work of the sprint and runs interference between the team and any distractions that may keep them from the work at hand. They also support the product owner in maintaining the backlog, prioritizing work, and defining when work is done.

125. D. The question describes technical project management skills, which is one of three categories of skill set that make up the PMI Talent Triangle®. The *PMBOK® Guide – Sixth Edition* defines technical project management skills as the knowledge, skills, and behaviors related to specific domains of project, program, and portfolio management.

126. C, D. Lateral thinking is a form of alternatives analysis often used to determine a project's scope. It was created by Edward de Bono and serves as a means of reasoning and thinking about problems differently than what can be classified as evident.

127. C. Defining the requirements and obtaining sign-off on the requirements will help you to ensure customer satisfaction. When stakeholders are aware of and agree to the requirements, they know exactly what the project is expected to deliver as well as what is not part of the deliverables.

128. B. Honesty and truthful reporting are required of PMP credential holders. In this situation, you would inform the customer of everything you know regarding the problem and work to find alternative solutions.

129. D. The formula for calculating lines of communication is as follows, where n represents the total number of stakeholders (you are already assumed to have been included in the number):

Plug in the numbers to get the following: $35(35 - 1) \div 2 = 595$.

130. B. The project team is using the product analysis technique to define the scope of the project.

131. B, C. The Agile Manifesto highlights how important individuals and their interactions are. As a result, Agile approaches stress the importance of optimizing flow to achieve ongoing value. Key benefits include the following: people are more likely to collaborate, teams produce *valuable* work faster, and teams waste less time.

132. C. Respect involves several areas, including the way we conduct ourselves, the way we treat others, listening to other viewpoints, and conducting ourselves in a professional manner. According to the *PMI Code of Ethics and Professional Conduct*, an environment of respect generates trust and confidence and fosters mutual cooperation.

133. B. When people work in unfamiliar environments, culture shock can occur. Training and researching information about the country you'll be working in can help counteract this.

134. C. A burndown chart shows the time remaining for the sprint and displays the time period of the sprint on the horizontal axis and the backlog items on the vertical axis.

135. B. Trudy and Roy are carrying out activities associated with planning stakeholder engagement, which involves developing the approaches to engage stakeholders based on their interests, impact on the project, needs, and expectations.

136. C. Expert power occurs when someone has a considerable amount of knowledge about a subject or has special abilities.

137. A. Engaging in development activities for the team allows the project manager to improve team competencies, team member interaction, and the overall team environment to enhance project performance.

138. C. The project manager is performing activities related to the Manage Stakeholder Engagement process. Interpersonal and team skills, a tool and technique of this process, involves cultural awareness.

139. A. These team members are confrontational with each other and are trying to find their position within the team and their standing with you. This describes the storming stage of team development.

140. C. This question describes a transactional leadership style. Transactional leaders are autocratic, activity focused, and autonomous; they use contingent reward systems and manage by exception.

141. C. While all options listed may help the situation, interpersonal and team skills is the prominent area that the offending team member lacks.

142. D. The most appropriate response is to tell the customer about the remaining tasks and work with them to modify the schedule date or modify the agreement regarding the payment date.

143. B. A conflict of interest is when you put your personal interests above the interests of the project or when you use your influence to cause others to make decisions in your favor without regard for the project outcome. Violating the procurement policy to improve the budget situation was not the appropriate action to take.

144. A. When building your team, it is important to consider things such as the organization's recruitment and procurement procedures and processes. You hired your friend on the spot, so important steps in the process could have been missed. Pre-assignment is when resources are assigned prior to the project start.

145. A. The formula for calculating lines of communication is as follows, where n represents the total number of stakeholders (you are already assumed to have been included in the number):

$$n\,(n-1) \div 2$$

Plug in the numbers to get the following: $12(12 - 1) \div 2 = 66$.

146. B. Expert power occurs when the person being influenced believes the person doing the influencing, typically because they are knowledgeable about the subject or have special abilities that make them an expert.

147. C. The stages of team development are as follows: forming, storming, norming, and performing. This model was developed by Tuckman-Jensen, and whenever a new member is added, the team reverts to the forming stage of development.

148. A. This team member is describing the self-actualization level of Maslow's Hierarchy of Needs.

149. B. Given that the project manager contributed to the handbook while under assignment by the contracting organization and was just one of multiple contributors, it is likely that his actions would be viewed as a violation of the organization's policies on intellectual property. This would be verified by reviewing the project manager's contractual agreement.

150. B. Rather than asking how the team can act in a predictable manner, a team looking to adopt an Agile mind-set may instead ask how the team can act in a more Agile or transparent manner.

Chapter 2: Process (Domain 2.0)

1. B. Rita is in the process of refining the backlog in order to prepare for the next iteration. Engaging the team allows everyone to be aligned on the stories, relative to one another.

2. C. The project manager is typically responsible for authoring the final report. The project's final report contains a summary of what occurred on the project and may include information on scope, cost, schedule/burn down of work, risk, and quality outcomes.

3. B. Risk strategy, methodology, and risk-related roles and responsibilities are all elements of the risk management plan. Other areas covered by the plan include the following: risk-related funding, timing, risk categories, stakeholder risk appetite, definitions of risk probability and impacts, probability and impact matrix, reporting formats, and tracking.

4. C. The Agile Manifesto identifies 12 principles that describe the Agile approach. It came about through a group of software developers who came together in 2001 to formalize the Agile approach.

5. C. According to PMI, a good project manager spends up to 90 percent of their time communicating. Communication skills are essential for a successful project manager.

6. A. Change-driven life cycles are also known as Agile or adaptive life cycles.

7. B. Project Communications Management involves every member of the project team, including all the stakeholders. Everyone involved in the project will send or receive project information or both. Project Resources involve all the human and physical resources assigned to the work of the project. Although all the folks working on the project are involved, only the project manager and perhaps a few others are involved in performing the processes within this Knowledge Area.

8. A, C, D. A highly predictive (waterfall) life cycle typically has detailed specifications, while a highly adaptive life cycle (Agile) has requirements that are progressively elaborated. All other statements are true.

9. A-5, B-1, C-4, D-2, E-3. There are a total of 10 Project Management Knowledge Areas. The best indicator of its description is identifying key words that tie it back to the name of the Knowledge Area.

10. A, C. According to the *PMI Code of Ethics and Professional Conduct*, you should always report the truth regarding project status. This question refers to activities associated with the Manage Communications process.

11. B. Using an Agile approach, a project team can assess results and adjust processes to meet new or modified requirements.

12. B. Incremental life cycles focus on speed of delivery as an optimization method. In this type of life cycle, the project yields frequent smaller deliverables to avoid waiting for everything to be completed before a solution exists. In other words, a subset of the overall solution becomes available sooner.

13. B. Since the scenario outlined that the final deliverable of the project was completed, it implies that closing activities would follow. Administrative closure, which occurs as part of the Close Project or Phase process, consists of activities such as ensuring that exit criteria have been met and contractual agreements were properly closed out, measuring stakeholder satisfaction, and ensuring that ongoing operational or sustainment activities are transferred to operations.

14. B. In Scrum, iterations are also known as *sprints*. Iterations or sprints are always time-bound and can be any short period of time defined and agreed upon by the team.

15. D. The milestone list contains the final dates that the project milestones have been accomplished. This is used as an input to the Close Project or Phase process, which is where the final report is produced.

16. C. Project communications is an input of the Close Project or Phase process as part of project documents. It includes all communications that have been generated throughout the project.

17. B. The project team is performing administrative closure activities associated with the Close Project or Phase process. While information captured will be added to the lessons learned register, administrative closure is a broader choice that captures additional activities noted in the question, such as archiving information and creating the final report.

18. B. According to the *Agile Practice Guide*, all project life cycles share the element of planning. What differs across predictive, iterative, incremental, and Agile life cycles is the degree to which planning is done, and when.

19. B, C. Remember that all questions on the exam will refer to specific terminology used in the *PMBOK® Guide – Sixth Edition*. Although the other options presented may seem correct, the *PMBOK® Guide* calls this process by any of these names: stage gates, phase reviews, phase gates, phase exit, or kill points.

20. C. The Monitoring and Controlling process group is where project performance measurements are taken and analyzed to determine whether the project is progressing according to the plan.

21. D. Agile project management is a methodology that manages projects through iterations of work; it allows the team to quickly adapt to new requirements and allows for continual assessment of goals, deliverables, and functionality of the product, service, or result of the project.

22. D. Within the Agile methodology, a sprint or iteration refers to a short, time-bound period of work, which always starts with a sprint-planning meeting. It is also known as an iteration.

23. D. A project is considered successful when it achieves its objectives and the stakeholder needs and expectations are met.

24. A. Information included within the project charter is high level versus detailed. While the charter may include a list of high-level risks, it is unlikely that a detailed list can be compiled at this early stage of the project.

25. A. The chances for successful completion during the Executing phase are medium to high. Since the project is nearing the end of execution and is currently on track, the likelihood of success is high.

26. A. There are two types of risk acceptance in which no proactive risk response strategy is selected: passive and active acceptance. Passive acceptance means that no action will be taken other than to periodically monitor the risk.

27. C. The project manager is putting together the cost management plan, which is an activity carried out through the Plan Cost Management process. The cost management plan documents the rules of performance measurement, level of precision and accuracy, units of measure, organizational procedures links, control thresholds, reporting formats, process descriptions, and other budget-related details necessary to develop, manage, and control the budget.

28. B. Appraisal costs are associated with the cost of quality and are the costs expended to examine the product or process and make certain the requirements are being met. Inspection and testing are examples of appraisal costs.

29. B. The best answer is the communications management plan, which is a subsidiary of the project management plan. While project management plan is also a correct answer, the communications management plan is a more specific choice and therefore a better answer. Stakeholder communication requirements, escalation processes, and methods for receiving/obtaining information are all elements addressed within the communications management plan.

30. B, C, D. The product scope description is a component of the project charter and of the project scope statement, but it is not an input to this process.

31. A, B, D. This statement does describe some objectives but *not* adequately. Objectives are quantifiable criteria used to measure project success and should include schedule, cost, and quality metrics. There are no measures of time, cost, or quality mentioned in this statement. Requirements describe the specifications of the objectives and typically wouldn't be mixed into an objective statement. The objective should be clear and concise.

32. C. As part of carrying out the Perform Quantitative Risk Analysis process, updates are made to the risk register. Among the updates are an assessment of overall project risk exposure and detailed probabilistic analysis of the project.

33. B. To determine the total duration of the project, you add up the expected value for each activity. Note, you calculate expected value only for activities that have zero float.

34. A. Philip Crosby is the quality theorist behind the Zero Defects practice, which promotes doing it right the first time.

35. B. Carina is performing the Identify Risks process. The purpose of the process is to identify individual project risks, as well as sources of overall project risk, and document their characteristics.

36. A. Low-priority risks are added to a watch list within the risk register, where they will be monitored for possible changes.

37. A. There are 10 channels of communication, which is taken into consideration when using the communications requirement analysis tool and technique of the Plan Communications Management process. The formula for this is $5(5 - 1) \div 2$.

38. B. The greatest expense for most projects is resources, both human and material and supplies.

39. C. Parametric estimating is a quantitatively based estimating method that multiplies the quantity of work by the rate or uses an algorithm in conjunction with historical data to determine cost, budget, or duration estimates. When the information is reliable, it yields an estimate that is high in accuracy.

40. C. According to the *PMBOK® Guide*, there are two levels of risk: individual project risk and overall project risk. An overall project risk is the effect of uncertainty on the project as a whole, arising from all sources of uncertainty.

41. B. The funding requirements are derived from the cost baseline. Management reserve is released in increments throughout the project, and the funding requirements are an output of the Determine Budget process.

42. D. Make-or-buy analysis is a tool and technique of the Plan Procurement Management process.

43. D. The Daily Scrum is intended to keep the team functioning on the same page, microcommit to each other, and address any impediments immediately. In her role as Scrum master, Chu attends to support the team and ensure they understand their roles and Scrum processes.

44. D. According to the *PMBOK® Guide*, the purpose of the Plan Stakeholder Engagement process is to develop approaches to involve project stakeholders based on their needs, expectations, interests, and potential impacts on the project. This is the second process of the Project Stakeholder Management Knowledge Area.

45. B. Direct and Manage Project Work, Manage Quality, and Conduct Procurements are 3 of the 10 processes that make up the Executing process group.

46. D. During Closing, a project has the highest probability of completing successfully.

47. D. Since EAC is based on actual costs to date and assuming ETC work will be completed at the budgeted rate, the equation to use for EAC is EAC = AC + (BAC − EV). In this case, your formula looks like this: $425 + ($900 − $475) = $850.

48. B. The project management plan contains the resource management plan, which addresses how resources will be obtained, managed, and released.

49. C. An Agile life cycle consists of a blend of iterative and incremental approaches, which focuses on refining the work to deliver outcomes more frequently. An Agile life cycle has dynamic requirements that focus on customer value.

50. C. Integration occurs when the resources of the project are distributed to other areas in the organization or are assigned to other projects. In this case, the functional manager is reassigning resources to another project.

51. C. Waterfall is a methodology that follows a predictive life cycle. While there are many Agile and Lean frameworks, the *Agile Practice Guide* addresses the following: Scrum, eXtreme Programming, Kanban Method, Crystal Methods, Scrumban, Feature-Driven Development, Dynamic Systems Development Method, and Agile Unified Process.

52. B. Reserve analysis is a technique used as part of the Control Costs and Monitor Risks process. This technique involves the analysis of how much reserves have been consumed to date and whether sufficient reserves remain to address current and future risks.

53. C. Data analysis is a tool and technique of multiple project management processes, including the Control Schedule process, where it encompasses the use of earned value analysis, iteration burndown charts, performance reviews, trend analysis, variance analysis, and what-if scenario analysis.

54. B. Planned value is the authorized budget assigned to the scheduled work; in other words, it refers to the value of the work to be completed.

55. C. Status review meetings are considered one of the most important types of meetings a project manager holds throughout the project. These types of meetings use interactive communication, where communication occurs between stakeholders and is live.

56. B. When performing activities relating to controlling resources, data analysis may be used to evaluate what alternatives exist to completing activities with resources, such as alternate resources. Data analysis also includes performing cost-benefit analysis, performance reviews, and trend analysis.

57. C. An iteration burndown chart is a data analysis tool and technique of the Control Schedule process. This chart is used to track the remaining work to be completed against the backlog.

58. B. If the critical path tasks have variances, your schedule is at risk. You will use corrective actions at this point (not preventive actions) to get the project back on track, such as adjusting the amount of buffer. Significant delays to noncritical-path tasks can make them become part of the critical path.

59. A. According to the *PMBOK® Guide*, scope creep refers to the uncontrolled expansion of product or project scope without adjustments to time, cost, and resources; in other words, it is scope that has not been approved.

60. A. To determine performance against the budget, you must first calculate variance at completion. To calculate variance at completion, subtract the estimate at completion from the budget at completion (BAC – EAC): $550,000 – $525,000 = $25,000. A positive VAC means that the project is performing under the planned costs.

61. A, B, D. Scope changes might affect the schedule, cost, quality, and other processes and should be thoroughly integrated with all the Monitoring and Controlling processes. Scope changes may reduce the project requirements and thus reduce the number or hours needed to complete the project. This, in turn, could cause a reduction in the project budget.

62. B. Work performance information is a key input that the project manager needs to evaluate performance against the plan (another key input in and of itself). Work performance data, on the other hand, represents raw data that is used in executing the work; it later becomes information as it is analyzed against baselines through other processes that belong to the Monitoring and Controlling process group. The remaining two options are tools and techniques of the process, not inputs.

63. A-1, B-4, C-3, D-2. There are generally three types of delivery methods: predictive, adaptive, and hybrid. Another layer to consider is the project life cycle, of which there are generally four: predictive, iterative, incremental, and Agile.

64. B. In a predictive life cycle, the project's scope, time, and cost are determined during the early phases of the project, meaning that the majority of planning occurs up front. Changes are closely managed following a change control process.

65. B. Status review meetings occur throughout the Monitoring and Controlling phase of the project. The purpose of these meetings is to provide stakeholders with updated information on the progress of the project in a formal manner. Attendees may include a variety of predetermined stakeholders, such as the sponsor, project team members, users, or customers.

66. B. Identify Stakeholders belongs to the Project Stakeholder Management Knowledge Area. The Project Integration Management Knowledge Area contains the following processes: Develop Project Charter, Develop Project Management Plan, Direct and Manage Project Work, Manage Project Knowledge, Monitor and Control Project Work, Perform Integrated Changed Control, and Close Project or Phase.

67. D. Face-to-face meetings are effective, but this statement is not true regarding status review meetings.

68. A. Fixed-price incentive fee contracts are the best option when you need a well-defined set of deliverables for a set price and are including a bonus or incentive for early completion or exceeding expectations.

69. B. Completing a quality audit may lead you to the conclusion that a change request is needed, but you must submit a change request and/or take corrective action to implement the quality improvement.

70. C. Managing quality is sometimes referred to as quality assurance. Manage Quality is a process within the Project Quality Management Knowledge Area. According to the *PMBOK® Guide*, the term *manage quality* is meant to encompass a broader meaning, including representing nonproject work.

71. C. The project manager is using a highly adaptive (Agile) life cycle, where Closing activities involve addressing the highest business value items first versus closing out the project or phase as in a highly predictive life cycle.

72. B. The risk register contains the list of identified risks and all information documented about them, including the risk response plans. As risk triggers occur, they will need to refer to the risk register for information about the risk response plans.

73. A. This process is used only if you are obtaining goods and services outside the organization.

74. C. Quality assurance may be provided by a third party from outside the organization, by an internal QA department, or by the project team. There is no general rule that it is generally provided by outside sources. According to the *PMBOK® Guide*, project managers have the greatest impact on quality during this process.

75. B. Project Scope Management is concerned with product scope and project scope. Product scope is concerned with the characteristics of the product or service of the project and is measured against the project requirements. Project scope is concerned with the work of the project and is measured against the project plan.

76. B. In 2001, several software developers converged to formalize the Agile approach. They published the manifesto for Agile software development and identified 12 principles that are the focus of any Agile approach.

77. B. The *PMBOK® Guide* addresses four project life cycles: predictive, iterative, incremental, and Agile.

78. B. The question describes activities associated with risk management. Kaylee and Alyssa are determining how best to address a positive risk (opportunity) that has been identified.

79. B. In an Agile life cycle, Planning activities involve the progressive elaboration of scope, based on continuous feedback from stakeholders.

80. C. Fast-tracking refers to compressing or shortening the project schedule. In this scenario, you are attempting to compress the phase.

81. B. The question describes a sprint retrospective meeting, which helps the team plan for the next sprint and determine overall progress.

82. A. Yasmin is using a Waterfall approach, which involves a greater level of up-front planning during the early stages of the project life cycle. In this approach, changes to requirements tend to follow a change control process.

83. B. There are three network paths: A-B-E, A-C-E, and A-D-E. Figure 2.1 shows the network diagram for the information displayed within the table of the question. The duration value is not needed to calculate the answer.

FIGURE 2.1   Network diagram: network path calculation

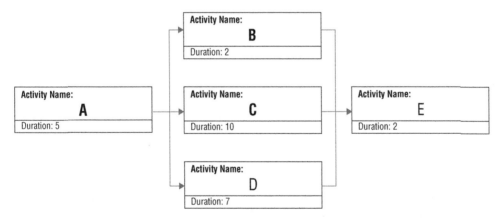

84. B. To calculate the critical path (which is the longest path through the network diagram), add the duration of activities that fall within each network path. The path with the greatest duration is the critical path. Figure 2.2 shows the network diagram, based on the information provided within the table. The duration of each network path is as follows:

A-B-E: 9

A-C-E: 17

A-D-E: 14

FIGURE 2.2   Network diagram: critical path calculation

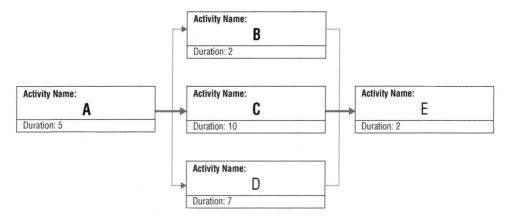

85. C. To calculate the near critical path (which is the second longest path through the network diagram), add the duration of activities that fall within each network path. The path with the second greatest duration is the near critical path. Figure 2.3 shows the network diagram, based on the information provided within the table. The duration of each network path is as follows:

A-B-E: 9

A-C-E: 17

A-D-E: 14

FIGURE 2.3   Network diagram: near critical path calculation

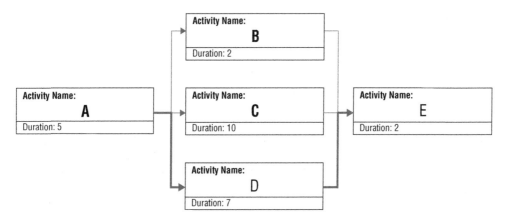

86. D. Purchasing insurance is an example of the transfer risk response. This involves shifting ownership of a threat to a third party to manage the risk and to own the impact if the threat occurs.

87. C. The project objectives should include quantifiable criteria that can be used to help measure project success. Project objectives should include schedule, cost, and quality measurements.

88. C. The purpose of the Perform Qualitative Risk Analysis process is to prioritize individual project risks for further analysis or action by assessing their probability of occurrence and impact as well as other characteristics.

89. A-4, B-1, C-2, D-3. Philip Crosby is the quality theorist behind the Zero Defects practice, which promotes doing it right the first time; Joseph Juran popularized the Pareto Principle, also referred to as the 80/20 principle; and W. Edwards Deming popularized the Shewhart Cycle, which he evolved into the Plan-Do-Check-Act Cycle. Walter Shewhart is considered to be the grandfather of TQM; he developed statistical tools to examine when a corrective action must be applied to a process.

90. B. Email is a form of push communication, which is one-way and refers to sending information to the intended receivers.

91. D. Functional requirements describe the behaviors of the product, including actions, processes, data, and interactions that the product should execute.

92. B. According to the *PMBOK® Guide*, there are two levels of risk: individual project risk and overall project risk. An individual project risk is an uncertain event or condition that, if it occurs, has a positive or negative effect on one or more project objectives.

93. B. Three-point estimating is the technique to use when you want to improve your estimates and account for risk and estimation uncertainty.

94. D. To calculate schedule variance, subtract planned value from earned value (CV = EV − AC): $500 − $450 = $50. A positive cost variance means that the project is under budget.

95. D. One of the benefits of Agile approaches is the ability to obtain feedback continuously throughout the project. This allows the team to incorporate the feedback early.

96. D. You should develop a mitigation plan for installation and setup to reduce the probability and/or impact of this risk to the project. Option A is not correct because the sharing response strategy is a strategy for positive risks. This is a negative risk to the project.

97. C. Tracking includes a description of how you'll document the history of the risk activities for the current project and how the risk processes will be audited. This section of the risk management plan is also helpful for lessons learned.

98. A, D. The procurement SOW can be prepared by either the buyer or the seller, but it is progressively elaborated throughout the procurement processes and will likely change prior to the contract award.

99. A. The project team is participating in bottom-up estimating, which will produce activity cost estimates. This activity is associated with the Estimate Costs process. Basis of estimates may also be generated through this session; cost estimates, however, are the primary end outcome of the activity.

100. B. Hybrid life cycles combine elements of different life cycles to achieve a certain goal. A hybrid approach may contain a combination of iterative, predictive, incremental, and/or Agile approaches.

101. A. The sponsor is requesting the earned value of the project. Earned value represents the measure of work performed expressed in terms of the budget authorized for that work; in other words, it is the sum of the planned value of completed work.

102. C. Reserve analysis is a data analysis technique of the Monitor Risks process. Reserve analysis compares the amount of contingency reserve remaining to address the risk that remains. Contingency reserves (used to deal with known risks) are considered part of the project budget, while management reserves (used to deal with unknown risks) are not.

103. B. To calculate EAC when the future work will be accomplished at the planned rate, use the following formula: AC + BAC − EV. Plug in the values provided in the question to arrive at the following: $15,000 + $20,000 − $18,000 = $17,000.

104. C. The elements of communication involve senders, receivers, and messages. The communication model, a tool and technique of the Manage Communications process, includes encoding, decoding, acknowledging, and feedback/response. Verbal and written are forms of communication.

105. D. The scenario notes that two critical activities are already delayed, meaning that an issue has been identified and must be addressed. While updates to the plan are likely, they will be the result of corrective action taken.

106. A. According to the *PMBOK® Guide*, quality assurance is most concerned with using project processes effectively. This includes assuring stakeholders that the end result of the project will meet their needs and expectations.

107. A, C, D. The requisition stage is where the procurement documents are prepared (not the responses to them) and is associated with the Plan Procurement Management process. The two outputs that become inputs are procurement documentation and source selection criteria.

108. D. The project team members, project manager, and the stakeholders are all equally responsible for the quality assurance of the project.

109. C. One of the most important criteria for evaluating sellers is to determine whether they have a clear understanding of what you're asking them to do or perform. Information such as past performance, financial records, and predetermined performance criteria are also important, but only after you are sure they have a clear understanding of what you're asking them to do.

110. A. A sprint retrospective is held at the end of an iteration/sprint to identify what the team learned over the last sprint, including what went well and what did not. The intent is to continue improving the overall process so that the team continues to become more effective as a unit.

111. B. The lessons learned register, created out of the Manage Project Knowledge process, records information about situations that have occurred within the project, including recording challenges, problems, realized risks and opportunities, and other information relevant for future reference. While "project documents" is a technically accurate answer, "lessons learned register" is a more specific answer.

112. D. The Manage Communications process is concerned with ensuring timely and appropriate collection, creation, distribution, storage, retrieval, management, monitoring, and the ultimate disposition of project information.

113. B. The five steps of decomposition are to identify major deliverables, organize the WBS, decompose the WBS components into lower-level components, assign identification codes, and validate the WBS. No mention was made in the question of assigning identification codes or validating the correctness of decomposition, so not all of the steps have been performed. The first three steps of the decomposition process for the Design deliverable have been performed.

114. A. The project scope statement contains the project scope description, project deliverables, acceptance criteria, and project exclusions.

115. B. This question describes an iteration review meeting, which can go by other names such as sprint demo. The intent of the meeting is to review the working product to obtain feedback directly from the product owner and other key stakeholders early so that any course corrections can be made. In iteration-based Agile, this meeting is held at the end of a sprint/iteration, whereas flow-based Agile encourages reviews to occur at least once every two weeks.

116. B. Marysil will need to add a lag between the activities. A lag occurs when time must elapse between two activities, where the delay is added to the successor activity. A lead, on the other hand, speeds up the successor activity.

117. C. The product scope defines the features and characteristics that describe the product, service, or result of the project.

118. B. According to the *PMBOK® Guide*, a definitive range of estimates is –5 percent to +10 percent.

119. D. Carrie used the analogous estimating technique, which is a form of expert judgment. It is a tool and technique of the Estimate Activity Durations process. Analogous estimating bases estimates on previous activities that are similar in fact, and they require the person estimating them to have expertise in the activity. Analogous estimating techniques are typically used to estimate project duration when there is a limited amount of information about the project.

120. C. Schedule compression shortens the project schedule without changing the project scope. Crashing doesn't always give you a good alternative and typically increases project costs. Fast-tracking typically increases risk and necessitates rework.

121. D. The duration of a milestone is zero, marking a significant point in time—typically the start or completion of a major deliverable. Therefore, "Finish GUI" is not a milestone.

122. A. A fallback plan, also referred to as a contingency plan, is a risk response strategy that is used when the initial response is not fully effective.

123. C. When using price alone as a criterion for selection, there should be more than one vendor who can supply the goods or services you are procuring. However, that doesn't mean you can't use additional criteria for source selection. You should include costs such as delivery and setup in the purchase price criterion.

124. A-1, B-4, C-2, D-3. The definitions provided are taken from *Agile Practice Guide*.

125. C. This question describes the Manage Communications and Manage Stakeholder Engagement processes, respectively. There is no process called Information Distribution.

126. D. Since an issue has not occurred as of yet, the project manager is likely to take preventive actions. Preventive actions are submitted through a change request, which is then evaluated and dispositioned through the project's change control board.

127. A. Claims administration is a tool and technique of the Control Procurements process. Claims administration involves addressing contested changes between the buyer and seller, which then converts into a claim.

128. D. Swarming is a strategy where the team, or several team members, focus collectively on resolving a blocker.

129. B. Weekly status updates are an example of work performance reports, which are produced out of the Monitor and Control Project Work process.

130. B. The Project Integration Management Knowledge Area is the only Knowledge Area that has processes across all five process groups. It contains the high-level processes that bring the results of the remaining Knowledge Areas together, unifying and coordinating all project management activities.

131. D. Julie is looking at a product backlog, which contains a prioritized list of user-centric requirements that she and the team maintain for the smart water bottle product.

132. B. The cost management plan contains the approved approach for determining the budget, managing it, and controlling it. It also captures additional key details, such as the rules of performance measurement, control thresholds, units of measure and levels of precision used, and so on.

133. C. Schedule compression uses fast-tracking or crashing compression techniques to bring delayed activities back in line with the plan. Allocating additional resources to critical activities describes the crashing technique; fast-tracking is where you complete two activities in parallel in order to complete the work faster.

134. C. The project manager is performing the Validate Scope process in this scenario, where a key output is the accepted deliverables. To accept deliverables, the committee would need to confirm that they have been verified through quality control activities. Verified deliverables is an input of the process.

135. A. Backlog refinement, also referred to as backlog grooming, is where the product owner works with the team to ensure that the stories are prepped and ready for the upcoming iteration. Stories should be clear enough for the team to understand the work, and they should be appropriately sized relative to each other.

136. A. Management reserves are funds set aside for unexpected situations and are used at the discretion of management (hence the name). Management reserves are not considered to be part of the cost baseline but are part of the overall project budget.

137. C. A rough order of magnitude ranges from −25 percent to +75 percent, whereas a definitive range spans −5 percent to +10 percent.

138. B. The recommended size of an Agile team is three to nine team members. It is recommended that Agile teams be colocated and dedicated to the project when possible.

139. A. Statistical sampling involves taking a sample number of parts from the whole population and inspecting them to determine whether they fall within acceptable variances.

140. C. A beta distribution calculation involves giving a greater weight to the most likely estimate. Simply multiply the most likely estimate by four, add the result with the other two estimates, and divide by six: (4 × (ML) $72 + (O) $55 + (P) $85) ÷ 6 = $71.3.

141. A-5, B-1, C-4, D-2, E-3. There are many variations of Agile approaches, including hybrid/combination approaches (i.e., ScrumBan). Descriptions provided are derived from the *Agile Practice Guide*, which offers several descriptions and examples of a wide range of Agile approaches.

142. A-3, B-2, C-1, D-4. Predictive and iterative life cycles tend to have low frequencies of delivery, whereas incremental and agile have a high frequency of finished deliverables; both predictive and incremental experience few changes, while iterative and Agile experience very frequent changes based on customer feedback.

143. A. The purpose of the daily stand-up meetings, one of three key meetings used within Scrum, is not planning. Instead, daily stand-up meetings are used to uncover any obstacles to committed work and as a way to ensure that work is progressing smoothly.

144. C, D. The Scrum team held a sprint retrospective. In Scrum, this meeting is held at the end of every sprint and allows the team to identify what went well in the process during the recent sprint and what could have gone better, and they commit to improving at least one thing in the upcoming sprint. They are a combination of lessons learned and process improvement.

145. D. Velocity refers to the total story points that the team is completing on average per iteration. Velocity allows the team to forecast the rate at which they are burning down the work of the project. A velocity chart shows the sum of the estimates of work delivered across all iterations.

146. A. The Plan-Do-Check-Act cycle was developed by Shewhart and later refined by Deming. It reflects the iterative, results-oriented, and interactive nature of the project process groups.

147. A. There are three series of project life cycles within the basic framework for managing projects: sequential, iterative, and overlapping. In a sequential life cycle, one phase must finish before the next phase can begin.

148. B. Phase endings are characterized by the completion, review, and approval of a deliverable.

149. A. The *PMBOK® Guide* describes 49 project management processes that can be grouped in five process groups, which are as follows: Initiating, Planning, Executing, Monitoring and Controlling, and Closing.

150. C. Agile project management is a method of managing projects in small, incremental portions of work that can be easily assigned, easily managed, and completed within a short period of time.

Chapter 3: Business Environment (Domain 3.0)

1. B. The business case is an economic feasibility study used to understand the business need for the project and determine whether the investment is worthwhile. In short, it justifies the need for the project and contains information such as the project description, high-level description of scope, analysis of the problem, financial analysis, and success factors.

2. B. Project management is defined as the application of knowledge, skills, tools, and techniques to project activities to meet the project requirements.

3. D. Since the marketing company where Bill works is a customer of Reasons to Lyv, the project being managed within his organization is a result of a customer request.

4. D. Respect, not fairness, is the value that addresses culture shock and diversity training. Accepting vendor gifts is acceptable when the gift or situation complies with a company's stated policies.

5. D. All the options are part of the organizational process assets updates output of this process. Feedback from stakeholders can be used on the current project as well as future projects.

6. D. The best answer to this question is D. This is a high-risk project, and a feasibility study should be conducted as a separate project because the outcome is unknown.

7. A. Don't accept gifts that might be construed as conflicts of interest. If your organization does not have a policy regarding vendor gifts, set limits for yourself depending on the situation, the history of gift acceptance by the organization in the past, and the complexity of the project. It's always better to decline a gift you're unsure about than to accept it and later lose your credibility, your reputation, or your PMP status because of bad judgment.

8. B. Marketplace conditions and financial management and accounts payable systems are examples of enterprise environmental factors versus organizational process assets. When performing the Close Project or Phase process, project or phase closure guidelines or requirements, along with the configuration management knowledge base, serve as valuable inputs. The configuration management knowledge base contains versions and baselines of standards, policies, procedures, and project documents belonging to the organization.

9. B. Linear, multi-objective programming, and nonlinear are all examples of constrained optimization methods, not benefit measurement methods. Benefit measurement methods include benefit-cost ratio analysis, scoring models, and benefit contribution methods.

10. D. Project selection methods include benefit measurement methods and mathematical models (also known as *constrained optimization methods*). Benefit measurement methods might include cost-benefit analysis and cash flow analysis.

11. A. The title of project coordinator indicates this is a weak matrix organization and that you are working within one of the business units rather than under the PMO (as you would if you were in a strong matrix organization). The question also states that the work of the project has begun, so you are in the Executing phase of the project.

12. B. According to PMI, business value is defined as the net quantifiable benefit derived from a business endeavor. These benefits may be intangible, tangible, or both.

13. A, B, C. A benefits management plan describes how and when the benefits of a project will be delivered. It also describes what mechanisms should be in place to measure those benefits. Examples of key elements that make up a benefits management plan include target benefits, strategic alignment, timeframe for realizing benefits, benefits owner, metrics, assumptions, and risks. Business need is captured within a business case.

14. A. In a weak-matrix organization, the project coordinator has a low degree of authority, which can be viewed as a disadvantage.

15. A, C, D. According to the *PMBOK® Guide*, the three types of PMOs are directive, supportive, and controlling.

16. A. Project A has the highest score based on the values provided. To calculate the score for each project, multiply the score of each criterion against the weight of the criteria and then add up all of the scores. See the following table for the calculations:

Criterion	Weight	Project A Score	Project A Totals	Project B Score	Project B Totals	Project C Score	Project C Totals
Profit potential	5	5	25	2	10	1	5
Marketability	1	1	1	5	5	3	3
Ease of use	3	2	6	3	9	5	15
Weighted score	—	—	32	—	24	—	23

17. B. Examples of enterprise environmental factors that are used in the Identify Stakeholders process are company culture, organizational structure, governmental or industry standards, global trends, and geographic locations of resources and facilities. The other options included are organizational process assets.

18. A. Market research can be used to examine industry and seller capabilities. Information can be obtained in places such as conferences, online reviews, and other sources available in the market.

19. B. Teams working in a weak matrix organization tend to experience the least amount of stress during the Closing processes. This is because, in a weak matrix organization, the functional manager assigns all tasks (project-related tasks as well) so the team members have a job to return to once the project is completed and there's no change in reporting structure.

20. B, C, D. When considering Agile approaches, organizational leaders should evaluate the compatibility of those methods to determine whether the organization is ready and can support such change. This includes the willingness to change at the executive management level and at the broader organizational level. There must be a willingness to focus on short-term budgeting and metrics versus long-term goals.

21. C. Sue is describing organizational project management (OPM). The *PMBOK® Guide* defines OPM as a framework in which portfolio, program, and project management are integrated with organizational enablers to achieve strategic objectives.

22. B. Enterprise environmental factors are the factors both internal and external to the organization that can influence the project. Marketplace conditions is one example, as are organizational culture, structure, and governance. Enterprise environmental factors is a frequent input of the project management processes.

23. D. Portfolio management groups projects, programs, portfolios, and other work that is similar in scope and weighs the value of each project against the business's strategic objectives. Portfolio management also monitors projects to make certain they adhere to the objectives and make efficient use of resources. Portfolio management is usually handled by a senior manager with many years of experience in project and program management.

24. D. Benefit-cost ratio can be referred to as cost-benefit analysis. It is a common benefit measurement method that compares the cost to produce the product, service, or result of the project to the benefit that the organization will receive after executing the project.

25. D. Projects are temporary endeavors undertaken to produce a unique product, service, or result. Operations, on the other hand, are ongoing and repetitive and do not have an ending date.

26. A. Payback period is considered to be the least precise project selection method.

27. C. Because Reasons to Lyv is attempting to exploit new GPS technology that is available, the project is a result of technological advance.

28. D. This project came about as a result of social need. Social need is one of seven typical reasons that trigger the need for a project, as noted by the *PMBOK® Guide*.

29. B. Honesty can include a lot of topics: reporting the truth regarding project status, being honest about your own experience, not deceiving others, not making false statements, and so on. As a project manager, you are responsible for truthfully reporting all information in your possession to stakeholders, customers, the project sponsor, and the public when required.

30. A. Responsibility is the act of making decisions that are for the good of the organization rather than yourself, admitting your mistakes, being responsible for the decisions you make (or those you don't make), and the consequences that result, along with other actions.

31. B. A program is defined as related projects, subsidiary programs, and program activities managed in a coordinated manner to obtain benefits not available when managing them individually. The other options provide the definition of a project, progressive elaboration, and product life cycle.

32. B. Projects exist to create a unique product, service, or result. What the director in the scenario describes is shifting the backend of an existing app to technology that also already exists within the company. This would reflect operations, which are considered to be ongoing and repetitive, versus the creation of new capabilities.

33. A. Economic models are an example of a benefit measurement method, not a constrained optimization method. These are project selection techniques that can be used to measure the advantages or merits of the product of the project.

34. A. Although the lessons learned register is a tempting choice and is an artifact of the project, the correct answer is organizational process assets. Organizational process assets are the organization's policies, guidelines, processes, procedures, plans, approaches, and standards for conducting work, including project work. They are a frequent input to the project management processes.

35. C. Honesty involves not only information regarding your own background and experience but information regarding the project circumstances as well.

36. C. Answer C is stated backwards. IRR is the discount rate when NPV equals zero.

37. A. Hybrid organizations are a combination of various organizational types and typically involve a project-oriented structure coexisting within a functional organization.

38. A. A megaproject is defined as a large multiyear project that costs more than $1 billion and affects 1 million or more people.

39. B. Projects with NPV greater than 0 should be recommended; the key determining factor in selecting Project Fun is that the NPV is positive. Had both NPVs been positive, then the determining factor would have been the greater NPV number, since the scenario notes that funding exists for only one project. Payback period is considered the least precise selection method and is not typically the sole determining factor.

40. A. A positive value for NPV means the project will earn a return at least equal to or greater than the cost of capital. Since NPV for Alternative A is positive, this alternative will earn at least a 12 percent return.

41. B. This is a false statement. Projects using an Adaptive approach prioritize work based on the highest business value items first. This reduces the failure of premature closure due to sunk costs because early benefits realization occurs.

42. C. The requirements traceability matrix links the requirements to the business and project objectives. This ensures that requirements add business value.

43. B. As a project manager, you are responsible for truthfully reporting all information in your possession to stakeholders, customers, the project sponsor, and the public when required. Always be up front regarding the project's progress.

44. C. Organizational structures are the forms that an organization can take and their influence on projects. They describe the style, culture, and way of communicating that influence how project work is performed.

45. A. Within a project-oriented organization, the project manager has a high degree of authority, and projects are treated with priority. A project manager has high to almost total resource access/availability, since team members are often dedicated to the project.

46. B. The question describes a hybrid organizational type, likely a mixture of a weak and a strong matrix. A clue is that your title is project manager, which does not typically exist in a purely functional organization; another is that the functional manager manages the project budget, which is not typical in a project-oriented or PMO organizational type.

47. A, B, D. According to the *PMBOK® Guide*, projects are initiated by business leaders because of the following categories or factors: regulatory compliance, legal requirements, or social requirements; stakeholder needs and requests; changing technology needs of the organization; create or improve processes, services, or products.

48. B. The formula for present value is $PV = FV / (1 + i)^n$. Plugging in the information from the question, the formula becomes $\$8{,}000 / (1 + .07)^3 = \$6{,}530$.

49. A. This came about because of a business need. Staff members were spending unproductive hours converting information, causing the company loss. The time the employees spent converting the information could have been spent doing something more productive.

50. D. The Project Management Institute is the industry-recognized standard for project management practices. PMI is active and recognized around the globe, although it is headquartered within the United States.

51. D. The *Code of Ethics and Professional Conduct* is published by PMI, and all PMP credential holders are expected to adhere to its standards.

52. B. When resources are cut off from the project and the project is starved prior to completing all requirements, it often leads to an unfinished project. Resources in this case can be money (such as in Yasmin's case), human resources, equipment, or supplies. This type of project ending is referred to as *starvation*.

53. C. An organization breakdown structure is a form of organization chart that shows the departments, work units, or teams within an organization and their respective work packages.

54. A. In a weak matrix organization, the functional manager has greater authority than the project manager. Based only on the information provided within the question, it is likely that resources will be reassigned to another project.

55. A, D. According to *Managing Change in Organizations: A Practice Guide*, published by PMI, there are three recommendations to consider when applying organizational change management at a comprehensive level: 1) models for describing change dynamics, 2) framework for achieving change, and 3) application of change management practices at the project, program, and portfolio levels.

56. A. According to the *PMBOK® Guide*, project benefits are defined as outcomes of actions, behaviors, products, services, or results that provide value to the sponsoring organization as well as to the project's intended beneficiaries.

57. B. Tailoring refers to determining which project management processes to use when managing and conducting the project.

58. A. While PMOs may facilitate the selection of projects that support a company's strategic objectives, they are not typically responsible for establishing the objectives and selecting projects. All other options describe the types of support that a PMO typically offers within an organization.

59. C. Antwon is performing portfolio management activities. Portfolio management is defined as the centralized management of one or more portfolios to achieve strategic objectives; it involves guiding the investment decisions of the organization to meet the organization's strategic goals.

60. C. Progressive elaboration is not necessarily a deferral in planning; it refers to progressively determining the characteristics of the product, service, or result incrementally, as more detail becomes available.

61. D. In a functional organization, the role of project manager typically does not exist. Instead, it may be a part-time role or a similar role such as a project coordinator.

62. B. The change control board (CCB) is responsible for reviewing all change requests and approving them or denying them. It is sometimes also known as a *technical assessment board*, *technical review board*, or *engineering review board*.

63. B. In this instance, Joe is correct. When resources are cut off from the project or are no longer provided to the project, it's starved prior to completing all requirements. Integration, on the other hand, is when resources of the project are distributed to other areas in the organization or are assigned to other projects.

64. C. Weak matrix organizational structures tend to experience the least amount of stress during the project closeout processes.

65. A. The business case is a feasibility study that lists objectives and reasons for a project. It identifies critical success factors for the project, why the project was undertaken, an analysis of the situation, and recommendations.

66. C. The product owner is responsible for guiding the vision and direction of the product. This includes owning the product backlog and prioritizing the work reflected in the backlog based on its business value.

67. B. Project selection methods are used prior to the Develop Project Charter process to choose which projects the organization should undertake or to choose among alternative ways of doing a project. According to the *PMBOK® Guide*, the project manager is not involved in project selection.

68. A. The new series is unique and hasn't been done before. There is a definite end date—sweeps week in November—and the beginning date was the start of the project creation. After the series has started, the project itself is over, and the series becomes an ongoing operation.

69. C. Directive PMOs tend to have a high degree of control over projects, with project managers assigned by and directly reporting to the PMO. The PMO typically controls and manages projects directly.

70. C. The best answer in this situation is to get the facts before taking any action. A violation based only on suspicion should not be reported. You can get the facts by telling your friend you're concerned about the appearance of impropriety and ask her whether the vendor gave her these items. It could be that these are the first of several samples that will be coming from all the vendors bidding on the project so the equipment can be evaluated in light of the project objectives. Or she could have accepted them as gifts, which is not appropriate. Never jump to conclusions. Always ask and get the facts straight before reporting a conflict-of-interest situation.

71. A. Addition is a project ending where a project evolves into ongoing operations. In these cases, a full-time staff can be required to support ongoing operations, maintenance, and monitoring of a project's deliverable.

72. B. The *Code of Ethics and Professional Conduct* addresses core values that project management practitioners should and must uphold. Specifically, it applies to all PMI members, PMI volunteers, those certified through PMI, and those going through the PMI certification process.

73. A. Preparing stories for the next iteration refers to backlog refinement or backlog grooming. The intent is to refine stories sufficiently so that the team understands what work must be accomplished.

74. A-2, B-3, C-1. According to the *PMBOK® Guide*, there are three types of PMOs: supportive, controlling, and directive. Supportive PMOs have a low degree of control, controlling PMOs have a moderate degree of control, and directive PMOs have a high degree of control.

75. D. Phase gates serve as important checkpoints throughout a project's life that allow the project team to compare the project's performance against the plan and decide whether the project should proceed to the next phase. The primary purpose of phase gates is not intended as an audit function against regulatory compliance.

76. C. The benefits management plan outlines the target benefits of the project and is used to measure both the tangible and intangible benefits. As part of project integration management activities, project managers should report progress against this plan to project stakeholders.

77. D. The benefits management plan describes how and when the benefits of the project will be delivered. It captures the target benefits, strategic alignment, timeframe for realizing benefits, and the metrics of how the benefits will be measured, along with other key information relating to business value delivered.

78. B. The project is being driven by legal requirements. New projects can occur as a result of laws passed, as in the case seen in this scenario.

79. C. The change control board is officially chartered and given the authority to approve or deny change requests as defined by the organization and as outlined within the project management plan. The authority level (including exception or emergency process) should be detailed within the project management plan.

80. A. Part of the *Code of Ethics and Professional Conduct* requires that you cooperate in any investigation concerning ethics violations and in collecting information related to the violation.

81. B. In a project-oriented organization, the project team is dedicated to the project. When a project is complete, they either transition to another project or are released.

82. E. According to the *Agile Practice Guide*, stakeholders should be educated on why and how to be Agile. This includes understanding the benefits of business value based on prioritization, greater accountability and productivity of empowered teams, and improved quality.

83. D. While most (if not all!) project managers hope that *all* project team members are held accountable to the core values identified within the *Code of Ethics and Professional Conduct*, it is written with project management practitioners in mind. This includes the following individuals: all PMI members, those who hold a PMI certification, those who begin the PMI certification process, and those who volunteer through PMI.

84. A. Responsibility entails ensuring integrity, accepting assignments we are qualified for, abiding by laws and regulations, and maintaining confidential information.

85. B. An organization's culture heavily influences the type of project management approaches adopted by project teams and how Agile approaches are used. For example, startup environments tend to operate in a lean fashion, opting to fail fast and iterate to produce results quickly.

86. D. Planned value in this scenario refers to the project's benefits. The benefits management plan describes how and when the project's benefits will be delivered. According to the *PMBOK® Guide*, benefits are an outcome of actions, behaviors, products, services, or results that provide value to the sponsoring organization as well as to the project's intended beneficiaries.

87. B. A controlling PMO is focused on two key areas: providing the organization with support in its application of project management practices and requiring compliance against those practices.

88. D. Project managers must remain alert to changes occurring across the internal and external business landscape to understand the impact to their projects. When this occurs, such as in Kaylee's case, project managers should assess and prioritize the impacts of these changes on their project and then adjust the backlog accordingly.

89. D. According to the *Agile Practice Guide*, backlog refinement is defined as the progressive elaboration of project requirements and/or the ongoing activity in which the team collaboratively reviews, updates, and writes requirements to satisfy the need of the customer request.

90. A. According to the *PMBOK® Guide*, phase reviews are also called *phase gates*, *phase entrances*, *phase exits*, *stage gates*, and *kill points*. Phase reviews typically serve as checkpoints at the end of a phase where performance or progress is evaluated against the project charter or plan. Once completed, the project progresses to the next phase.

91. B. Tailoring involves determining which project management processes to use when managing and conducting the project.

92. A. Projects using an iterative and incremental approach to managing the project life cycle tend to experience short feedback loops and reprioritization of the backlog. Frequent delivery and feedback allow the team to adapt and adjust to changes quickly, as well as prioritize appropriately.

93. D. According to the *PMBOK® Guide*, most projects fit one of seven needs and demands that result in their creation: market demand, organizational need, customer request, technological advance, legal requirement, ecological impacts, or social need.

94. C. Honesty entails acting in a truthful manner in both our communications and conduct. Although the project manager's intentions seemed to result from positive intentions, the act of forging survey responses—even if he felt that they reflected truthful feedback received—does not represent truthful actions.

95. D. Honesty can include a lot of topics: reporting the truth regarding project status, being honest about your own experience, not deceiving others, not making false statements, and so on. According to the *Code of Ethics and Professional Conduct*, honesty is your duty to understand the truth and act in a truthful manner, both in your communications and in your conduct.

96. A-1, B-2. Organizational process assets are factors that are internal to the organization, such as internal policies, processes, templates, and lessons learned repositories; enterprise environmental factors are external to the organization, such as laws, regulations, published standards, and marketplace conditions.

97. A. According to the *PMBOK® Guide*, quality assurance, which occurs through the Manage Quality project management process, is most concerned with using project processes effectively. This includes assuring stakeholders that the end result of the project will meet their needs and expectations and that quality requirements are met.

98. A. Brainstorming is a form of data gathering, a technique of the Develop Project Charter process. Other examples of data gathering include focus groups and interviews.

99. C. The organization's culture, structure, and governance are considered to be part of enterprise environmental factors. Enterprise environmental factors are conditions or capabilities that are not under the direct control of the project team but that influence or constrain the project.

100. C. When joining a new organization, it is important that a project manager familiarize themselves with the organization's culture. Understanding how the organization operates, its tolerance level, and its appetite for risk, among other things, is important to tailoring the project management approach.

Chapter 4: Full-Length Practice Exam 1

1. B. There are four development life cycles: predictive, iterative, incremental, and hybrid. The iterative development life cycle defines project deliverables early in the development life cycle and progressively elaborates them as the project or life cycle progresses.

2. D. According to the *PMBOK® Guide*, decomposition of the total project work into work packages involves the following five steps: 1) identifying and analyzing the deliverables, 2) structuring and organizing the WBS, 3) decomposing the WBS into lower-level components, 4) developing and assigning the identification codes, and 5) verifying the degree of decomposition of the deliverables.

3. A-3, B-4, C-1, D-2. The project manager's level of authority varies, based on the organizational structure that they work within. It is lowest in a functional type and highest in a project-oriented type. Matrixed structures tend to fall in the middle, with weak matrix closest to functional, and strong matrix closest to project-oriented.

4. A. The scenario describes the early stages of a project, where the project has just been selected and a project manager has been assigned. This occurs in the Initiating process group.

5. A. The Plan-Do-Check-Act cycle was developed by Shewhart and later refined by Deming. It reflects the iterative, results-oriented, and interactive nature of the project process groups.

6. A. Requirements are the specifications of the deliverables and tell you how you know the deliverable was completed successfully.

7. A. The Expectancy Theory, proposed by Victor Vroom, states that the expectation of a positive outcome drives motivation. In other words, people will behave in certain ways if they think there will be good rewards for doing so.

8. A. The question is asking for an input that can be used to address the engagement level of stakeholders. The scenario involves the Monitor Stakeholder Engagement process. Interpersonal and team skills and decision-making are tools and techniques and therefore not the correct choices. Since the project management plan contains the stakeholder engagement plan, which documents the strategy for engagement stakeholders, this is the best option. Other useful components of the project management plan also include the communications management plan and resource management plan.

9. D. Albert is attempting to manage the project using a predictive approach, which aims to identify the majority of requirements early on in the project's life cycle. A technology startup environment, coupled with a high-uncertainty project, is likely to lean toward an adaptive approach to managing projects.

10. C. The product manager is using an incremental approach to carry out the project. This method generates incremental value to the customer through its frequent delivery cadence, short and frequent feedback loops, and ability to reprioritize and adapt based on changing or clarified requirements.

11. B. The project manager is currently performing the Direct and Manage Project Work process. Of the options provided, project management information system (PMIS) is the only tool or technique listed. The change log and approved change requests are inputs to the process, while work performance data is an output.

12. D. A project manager or other stakeholders may use various types of power to get work done. Punishment, expert, legitimate, and referent are all types of power.

13. B. It is important to monitor ongoing changes to the external business environment that may impact current or future projects. This is an element of enterprise environmental factors, a key input to many project management activities.

14. D. To calculate variance at completion, subtract the estimate at completion from the budget at completion (BAC – EAC): $550,000 – $525,000 = $25,000.

15. B. The cost plus fixed fee contract reimburses the seller for the allowable costs and includes a fixed fee for completing the project as outlined in the terms of the contract.

16. C. Both senders and receivers transmit information they receive through their knowledge of the subject, cultural influences, language, emotions, attitudes, and geographic locations. Senders should keep this in mind when preparing their messages. Senders are responsible for communicating the information clearly and concisely, and receivers are responsible for understanding the information correctly.

17. C. Payback period is the least precise of all cash flow calculations, so you shouldn't give this a lot of consideration if NPV is positive and IRR is greater than 0. Since Project B and Project D both have a negative NPV, they shouldn't be chosen. Project C has a higher IRR value than Project A and should be the project you choose, even though its payback period is longer than that of Project A.

18. D. Agile teams tend to place greater importance on delivering business value often. For this reason, emphasis is placed on frequent feedback, frequent delivery, and remaining adaptable to changing or evolving requirements.

19. B. The greatest expense for most projects is resources, both human and material and supplies.

20. D. Analogous estimating is also referred to as *top-down estimating*. This technique uses the actual duration of a similar activity completed on a previous project to determine the duration of a current activity.

21. C. The project charter not only authorizes the existence of a project but also provides the project manager with authority to begin applying organizational resources to project activities.

22. D. Quality reports, an output of the Manage Quality process, typically include quality management issues escalated; recommendations for process, project, and product improvements; corrective actions recommendations; and summary of quality control findings.

23. D. The project manager is in the process of carrying out the Identify Stakeholders process. The stakeholder register, the primary output, captures the list of stakeholders and documents information about them, including any assessment information.

24. D. During the Planning phase of the project life cycle, stakeholder influence tends to be high, although it is highest during Initiating; costs, staffing, and chances for successful project completion tend to be low during Planning.

25. A. IRR is the discount rate when the present value of the cash inflows equals the original investment. Project C's original investment equals the present value of its cash inflows at a discount rate of 7 percent. Therefore, Project A has the highest IRR and should be chosen above the other two.

26. A. According to the *PMBOK® Guide*, a project manager is likely to leverage the following tools and techniques to manage stakeholder engagement: expert judgment, communication skills (feedback), interpersonal and team skills (conflict management, cultural awareness, negotiation, observation/conversation, political awareness), ground rules, and meetings. Decision-making, while valuable, is a tool and technique used to monitor stakeholder engagement.

27. B, C, D. The *Agile Manifesto for Software Development* was published in 2001 by thought leaders in the software industry. The intent was to propose a new way of developing software. It consists of 12 principles and 4 key values.

28. B. Work performance information includes information regarding the status of risks (in the case of the Monitor Risks process), the status of change requests, and more. Work performance data and work performance reports are both inputs to this process.

29. C, D. According to the *Agile Practice Guide*, the goal of project management is to produce business value. The method that a team uses to deliver value should be based on which would yield the most successful outcome. This is often driven by the nature of the project and the circumstances surrounding the project.

30. B. Data analysis is a tool and technique used within the Perform Integrated Change Control process, where change requests are evaluated by the change control board. As part of performing data analysis, alternatives are considered, and a cost-benefit analysis is performed to determine whether the changes proposed are worth the associated costs.

31. B. Approved change requests are an output of the Perform Integrated Change Control process but not of the Monitor Risks process.

32. D. This question describes the Direct and Manage Project Work process. Approved changes are one of the inputs of this process. The daydream involves a conflict-of-interest situation. Thank goodness it was only a dream.

33. A. The question describes two different levels of Maslow's Hierarchy of Needs: social needs and self-esteem needs.

34. A. The project manager has performed the Define Activities, Sequence Activities, and Estimate Activity Resources processes. Next, she is likely to perform the Estimate Activity Durations process to determine how long each activity will take.

35. B. The solicitation stage is where vendors respond to the RFP.

36. A, B, C. The *Agile Manifesto for Software Development* was published in 2001 by thought leaders in the software industry. The intent was to propose a new way of developing software. It consists of 12 principles and 4 key values.

37. B. Information management systems are ways of distributing project information to the team. Electronic files are a method to store files and are not a distribution method.

38. C. You are performing the Determine Budget process. The purpose of this process is to aggregate the estimated costs of individual activities or work packages to establish an authorized cost baseline.

39. C. The collective phases a project progresses through are known as the project life cycle.

40. B. The minimum viable product reflects the minimum number of features intended to roll out a product to a limited number of customers. In some cases, the MVP is a prototype that can yield feedback that will be incorporated into the finished product.

41. A, B, C. The most effective Agile teams tend to range from three to nine team members in size, are colocated, and are able to dedicate 100 percent of their time to the team and work at hand. Agile teams typically have daily stand-up meetings versus daily status meetings.

42. A. Claims administration is a tool and technique of the Control Procurements process. This involves documenting, monitoring, and managing contested changes to the contract. Specifically, the project manager in this scenario is using arbitration, which involves bringing all parties to the table with a third, disinterested party who is not a participant in the contract to try to reach an agreement.

43. C. The project manager will need to analyze the impact of the scope change and what options exist, such as whether to undo what has been completed, or analyze whether the scope change should be approved. This should occur through the formal change control process via a change request.

44. D. The project charter identifies the purpose of the project and the project or product description. It includes a summary budget and summary milestone schedule. A detailed project schedule is not part of the project charter.

45. C. According to the *PMBOK® Guide*, project teams spend effort in identifying and analyzing risks and developing risk responses but then take no action in managing the risk.

46. B. The question describes the Monitor Communications process. This process involves ensuring the information needs of the project and its stakeholders are met; the project manager determines whether the communications planned are achieving the desired results.

47. D. A team using a flow-based agile approach, such as Kanban, focuses on developing prioritized features from the backlog. As capacity opens, the team pulls the next feature from the backlog and shifts it to the next column of the task board. They work on the feature until it is complete and then move on to the next one.

48. C. Rianna is currently performing the Manage Team process. This process is concerned with tracking team member performance, providing feedback, resolving issues, and managing team changes to optimize project performance.

49. B. The changes to the project management plan (and subsidiary plans within it) are dispositioned and managed through the Perform Integrated Change Control process.

50. B. Stakeholders have the greatest chance of influence over the project and the characteristics of the product, service, or results of the project in the early phases of the project, not the end. All other statements are true.

51. A. The project manager and team are likely to execute the work associated with the approved change requests. These approved change requests are implemented through the Direct and Manage Project Work process.

52. C. Roshoud and Sally are performing the Plan Resource Management process, where roles and responsibilities are identified and documented, which is a process that belongs to the Project Resource Management Knowledge Area.

53. A. The scenario describes the early stages of a project, which has just been selected and a project manager assigned. This occurs in the Initiating process group.

54. A. This is the estimate to complete (ETC) calculation, which will estimate the remaining work of the project. The ETC calculation is part of the forecasting tool and technique of the Control Costs process.

55. C. As uncertainty in projects increases, the likelihood of change also increases. Depending on the project management approach used, wasted work and the need for rework may also increase.

56. C. A master service agreement allows the project manager and procurement team to create a multitiered structure when formalizing a contracting relationship. This is especially useful for hybrid project approaches, where some items will be fixed (i.e., warranties) and others will be more dynamic.

57. D. The project manager and project team together are responsible for determining how best to tailor the project management processes, based on the needs of the project.

58. B. According to the *PMBOK® Guide*, assumptions are factors in the planning process considered to be true, real, or certain, without proof or demonstration. They are factors expected to be in place or to be in evidence.

59. B. Kaylee has just carried out the Collect Requirements process and is likely to carry out the Define Scope process next.

60. A. The Initiating processes are characterized by low costs, low staffing levels, decreased chances for a successful completion, high risk, and the greatest amount of stakeholder influence concerning the characteristics of the product or service of the project. Initiating acknowledges that the project or next phase of the project should begin and authorizes the assignment of resources.

61. A-4, B-1, C-5, D-2, E-3. Measuring ongoing progress against committed work is important for predictive, adaptive, and hybrid project delivery approaches. There are various methods of measuring and displaying progress.

62. D. Purchase order, memorandum of understanding, and agreement are all terms used for a contract according to the *PMBOK® Guide*. A procurement order is different.

63. C. Douglas McGregor defined two models of worker behavior, Theory X and Theory Y, that attempt to explain how different managers deal with their team members. Theory X managers believe most people do not like work and will try to steer clear of it; they believe people have little to no ambition, need constant supervision, and won't actually perform the duties of their job unless threatened.

64. B. According to the *PMBOK® Guide*, work performance data refers to the raw observations and measurements identified during activities being performed to carry out the project work. This occurs as a result of processes belonging to the Executing process group.

65. B. Change requests may take the form of preventive or corrective actions or workarounds. It's not too late to take preventive action in the Monitoring and Controlling process group.

66. A-2, B-3, C-1. There are a variety of project management office (PMO) types. The *PMBOK® Guide* provides an example of three distinct types: supportive, controlling, and directive.

67. D. The project manager is in the process of carrying out stakeholder analysis and is evaluating the level of interest and influence of stakeholders. In this scenario, the project manager is carrying out the Identify Stakeholders process.

68. A. According to the *PMBOK® Guide*, phase reviews are also called *phase gates*, *phase entrances*, *phase exits*, *stage gates*, and *kill points*. Phase reviews typically serve as checkpoints at the end of a phase where performance or progress is evaluated against the project charter or plan. Once completed, the project progresses to the next phase.

69. D. The purpose of the Monitor Risks process is to monitor risk response plans, track identified risks, identify and analyze new risks, and evaluate the effectiveness of the risk processes. As part of carrying out this process, risk review meetings may be held to examine and document the effectiveness of risk responses in dealing with overall project risks and individual project risks.

70. B. Manage Communications is concerned with ensuring the timely and appropriate collection, creation, distribution, storage, retrieval, management, monitoring, and ultimate disposition of project information. In this scenario, the project manager is utilizing communication skills.

71. D. Deliverables are measurable outcomes, measurable results, or specific items that must be produced before the project or project phase is considered complete. Requirements are the specifications of the deliverables and tell you how you know the deliverables were completed successfully.

72. C. The Acquire Resources process is concerned with all resources for the project, both existing staff members and consultants or external staff. The procurement processes are used to obtain the staff members, and the Acquire Resources process involves attaining and assigning resources.

73. C. The project will recoup its investment by month 18. To calculate, simply total the cash inflow for every quarter as indicated; payback is reached when you hit the amount of total investment.

74. A. Robert is correct in stating that project managers should consider all project management processes as they are managing projects. This does not mean that all project management processes must be carried out, but they must be evaluated and considered for their applicability.

75. B. This question describes the characteristics of an effective team.

76. D. The procurement documentation contains a variety of useful information relating to the agreement signed with a vendor, including the statement of work, payment information, performance information, and any other correspondence with the vendor. While the project management plan and agreement are two other key inputs, they alone do not provide sufficient information for the meeting with Nicolas. This type of discussion and analysis occurs as part of performing the Control Procurements process, and procurement documentation is a key input of the process.

77. B. Sally failed to keep Roshoud, as the project sponsor, informed and up to date. The scenario notes that he heard of the resource gaps and had to approach Sally to get clarification.

78. C. The elements of communication involve senders, receivers, and messages. The communication model, a tool and technique of the Manage Communications process, includes encoding, decoding, acknowledging, and feedback/response. Verbal and written are forms of communication.

79. A. The project manager is in the process of carrying out the Identify Stakeholders process. As part of this process, stakeholder analysis is performed. Stakeholder analysis and identification should occur regularly throughout the project's life cycle.

80. C. The configuration management system, used in the Perform Integrated Change Control process, documents the physical characteristics of the product of the project and ensures that the description is accurate and complete.

81. B. This is describing a weighting system technique. Vendor B had a final score of 37, and vendor A had a final score of 26. For each vendor, multiply each score by its weight, and add the results to obtain that vendor's final score.

82. B. While the project management plan is technically a correct answer, the question specifically refers to the resource management plan (a component of the project management plan).

83. B. Plan Stakeholder Engagement is concerned with effectively engaging stakeholders, understanding their needs and interests, understanding the good and bad things they bring to the project, and understanding how the project will affect them.

84. B. The performance measurement baseline consists of the schedule, scope, and cost baseline. The cost baseline does not include management reserves; therefore, the PMB does not include them.

85. C. Plan Schedule Management, Estimate Activity Durations, and Control Schedule are processes that belong to the Project Schedule Management Knowledge Area. Other processes belonging to this Knowledge Area include Define Activities, Sequence Activities, and Develop Schedule.

86. B. Alyssa is carrying out the Plan Scope Management process and is using the expert judgment technique to help produce the scope management plan.

87. D. NPV and IRR will generally bring you to the same accept/reject decision.

88. D. Fast-tracking is the best answer in this scenario. Budget was the original constraint on this project, so it's highly unlikely the project manager would get more resources to assist with the project. The next best thing is to compress phases to shorten the project duration.

89. B. The scenario describes activities associated with the Acquire Resources and Conduct Procurements processes, which are processes that belong to the Executing process group.

90. B. You are in the Manage Quality process and have performed a quality audit. Quality audits are performed to determine inefficient or ineffective processes, policies, procedures, and guidelines, and, when performed correctly, to determine if the product is fit for use, if applicable laws and standards are followed, if corrective actions are necessary, and more.

91. A, B, C, E. A RACI is a type of responsibility assignment matrix that captures resources assigned and how they are associated with the work of the project. RACI stands for responsible, accountable, consult, inform.

92. A. You have just performed a quality audit and identified a need for a corrective action.

93. C. The Manage Project Knowledge process, like most processes, is performed iteratively throughout the project's life cycle.

94. A. This Knowledge Area is responsible for both human and physical resources.

95. B. The Tuckman ladder, developed by Dr. Bruce Tuckman, is a team development model that identifies the various stages of development that a team goes through together.

96. A. Enterprise environmental factors are both internal and external factors that can influence or impact a project. In the Acquire Resources process, enterprise environmental factors is a key input that represents existing information on organizational resources, such as availability, experience levels, interests, costs, and competence levels.

97. A. Cost-reimbursable contracts go by various names, depending on certain terms used. They include cost plus incentive fee, cost plus award fee, cost plus percentage of cost, and cost plus fixed fee.

98. A. This question describes activities associated with monitoring stakeholder engagement, which is part of the Monitor Stakeholder Engagement process. Keeping stakeholders engaged will help overall project success, and it will keep them up to date on issues and status.

99. C. Schedule variance tells you whether the schedule is ahead or behind what was planned for this period and is calculated by subtracting PV from EV. In this case, the formula looks like this: 95 – 85 = 10. The resulting number is positive, which means the project is ahead of schedule for this time period.

100. D. The project manager and project team together are responsible for determining how best to tailor the project management processes, based on the needs of the project.

101. B. Bottom-up estimating is carried out by obtaining individual estimates for each project activity and then adding all of them up together to come up with a total estimate for the work package or the project. It is generally an accurate means of estimating, although it's more time-consuming and costly to perform.

102. C. This describes a risk review, which is a tool and technique used within the Monitor Risks process, as part of "meetings" held. According to the *PMBOK® Guide*, risk reviews are scheduled regularly and should evaluate and capture whether risk responses implemented are effective in dealing with identified project and individual risks.

103. D. Project phases generally produce at least one deliverable by the end of the phase.

104. A. The Tuckman ladder, developed by Dr. Bruce Tuckman, is a team development model that identifies the various stages of development that a team goes through together.

105. C. The addition of two stakeholders brought the total number of communication channels to 66. Remember that you must apply the formula for calculating communication channels, which is as follows:

$$n\ (n\text{-}1) \div 2$$

The question, however, asks how many more communication channels you will need to manage, meaning that you must now subtract the original number of channels from the new number of channels to get the answer (66 – 45). The answer is 21.

106. B. According to the *PMBOK® Guide*, the issue log is used to promote communication with stakeholders. The issue log is part of the project documents updates output of this process.

107. B. Nicolas used the stakeholder engagement plan as part of carrying out the Manage Stakeholder Engagement process activities. The stakeholder engagement plan is a key input to this process, and it documents identified strategies and actions required to promote the productive involvement of stakeholders.

108. B. Approved change requests are an input to the Direct and Manage Project Work process. This process will be repeated to implement the change. Approved change requests come about as a result of the approved change requests output of the Perform Integrated Change Control process. There is not enough information in the question to determine whether the scope has increased, so neither C nor D is correct.

109. B. Organizational process assets include historical documents from past projects, along with templates. Templates, in particular, can help expedite the preparation of network diagrams.

110. D. The WBS is a decomposition of the total scope of work to be carried out by the project team. As is implied, it represents 100 percent of the project's scope, as well as objectives to be accomplished to produce the required deliverables.

111. B. Carina is performing activities associated with the Planning process group.

112. D. Parametric estimating uses mathematical models to calculate cost estimates through historical data, resulting in a fairly accurate estimate.

113. B. This question requires discounted cash flow analysis to compare the value of Alternative A to Alternative B. Applying the present value formula to Alternative A, the formula is calculated this way: $\$21,000,000 / (1 + .05)^2 = \$19,047,619$. Alternative B is calculated this way: $\$29,000,000 / (1 + .05)^3 = \$25,051,831$.

114. B. Mandatory dependencies are also known as hard logic or hard dependencies. In a mandatory dependency, the nature of the work itself dictates the order in which activities should be performed.

115. A. Scope changes will cause schedule revisions, but schedule revisions do not change the project scope. Project requirements are part of the project scope statement, and therefore option D is one of the correct responses.

116. A. The question describes the Monitor Communications and Monitor Stakeholder Engagement processes. Both processes evaluate the results of communication and stakeholder engagement activities and compare them against the desired outcomes. Based on the comparison, adjustments to these activities may be made.

117. D. Trend analysis is a mathematical formula used to forecast future outcomes and predict project trends. It is not a tool for analyzing how problems occur. It is part of the data analysis tool and technique of the Control Costs process.

118. A. The triangular distribution formula using the three-point estimating technique is (Optimistic + Most Likely + Pessimistic) ÷ 3. Plugging in the values provided yields the following: ($2,500 + $3,500 + $7,200) ÷ 3 = $4,400.

119. C. There are four development life cycles: predictive, iterative, incremental, and hybrid. The incremental development life cycle uses predetermined periods of time called *iterations* to complete the deliverable (not to be confused with the iterative development life cycle).

120. A. Since the question states you are meeting to discuss details of the contract, you are using the procurement negotiation tool and technique, which is part of interpersonal and team skills. Proposal evaluation is used prior to deciding among multiple responses. Procurement negotiations are used to come to agreement on the contract; while the project manager may participate in contract negotiations, it is typically the procurement administrator who performs negotiations.

121. A. Getting this question correct involves knowing how to calculate the expected monetary value, as well as understanding decision tree analysis. The correct answer is $37,250. Based on the question, our focus is on the make scenario. To calculate the expected monetary value, take the impact of $15,000 and multiply it by the probability of 15 percent, and then add the initial investment of $35,000.

122. D. There isn't enough information in this question to determine an answer. Payback period is the least precise of cash flow analysis techniques, but in this question, the payback periods are all the same. Initial investment isn't enough information to help choose among the projects.

123. A. This question describes expert power on the part of the brilliant teammate and a democratic leadership style because team members were asked for input before a decision was made.

124. A. During the early stages of a project, risk probability of occurrence is at its highest; uncertainty is greatest during the Initiating phase of the project.

125. B. According to the *PMBOK® Guide*, there are three ways project life cycle phases could be performed: sequential, iterative, and overlapping.

126. A. The project manager has asked Yazzy to calculate estimate to complete (ETC). When the work is proceeding as planned, use the following ETC formula: EAC – AC. Plug in the values to get the following: $75,000 – $50,000 = $25,000.

127. C. The team is currently in the norming stage, where they are working together well and where team members adjust their work habits and behaviors to support the team.

128. A. To calculate schedule variance, subtract planned value from earned value (SV = EV – PV): $500 – $700 = –$200. A negative schedule variance means that the project is behind schedule.

129. B. Reporting templates, communication policies, communication technologies, and security issues surrounding data, communicating methods, and records retention policies are all part of the organizational process assets input of the Monitor Communications process, not the project communications input.

130. D. What-if scenario analysis is typically performed using the Monte Carlo technique, which simulates hundreds of scenarios by using existing project data and considering uncertainty. This is used as part of modeling techniques performed through the Develop Schedule and Control Schedule processes, as well as the Perform Quantitative Risk Analysis process.

131. B. You are in the process of carrying out the Collect Requirements process, which is part of the Planning process group.

132. D. The project charter authorizes the project to begin. Once approved, it gives the project manager authority to apply resources to the project.

133. B. The project manager has carried out the Develop Project Charter and Identify Stakeholders processes. He will likely begin to assemble the project management plan as a next step, by performing activities outlined within the Develop Project Management Plan process.

134. D. While Monitor and Control Project Work represents another great option, David is likely to place extra emphasis on the Control Scope process. This process ensures that the approved scope, and only the approved scope, is completed. Any changes are managed according to the formal change control process.

135. C. Only critical path activities will cause schedule delays unless one or more of the noncritical-path activities have used up all their float time. This question doesn't specify that a noncritical-path activity has used all its float time.

136. A. Completion of the product scope is measured against the product requirements, whereas completion of the project scope is measured against the project management plan. Although requirements documentation is technically a correct answer, product requirements is a far more specific answer.

137. A. According to the *PMBOK® Guide*, the project management plan describes how the project will be executed, monitored, controlled, and closed. It brings together all of the subsidiary management plans and baselines, as well as other information, to manage the project.

138. C. The project manager is performing the Manage Stakeholder Engagement process. This process includes activities such as engaging stakeholders at appropriate stages, managing their expectations through negotiation and communication, addressing risks or potential concerns related to their management and anticipating future issues, and clarifying and resolving issues identified.

139. D. The key pieces of information within the question reveal that you have accurate historical information and quantifiable parameters. Both are needed to utilize the parametric estimating technique.

140. C. The tools and techniques of the Acquire Resources process are pre-assignment, interpersonal and team skills (negotiation), virtual teams, and decision-making (multicriterion decision analysis). Resource calendars are an output of this process.

141. A. ETC when variances are atypical is BAC – EV.

142. A. Legitimate power, also known as formal power, comes about as a result of the influencer's position. For example, team members may agree to go along with an executive simply as a result of their position.

143. C. The project manager is performing the Manage Stakeholder Engagement process. This process includes activities such as engaging stakeholders at appropriate stages, managing their expectations through negotiation and communication, addressing risks or potential concerns related to their management and anticipating future issues, and clarifying and resolving issues identified.

144. A, C, D. Teams are made up of individuals, and individual development is a factor critical to project success.

145. A. Change requests are typically a means of taking corrective or preventive actions or performing defect repairs. Updates to project documents will typically occur as a result of implementing a change request.

146. B. Carina is concluding major activities associated with the Planning process group and is getting ready to enter into Executing. At this point in the project life cycle, costs are typically low.

147. C. Scope changes might affect the schedule, cost, quality, and other processes and should be thoroughly integrated with all the Monitoring and Controlling processes. Scope changes may reduce the project requirements and thus reduce the number or hours needed to complete the project. This, in turn, could cause a reduction in the project budget.

148. C. To calculate the project's performance using the information provided, you can use the cost performance index (CPI) earned value calculation. The formula for calculating CPI is CPI = EV ÷ AC. Plug in the values to calculate the following: $5,000 ÷ $7,500 = $0.67. A CPI of less than 1 means that the project is performing over budget.

149. C. Monte Carlo analysis examines risk from the perspective of the project as a whole.

150. D. To answer this question, you will need to calculate the cumulative SPI and CPI. All values needed to do this have been provided within the question. The formula for calculating SPI, which will tell us how the project is performing according to the schedule, is EV ÷ PV. Plug in the values provided to result in the following: ($59,000 / $70,200) = 0.84. Anything less than 1.0 means that the project is behind schedule. Now, calculate CPI by using the following formula: EV ÷ AC. Plug in the values provided to result in the following: ($59,000 / $64,500) = 0.91. A CPI under 1.0 means that the project is over budget. Therefore, the project is behind schedule and over budget.

151. C. As part of carrying out the Perform Quantitative Risk Analysis process, updates are made to the risk register. Among the updates are an assessment of overall project risk exposure and detailed probabilistic analysis of the project.

152. A. Analogous estimating involves the use of historical information from past similar projects as the basis for determining the activity duration estimates. This is what the project manager has done within the question by using the estimates from the past edition's project.

153. A. Carina will update risks identified and information about the risks within the risk register. While project documents is technically a correct answer (since the risk register is a project document), risk register is more specific and therefore a better choice. Her findings may also find their way into the risk report, although, again, that is a secondary choice.

154. B. A TCPI of 1.0 means that the project must continue performing at its current level of efficiency to complete within specified targets.

155. C. Maslow's Hierarchy of Needs notes that there are five sets of needs that must be met in the following hierarchical order: basic physical needs, safety and security needs, social needs, self-esteem needs, self-actualization. The idea is that these needs must be met before the person can move to the next level of needs in the hierarchy.

156. B. ADM only uses the finish-to-start dependency. Precedence diagramming method (PDM), on the other hand, uses all dependency types.

157. C. Total float refers to the amount of time you can delay the earliest start of an activity without delaying the ending of the project. To calculate total float, subtract either the early start from the late start or the early finish from the late finish (both give you the same answer).

158. C. According to the *Code of Ethics and Professional Conduct*, respect is our duty to show a high regard for ourselves, others, and the resources entrusted to us.

159. C. Work performance reports are an output of the Monitor and Control Project Work process. These reports can take many forms and are intended to create awareness of issues, provide information to make decisions, and take action regarding the issues.

160. C. Inspection is an important tool and technique of the Validate Scope process. The purpose is to inspect work and deliverables to ensure that they meet requirements and product acceptance criteria. If the deliverables pass inspection and receive sign-off, they are formally considered accepted deliverables—a major output of this process.

161. A. An agreement is a mutually binding document that obligates the seller to provide a specific set of products, services, or results. It typically contains a lot of information, such as the procurement statement of work or major deliverables, when the goods or services will be produced, reporting, associated terms, and other relevant information. Agreements are an output of the Conduct Procurements process.

162. A, B, D. Referent power refers to power that is inferred to the influencer by their subordinates. For example, project team members may have a high level of regard for their project manager and therefore willingly go along with a decision that the PM makes. Formal power is also known as legitimate power, not referent power.

163. D. Quality improvements come about as a result of quality audits, which are a tool and technique of the Manage Quality process. Quality improvements are implemented by submitting change requests and/or taking corrective action.

164. A. Supportive PMOs tend to have a low degree of control over projects and play more of a consultative role in projects. Typically, a supportive PMO provides best practices, templates, training, and other resources to support projects.

165. A. This describes the cost-benefit analysis tool and technique of the Plan Quality Management process.

166. C. Costs are highest during the Executing phase of the project life cycle, when resource usage is at its highest.

167. A. The formula for CPI is EV ÷ AC; therefore, 114 ÷ 103 = 1.1. The formula for SPI is EV ÷ PV; therefore, 114 ÷ 120 = .95.

168. A, C, D. A backlog contains a prioritized list of all work encapsulated in a project. It is used to track, review, and regulate work. The team generally pulls work from the top of the backlog, and the backlog is continuously refined over the course of the project. The product owner is responsible for maintaining the backlog and is a representative of the business.

169. A. The question is asking for an input that can be used to address the engagement level of stakeholders. The scenario involves the Monitor Stakeholder Engagement process. Interpersonal and team skills and decision-making are tools and techniques and therefore not the correct choices. Since the project management plan contains the stakeholder engagement plan, which documents the strategy for engagement stakeholders, this is the best option. Other useful components of the project management plan also include the communications management plan and resource management plan.

170. B. The team is engaged in the Estimate Costs process. The purpose of this process is to develop an approximation of the cost of resources needed to complete project work.

171. C. Project management processes are often revisited several times as the project is refined throughout its life and are therefore performed in an iterative fashion throughout the project's life cycle.

172. C. What the project sponsor is looking for is an updated project schedule that reflects where the project is currently at in terms of work accomplished. The schedule baseline contains the planned information, not actual work progress. Instead, the schedule baseline is typically compared to the current project schedule to determine what variances exist.

173. D. This question describes the process analysis tool and technique. Process analysis looks at process improvements from an organizational and technical perspective. It examines problems and constraints experienced while conducting the work of the project, and it identifies inefficient and ineffective processes.

174. B. The correct answer is contingency reserve, which are funds set aside for responding to risk that remain after carrying out the risk response plan. Management reserves are funds that have been set aside to cover unforeseen risks. Cost aggregation deals with aggregating cost estimates, so was a clear elimination, and cash flow refers to needed, or used, funds.

175. A. While it's true that gathering three-point estimates helps to generate estimates with higher accuracy, this is a technique that we use to generate duration estimates, not resource estimates. All other statements are accurate.

176. D. Estimate at completion (EAC) is the expected cost of the work when completed.

177. B. The project management plan contains the procurement management plan, which will serve as a guide to carrying out procurement-related activities.

178. D. The project manager has just completed the Direct and Manage Project Work process, eliminating this as the best option. Although the Executing and Monitoring and Controlling processes are iterative and overlap, the best choice of those presented is the Monitor and Control Project Work process. This process is responsible for tracking, reviewing, and reporting overall progress against the plan. In this case, results and performance of the deliverable produced will be evaluated against the plan. While it is possible that change control is another process that will be performed (many times on any given project), you do not have sufficient information to select this as the best option.

179. D. Communications requirements analysis, a tool and technique of the Plan Communications Management process, considers things such as company and departmental organization charts, stakeholder relationships, all the departments and disciplines involved in the project, the number of people associated with the project and their location, and any external needs like the media, government, or industry organizations requiring communication updates.

180. A. Corrective actions are taken as a result of comparing and monitoring project performance against the baseline. The baseline is the project management plan. Deviations that are discovered during the course of the project may or may not require corrective actions. Preventive actions are taken to reduce the probability of negative consequences, and defect repairs are submitted to correct product defects.

181. B. System or process flow charts show how the various elements of a system interrelate, which can reveal how a problem occurs. This is done by analyzing the steps of a system and is useful in identifying potential responses to risks.

182. D. The Closing process group encompasses only one process, not Initiating. Initiating has a total of 2 processes, Planning a total of 24, Executing a total of 10, and Monitoring and Controlling a total of 12.

183. D. Once a seller is selected, resource calendars will be generated for the resources procured. This displays the availability of those resources.

184. B. The risk manager has omitted the initial process of risk management, which involves creating the risk management plan. The risk management plan is an essential part of carrying out the other risk management processes, since it outlines how risks will be identified, analyzed, monitored, and so forth. Therefore, the project manager in this scenario has a low likelihood of developing a risk register that will be useful in carrying out risk management. For exam purposes, the risk management plan is a requirement.

185. B. Personal work styles, scheduling priorities, and scarce resources are the top three reasons for conflict. The correct answer is therefore personality clashes.

186. B. Velocity refers to the average cycle time or stories completed per iteration. This is used by the team to predict how long the project will take, assuming that the velocity calculated is reliable.

187. D. Both processes are responsible for carrying out closure activities when it comes to procurements. The closed procurements output is a result of Control Procurements, where completed requirements are validated against the contract; administrative closure of procurements occurs through the Close Project or Phase process, including archiving related documentation.

188. D. The project manager will need to measure scope completed against scope planned. To do this, they will need work performance data, a key input of the Control Scope process. Variance and trend analysis are tools and techniques of the process, not inputs.

189. A. The project scope statement contains a list of the project deliverables, their requirements, and the measurable criteria used to determine project completion. The project scope statement is an output of the Define Scope process and is used as an input to the Create WBS process.

190. B. Carina is using the earned value analysis technique of the Control Costs process. Earned value analysis compares the performance measurement baseline against actual performance, such as actual schedule progress and costs.

191. C. The project objectives should include quantifiable criteria that can be used to help measure project success. Project objectives should include schedule, cost, and quality measurements.

192. B. Waterfall, Agile, and PRINCE2 are examples of methodologies used to manage projects.

193. A. Expected value is calculated as follows: (Optimistic + Pessimistic + (4 × Most Likely)) ÷ 6. The formula is as follows: ($75 + $250 + (4 × $100)) ÷ 6 = $120.83.

194. A. According to the *Code of Ethics and Professional Conduct*, project management practitioners should adhere to the following four values: responsibility, respect, fairness, and honesty.

195. C. Weighted scoring models use the weight of the criteria multiplied by the score to derive an overall score. Project 1's score is 47, Project 2's score is 45, and Project 3's score is 42. Based on this information, Project 1 is the best choice.

196. C. The project manager is responsible for ensuring that changes are managed properly throughout the project's life cycle and that the organization's change control policies are followed.

197. A. With the Just in Time strategy, inventory costs are brought in just as they are needed. But to implement this type of strategy, a company must be highly efficient and have a high focus on quality, or the strategy won't work, and the goods will arrive either too early or too late.

198. C. A burndown chart shows how much work remains versus how much time is left within a timebox. Examples of timebox include time remaining for the current or a future iteration, or it may reflect time remaining for the project.

199. B. Attributes sampling is an inspection measurement technique with only two possibilities: conforming or nonconforming. In other words, the measurements conform (meet the requirement), or they do not conform. This can also be considered a pass/fail or go/no-go decision.

200. A-2, B-1, C-3. Project management always includes planning activities, regardless of the life cycle used to carry out the project. While all share planning as a key activity, when and how planning occurs varies for each.

Chapter 5: Full-Length Practice Exam 2

1. D. Virtual teams create opportunities to expand the resource pool across many geographic areas and increase the likelihood of acquiring special expertise. With team members engaging virtually, cost can be reduced by limiting travel and allowing team members to work remotely.

2. D. Within Agile there is a concept that describes the degree to which individuals can take on work, according to their depth and breadth. "I" shaped people are those who have deep specializations in one domain and rarely contribute to work outside of that domain; "T" shaped people are considered generalizing specialists who have expertise in an area but can also contribute to other areas.

3. B, D. PMOs may facilitate project audits as a means of monitoring compliance against published standards, policies, and procedures published by the PMO and/or the company. A key benefit of project audits is that they serve as a tool for identifying potential threats to compliance, such as legal or contractual requirements.

4. A-3, B-1, C-4, D-2. There are four types of project endings: integration, starvation, addition, and extinction. Extinction is the best type of ending.

5. B. Earned value (EV) is the value of the work that's actually been completed. Planned value (PV) is the budgeted amount planned for work to be completed during a given time period, and actual cost (AC) is the cost of work completed during a given time period. EAC is a forecasting technique that is an estimate of the expected total cost of a work component.

6. A. RACI charts are part of the organization charts and position. A RACI is a type of responsibility descriptions tool and technique of the Plan Resource Management process. They are matrix-based charts, but matrix-based charts are part of the organization charts and position descriptions tool and technique.

7. C. There are three common roles used in Agile teams: cross-functional team member, product owner, and team facilitator.

8. E. Diversity and inclusion are important elements to consider when acquiring project team members.

9. D. Since payback period is the least precise cash flow analysis technique, IRR values have a higher priority in determining go or no-go project decisions.

10. D. All team members, not just the project manager, should exhibit emotional intelligence. These skills enable the team to respond to changes and adapt to the work and each other.

11. B. The cost management technique used when evaluating various alternatives is called *life-cycle costing*. This technique considers acquisition, operating, and disposal costs.

12. A, D. Organizations interested in adopting Agile practices or other new cultural norms must foster and enable an environment that is safe, honest, and transparent. This type of environment encourages the team to move forward and avoid falling into old behaviors and practices.

13. C. Pre-assignments occur when team members are determined in advance. Typically, the pre-assignment is formally captured within the project charter or committed as part of a project proposal.

14. A-5, B-2, C-1, D-4, E-3. There are five conflict resolution techniques, all of which go by two different names: withdraw/avoid, smooth/accommodate, compromise/reconcile, force/ direct, collaborate/problem-solve.

15. C. Alyssa is performing the Develop Project Management Plan process. The only output of this process is the project management plan.

16. A, C, D. The activities list is a key element of the project schedule that will form the schedule baseline. According to the *PMBOK® Guide*, the scope baseline consists of the following: the project scope statement, WBS, work packages, planning packages, and WBS dictionary.

17. D. Walter Shewhart is considered to be the grandfather of TQM; he developed statistical tools to examine when a corrective action must be applied to a process.

18. D. Project managers can use a variety of individual and team assessments to gain insight into areas of strengths and weaknesses. Examples of this tool include surveys that capture team member preferences, structured interviews, ability tests, and focus groups.

19. C. There are three types of PMOs: supportive, controlling, and directive. Controlling PMOs are concerned with providing project teams with support, such as through published resources and templates, and ensuring compliance with published project management and governance frameworks.

20. A. The Perform Integrated Change Control process is carried out as part of monitoring and controlling the activities, which occurs in conjunction with execution activities but is not itself considered part of the Executing process group.

21. B. The project management plan describes how the project will be executed, monitored and controlled, and closed. It addresses the various elements of how the project will be managed, including any methodology that will be used.

22. A, B, D. Common causes of variance that fall outside the acceptable range are difficult to correct and usually require reorganization of the process. Decisions to change the process are not within the project manager's authority and always require management approval. The rule of seven refers to when seven or more processes fall on the same side of the median; this indicates that an external factor may be influencing the results.

23. B. At the end of the meeting, the project manager took a compromising approach, also referred to as reconciling. This is when an individual attempts to bring about some degree of satisfaction to all parties to partially resolve the conflict. The project manager did this by increasing the priority of user story #2 and allowing for the possibility of it being pulled into the iteration.

24. A. Legitimate power, also referred to as formal power, comes about as a result of someone's position or formal title. In this case, the division president's directive carries a heavy influence due to her position.

25. C. When building a team, project managers must take several factors into account. One tool used as part of the decision-making process is multicriteria decision analysis. Availability, cost, and ability are examples of team member selection criteria that a project manager may use. Availability, cost, and ability may be assumptions or constraints captured but are not considered ongoing.

26. D. The assumption log contains both assumptions and constraints and is first created during the Develop Project Charter process.

27. C. A fixed-price contract can either set a specific, firm price for the goods or services rendered or include incentives for meeting or exceeding certain contract deliverables. There are three types of fixed-price contracts: firm fixed-price, fixed-price incentive fee, and fixed-price with economic price adjustment.

28. B. The requisition stage is where the procurement documents are prepared (not the responses to them) and is associated with the Plan Procurement Management process. The two outputs that become inputs are procurement documentation and source selection criteria.

29. A-5, B-1, C-3, D-2, E-4. Classifying stakeholder engagement levels and documenting them helps plan and create action plans for those stakeholders who are not at the desired level of engagement.

30. C. The stakeholder engagement plan captures the strategies used to promote productive involvement of stakeholders throughout the project. While the stakeholder engagement plan is a component of the project management plan, identifying the component itself is a more specific and therefore better answer.

31. B. There are three common roles used in Agile teams: cross-functional team member, product owner, and team facilitator.

32. C. Generating status reports is an activity that belongs to the Monitor and Control Project Work process, which is part of the Monitoring and Controlling process group. The key output of this process is work performance reports.

33. D. Lack of executive buy-in occurs when leaders are accustomed to a predictive mindset and approaches. A new way of working may be difficult to understand without education and training. The *Agile Practice Guide* also recommends describing Agile terms using lean thinking, such as frequent reviews.

34. B, C, D. According to the *PMBOK® Guide*, there are three main categories to consider when choosing a methodology to manage the work of the project. They are culture of the organization, the project team, and the project itself.

35. D. Kanban follows a lean approach using a pull-based scheduling system, also referred to as on-demand scheduling, to maintain flexibility and focus on continuous delivery. This pull system involves moving work through a process in a visual manner using a Kanban board.

36. C. Proposal evaluation techniques are a tool and technique of this process. It is also an example of source selection criteria, which are an input to this process and may also include financial capacity and technical capability.

37. A. The sponsor is referring to benefits. According to the *PMBOK® Guide*, project benefits are defined as outcomes of actions, behaviors, products, services, or results that provide value to the sponsoring organization as well as to the project's intended beneficiaries.

38. D. Assessing risk probability is difficult because it relies on expert judgment; the other options listed are not used during this process.

39. D. Developing the project team sets up the team for success, but it is also a strategy that creates an open, encouraging environment that enables team members to contribute.

40. A, B, C. According to the *Agile Practice Guide*, colocation improves communication, increases knowledge sharing, enables team member commitment to each other and the project, and creates a low-cost continuous learning environment.

41. C. Expert power occurs when the person being influenced believes that the person doing the influencing is knowledgeable about the subject. In this case, the division president felt that your experience and knowledge gave merit to your advice.

42. C. The Executing process group is where you should execute the work defined within the plan and implement corrective and preventive actions as they are approved. The primary focus of the Monitoring and Controlling process group is to take measurements and perform inspections to find out whether there are variances in the plan.

43. D. This question describes the Conduct Procurements process. Make-or-buy decisions is one of the inputs of this process, and bidder conferences and proposal evaluation techniques are two of the tools and techniques of this process. Since you know the vendor, even though you haven't seen this person recently, you should be concerned about a conflict-of-interest situation.

44. A, B, D. Agile project management offices (PMOs) exist to guide the organization in continuously achieving business value. According to the *Agile Practice Guide*, an Agile PMO is value-driven, invitation-oriented, and multidisciplinary.

45. B, C, D. Project managers are continuously using interpersonal and team skills to perform their daily work. Among these skills, project managers often must use negotiation techniques to build the project team and acquire the skills and capabilities needed. Negotiation often occurs with functional managers, other project managers, and vendors/suppliers that are external to the organization.

46. A. Virtual teams often reduce project or organizational costs; while costs may be dispersed across regions, this is highly scenario-dependent and not always applicable or the case. All other options are valid benefits of using virtual teams.

47. C. Implementing approved changes occurs as part of the Direct and Manage Project Work process, which is part of the Executing process group.

48. C. This Agile methodology is grounded in governance framework that combines the iterative and incremental approaches. At the onset of the project, DDSM establishes the cost of the project, the quality standards, and the timeframe to completion and, as such, is constraint-driven.

49. B. The lowest level of the WBS is the work package. Work packages are later decomposed further into activities as part of developing the schedule. Activities, however, are not considered to be part of the WBS.

50. D. Within a strong matrix organization, project managers have moderate to high authority, report into a functional manager, and directly manage the project budget; they are full-time project managers with a job title that reflects the role.

51. C. This question describes the affinity diagram, which is a data representation tool and technique. Affinity diagrams pinpoint which areas should get the most focus by grouping related potential causes of defects.

52. B. Crystal methods refers to a family of methodologies designed to scale to the project needs. It is multifaceted, with each face representing a core value. The core values of Crystal are people, interaction, community, communication, skills, and talents.

53. A. The Role Delineation Study covered in the *PMI Code of Ethics and Professional Conduct* covers four areas, including promoting interaction among team members and other stakeholders. This question describes the purpose of the Manage Stakeholder Engagement process.

54. C. Ground rules refer to the expectations established by the team of acceptable behaviors they are to exhibit. Ground rules are typically captured as part of the team charter. They become an important tool to use when managing stakeholder engagement.

55. B. The sponsor is referring to benefits. The benefits management plan describes how and when the benefits of the project will be delivered. It captures the target benefits, strategic alignment, timeframe for realizing benefits, metrics of how the benefits will be measured, and benefit owners, among other key information relating to business value delivered.

56. D. Expected value can be calculated using a triangular distribution (simple average) or beta distribution (weighted average). The three-point estimating formula that uses a triangular distribution is as follows: (Optimistic + Pessimistic + Most Likely) ÷ 3. Plug in the values provided to calculate the following: ($25 + $50 + $35) ÷ 3 = $36.7, or 37 when rounded to the nearest whole number.

57. D. Data representation can include the use of a stakeholder engagement matrix to assess whether communication needs are being met. In this scenario, the Monitor Communications process is being carried out.

58. B. Interactional is a leadership style that encompasses a mixture of three styles: transactional, transformational, and charismatic. Transactional refers to a leader who focuses on goals, feedback, and accomplishments when determining rewards; transformational refers to a leader who empowers followers through idealized attributes and behaviors, and encourages innovation and creativity; and charismatic refers to a leader who leads by inspiring followers, who creates high energy around them, and who tends to hold strong convictions.

59. D. The Tuckman ladder, also referred to as stages of team development, consists of five stages that teams may go through: forming, storming, norming, performing, and adjourning. The performing stage is where the team experiences peak performance. They are most productive and effective during this stage.

60. A. The question refers to the Direct and Manage Project Work process, which is responsible for leading and performing the work defined in the project management plan and implementing any changes that have been approved. This is where the project manager provides the overall management of the work being executed. Inputs to this process include the project management plan, project documents, approved change requests, enterprise environmental factors, and organizational process assets. Expert judgment is a tool and technique, while issue log and work performance data are outputs of the process.

61. D. Project 1's payback period is 19 months. Year 1 inflows are $528,000. Year 2 inflows are $39,000 per month, making the total payback period 19 months. Project 2's payback period is 16 months. Year 1 inflows are $72,000. Year 2 inflows are $45,000 per month, which makes the payback period 16 months.

62. A. Since you've identified the risks, you've completed the Identify Risks process.

63. A. Options C and D are not viable responses because the question is asking for an estimate at completion, not an estimate to complete. When changes in performance or risks occur on the project, it may cause BAC to no longer make sense. When that is the case, switch to the EAC to project the cost at completion.

64. D. Knowledge can be split into two types: explicit or tacit. Explicit knowledge can be captured and expressed using words, pictures, and numbers; tacit knowledge is more difficult to capture or express, such as beliefs, experiences, and "know-how."

65. C. According to the *Agile Practice Guide*, servant leaders practice and exude Agile. They approach their work in the following order: purpose (work with the team to define the "why"), people (encourage the team to create an environment where all can succeed), and process (look for results).

66. C. Cross-cultural communication presents unique challenges, particularly in ensuring that the meaning of a message is understood. This occurs through differences in communication styles (i.e., age, nationality, ethnicity, gender), use of different languages, and varying processes and protocols.

67. D. A salience model is a method used to classify stakeholders based on an assessment of their degree of authority/power, urgency, and legitimacy.

68. A. The project management plan is a compilation of plans and baselines and is considered to represent the project baseline. Once work is executed, progress will be measured against this plan.

69. A, B. The question describes the Scrum framework, and the technique referenced is the facilitation of sprint retrospective meetings (in Scrum, iterations are referred to sprints). Sprint retrospectives are held to determine what went well, what could be improved for the next sprint, and any changes needed to the scope.

70. E. Teams that are geographically disbursed can still benefit from common virtual workspaces. The *Agile Practice Guide* provides two examples: creating a fishbowl window through an ongoing videoconferencing link between various locations, which is live through the workday, and setting up remote pairing through virtual conferencing tools that allow for screen, video, and audio sharing capabilities.

71. C. Precedence diagramming method (PDM) is the most frequently used diagramming method. PDM uses boxes to represent activities and connects the activities with arrows showing the dependencies between them. PDM is also known as *activity on node (AON)*.

72. B. Agile teams focus on measuring value and what the team delivers versus what the team predicted it would deliver. Measurements tend to be empirical and value-based in nature.

73. B. You are in the Manage Quality process. This process is responsible for translating the quality management plan into executable-quality activities that incorporate the organization's quality policies into the project.

74. B, C, D. The sender/receiver communication model includes three key components: encode, transmit, and decode. Encoding is where the sender puts the information into a language the receiver will understand; transmit refers to sending the message using an appropriate method; and decode is where the receiver translates the information that was sent.

75. C. The team charter, also referred to as the team's social contract, creates an Agile environment that enables team members to work to the best of their ability as a team.

76. C. Acquiring resources involves activities required to obtain team members, facilities, equipment, materials, supplies, and other resources necessary to complete the work of the project.

77. C. Analogous estimating is less time-consuming than other estimating techniques and can be used to estimate time for different phases on the project. Analogous estimating is not as accurate as other estimating techniques.

78. B. Late finish is calculated by subtracting the duration of the last activity (activity 4) from its start date. Since it is one day, that means the late finish is 6/4. Late start is 7 days prior to 6/4, which is 5/29.

79. C. To calculate the early start and early finish for activity 4, you need to perform a forward pass. This is done by adding the duration of activity 4 to the early finish date of activity 3.

80. A. First you need to calculate the standard deviation for this activity, which is 1.67. That is, (Pessimistic − Optimistic) ÷ 6. A 95.44 percent confidence factor is 3 standard deviations. That is, 1.67 × 3 = 5.01. The expected value is 23 days, so you have a 95.44 percent chance of completing the activity within between 18 and 28 days.

81. D. The resource management plan captures how resources will be categorized, allocated, managed, and released. As part of team management, the plan details training strategies needed for team members.

82. B. Agile practices are highly adaptable to change and regularly assess the need for change and evolving requirements. In this scenario, changing requirements would require an assessment and refinement of the backlog with the consultation of the team.

83. C. This question describes the Validate Scope process. The tools and techniques of this process are inspection and decision-making.

84. A. Agile release planning is a tool and technique of the Develop Schedule process. According to the *PMBOK® Guide*, it provides a high-level summary timeline of the release schedule and helps the team determine the number of iterations or sprints needed to complete the release.

85. C. Lateral thinking is a form of alternatives analysis often used to determine a project's scope. It was created by Edward de Bono and serves as a means of reasoning and thinking about problems differently than what can be classified as evident.

86. D. Collaborating, also known as problem-solving, is where individuals adopt a cooperative attitude and create open dialogue in order to reach consensus and commitment to resolving conflict. This type of approach leads to a win-win situation.

87. A, B, C. Good leaders use referent power, which is inferred to them by their subordinates. They are visionaries and are concerned with the big picture, or strategic direction and plans.

88. A-1, B-1, C-2, D-2, E-1. Projects are heavily influenced by the environment that they operate within. There are two major categories that influence projects: enterprise environmental factors and organizational process assets.

89. C. The formula for TCPI when targeting EAC is as follows: TCPI = (BAC − EV) ÷ (EAC − AC). Plug in the values to get the following: ($15,000 − $10,000) ÷ ($17,000 − $12,000) = $1.0.

90. C. According to the *Agile Practice Guide*, backlog refinement is defined as the progressive elaboration of project requirements and / or the ongoing activity in which the team reviews, updates, and writes requirements to satisfy the need of the customer. Other definitions provided refer to the product backlog, progressive elaboration, and sprint review.

91. B, C, D. According to the *PMBOK® Guide*, sources of conflict include scarce resources, scheduling priorities, and personal work styles. Having team ground rules, group norms, and project management practices (i.e., communication planning and role definition) are ways of reducing conflict.

92. D. Rewards and recognition systems are formal ways of promoting desirable behavior. In this scenario, the engineer has delivered against commitments but has not lived up to the team charter and exhibited behavior that benefits the team.

93. D. Paul's benefits management plan is lacking the implementation of a system that will track and measure benefits to ensure that value is achieved as expected.

94. B. The risk probability and impact assessment tool and technique is used to determine the likelihood the risk will occur and the potential effects on project objectives. After performing the assessment, you'll determine risk scores or conditions (red, yellow, green) using the probability and impact matrix.

95. B. To calculate lines of communication, use the following formula, where n represents total number of stakeholders: $n(n − 1) ÷ 2$. Next, plug in 15 in place of the n to get the answer: $15(15 − 1) ÷ 2 = 105$.

96. B. When joining a new organization, it is important that a project manager familiarize themselves with the organization's culture. Understanding how the organization operates, its tolerance level, and its appetite for risk, among other things, will help Kristin tailor her project management approach and better understand the behaviors and norms of the team.

97. A, B, D. When managing project teams, many conflicts come about as a result of scheduling issues, availability of resources, or personal work habits.

98. A. An incremental life cycle focuses on completing deliverables by the end of each iteration so that it may be turned over to the customer for use.

99. D. The formula for calculating lines of communication is as follows, where n represents the total number of stakeholders (you are already assumed to have been included in the number): $n(n - 1) \div 2$. Plug in the numbers to get the following: $45(45 - 1) \div 2 = 990$.

100. D. The RAM and RACI charts, which are included as a component of the Organization Charts and Position Descriptions tool and technique, are matrix-based charts.

101. D. The team charter provides the full team with an understanding of how they will work together. It aligns the team on team values, working agreements, ground rules, meeting guidelines, and other group norms.

102. C. Knowledge can be split into two types: explicit or tacit. Explicit knowledge can be captured and expressed using words, pictures, and numbers; tacit knowledge is more difficult to capture or express, such as beliefs, experiences, and "know-how."

103. B, C, D. Estimate Activity Resources is a process that belongs to the Project Resource Management Knowledge Area. All other statements are true.

104. A, D. In flow-based Agile, the focus is on the team's throughput. Questions posed during stand-ups include the following: What do we need to do to advance this piece of work? Is anyone working on anything that is not on the board? What do we need to finish as a team? Are there any bottlenecks or blockers to the flow of work?

105. C. The project manager is carrying out activities associated with the Estimate Activity Resources process. Activities of this process include estimating team resources and the type and quantities of material, equipment, and supplies needed to carry out the project work.

106. B. There are several viable options included, most notably controlling the schedule and resources. Since the project manager is currently negotiating for resources, the best option is controlling resources, which are activities that occur through a project management process called Control Resources. As part of this process, the project manager uses their interpersonal and team skills to influence and negotiate for resources.

107. D. While there may be multiple gaps within the team charter, one that is likely to emerge is the lack of decision-making criteria.

108. C. Although enterprise environmental factors (i.e., marketplace conditions, changing federal regulations) are out of a project manager's control, they may result in an outcome that affects a project. A project manager should be regularly surveying both internal and external changes to the business environment to appropriately identify and manage risk to the project.

109. A. Kaylee and Alyssa are using the Monte Carlo analysis, which simulates the combined effects of individual project risks and other sources of uncertainty to determine their potential impact on the project objectives.

110. C. In this scenario, you are using a combination of push and interactive communication methods to address team members. Push is one-way communication and refers to sending information to intended receivers (such as email, in this case); interactive communication involves multidirectional communication where two or more parties exchange thoughts or ideas (such as during meetings).

111. B. You can plot the degree of certainty (or agreement) about the complexity elements such as requirements or team skills on a Stacey Complexity Model. The degrees are measured from low uncertainty or agreement to high uncertainty or lack of agreement. This model displays levels of uncertainty from low to high on both the x- and y-axes, or it may show levels of uncertainty on the x-axis and agreement levels on the y-axis.

112. C. The Expectancy Theory was developed by Victor Vroom. He believed that the expectation of a positive outcome, in other words, individual values, drives motivation.

113. B. Claims administration involves documenting, monitoring, and managing contested changes. Contested changes are resolved using alternative dispute resolution processes, such as arbitration, when parties cannot reach an agreement.

114. C. Projects that have high degrees of ambiguity and change require frequent and quick communication. Communicating frequently and transparently is a common characteristic of Agile approaches.

115. A. Looking at the scenario from Bob's perspective, he conceded his position to maintain harmony within the meeting. This conflict resolution technique is referred to as smoothing or accommodating.

116. C. Douglas McGregor is responsible for defining two models of worker behavior, Theory X and Theory Y, which attempt to explain how different managers deal with employees.

117. B. Alyssa is performing the Develop Project Management Plan process. The purpose of this process is to define, prepare, and coordinate all plan components and consolidate them into an integrated project management plan. It is also at this critical point that a strategy for how the project will be managed is made.

118. C. When competencies or skills are lacking within the team, one option is to incorporate training to enhance the competencies. Examples of training include classroom, distance learning, on-the-job training, mentorship, and coaching.

119. D. When taking on a servant leadership approach, project managers shift to emphasize coaching those open to the help, fostering high collaboration across the team, aligning stakeholder needs, and encouraging the distribution of responsibility to the team.

120. D. Transitioning to Agile approaches can be difficult and confusing for those not familiar or accustomed to this way of working. One method of gaining adoption is to begin using hybrid approaches that combine both predictive and Agile approaches as a means of introducing the team to Agile.

121. A. The servant leadership approach centers around empowering the team. A leader using this approach focuses on addressing the needs and development of team members to yield the greatest team performance possible. A servant leader approaches project work by clarifying or creating purpose (the "why") for the project/work, focusing on people by encouraging an environment where all can be successful, and lastly, they focus on process by looking for results.

122. A. Douglas McGregor defined two models of worker behavior: Theory X and Theory Y. Your new manager exhibits characteristics of Theory X managers, who believe that most people do not like work, have little to no ambition, and need constant supervision.

123. C. The main purpose of the Control Quality process tools and techniques is to examine the product, service, or result as well as the project processes for conformity to standards. They are used with the Plan-Do-Check-Act cycle to help identify and resolve problems related to quality defects.

124. B. CPI = EV ÷ AC, or in this example, $2,100 ÷ $2,000 = $1.05. SPI = EV ÷ PV, or in this example, $2,100 ÷ $2,200 = $.95.

125. D. It is important to create an environment that fosters adherence to team ground rules. In this scenario, your colleague must manage and rectify the ground rule violations. As a first step, your colleague should address the issue with the engineer directly to understand why he or she is behaving in such a manner. If the issue does not resolve, then escalation may be a necessary next step.

126. D. Scrumban is a hybrid methodology that combines Scrum and Kanban. The idea is that the work is organized in sprints, as in traditional Scrum, but uses a Kanban board to display the work of the sprint and monitor work in progress.

127. D. There are five levels of classification of stakeholder engagement: unaware, resistant, neutral, supportive, and leading. A stakeholder that is neutral is neither supporting nor resisting the project and may be minimally engaged.

128. D. Maslow's Hierarchy of Needs suggests that once a lower-level need has been met, it no longer serves as a motivator, and the next higher level becomes the driving motivator in an individual's life. A person goes up and down the pyramid, depending on what they are experiencing in their life. The lowest level is basic physical needs (shelter, clothing, food), followed by safety and security, social needs, self-esteem needs, and self-actualization.

129. C. The SV for this project is –25, which means the project is behind schedule. The CV for this project is 50, which means the costs are lower than what you had planned for this point in time.

130. A, B. The Five-Factor Model, also known as the Big Five personality traits, is a personality survey that identifies five broad dimensions used to describe an individual's personality. The five factors are openness to experience, conscientiousness, extraversion, agreeableness, and neuroticism.

131. D. Enterprise environmental factors are defined as those factors that are internal and external to the organization that can influence the project. Examples include marketplace conditions, federal regulations, and the organization's culture and structure.

132. C. The team is using bottom-up estimating. This technique estimates costs associated with every activity individually and then rolls them up to derive either a more accurate activity-level estimate or a total project estimate.

133. A. The stakeholder register is the project artifact where information about identified stakeholders is captured. The stakeholder register typically includes identification information, assessment information, and stakeholder classification.

134. B, C, D. The stakeholder register contains the identified stakeholders and information about them. This includes identification information, assessment information, and stakeholder classification. The team ground rules are captured within the team charter.

135. E. According to the *PMBOK® Guide*, activities associated with Project Resource Management should be tailored to the unique needs of the project and organization, including diversity of the team, physical location of team members, industry-specific resources needed, acquisition of team members, management of the team, and life cycle approaches used.

136. D. Team-building activities help increase collaboration and cooperation within the working environment. These types of activities also help team members bond and build social relationships that help them work more effectively together, creating a win-win situation.

137. A. Screening systems use predefined performance criteria or a set of defined minimum requirements to screen out unsuitable vendors.

138. C. When projects end prematurely, the Validate Scope process is where the level of detail concerning the amount of work completed should be documented.

139. A, B, D. The underlying success factors in forming effective Agile teams are building a foundational trust and safe working environment, as well as an Agile mindset.

140. A. Culture can be considered by examining organizational bias. This relates to the values and preferences that characterize the organization and its culture. According to the *Agile Practice Guide*, the biases include exploring versus executing, speed versus stability, quality versus quantity, and flexibility versus predictability.

141. C. Tailoring is often a way to address obstacles and blockers for teams looking to adopt more Agile practices. When Agile terms and language do not fit the organizational norms, one way to overcome it is by modifying the terms so that team members understand and agree to the activities. To be successful, teams should clearly define terms in order to align with the meaning.

142. A. Low-priority risks are added to a watch list within the risk register, where they will be monitored for possible changes.

143. C. The schedule management plan documents the method and approach for developing, managing, and controlling the project schedule.

144. C. Jenny used the directing conflict resolution technique, also known as forcing. Directing is where one pushes their own viewpoint at the expense of others. In this scenario, Jenny did not fully acknowledge or recognize Bob's concerns and opinions about user story #2. This is considered to be a win-lose situation.

145. B. Cost variance tells you whether costs are above or below what was planned for this period and are calculated by subtracting AC from EV. In this case, the formula looks like this: $95 − $100 = −$5. The resulting number is negative, which means the project costs are lower than what was planned for this time period.

146. D. The business analyst and the project manager have carried out activities relating to the following processes: Collect Requirements, Define Scope, and Create WBS. These processes belong to the Project Scope Management Knowledge Area. Project Requirements Management is not an official Knowledge Area.

147. B, C, D. Project governance frameworks address governance at the project versus organizational level. According to the *PMBOK® Guide*, project governance is the framework, functions, and processes that guide project management activities to create a unique product, service, or result to meet intended goals.

148. D. The team charter is also referred to as the team's social contract. In addition to ground rules, this agreement captures team values, working agreements, and group norms. Ideally, the team formulates this together.

149. C. All of the options listed are benefits of using virtual teams. In this scenario, the team is lacking in the technical knowledge required to complete the set of features. Broadening the resource pool to include virtual team members increases the likelihood that the right skill set will be acquired.

150. B. This question references the Manage Communications process, which is responsible for ensuring the timely distribution of project information. Project management plan, project documents, work performance reports, enterprise environmental factors, and organizational process assets are all inputs of the process. The remaining options presented are tools and techniques of the process, not inputs.

151. B. Schedule network analysis is a tool and technique of the Develop Schedule process that's used in conjunction with other tools and techniques, including the critical path method, to produce the project schedule.

152. A-1, B-2, C-2, D-1, E-1. The resource management plan captures how resources will be categorized, allocated, managed, and released. The team charter captures and documents the guidelines for how the team will operate together, and it also captures the team values and agreements.

153. B. The risk report contains a summary of identified project risks and sources of overall project risk.

154. A. Change control systems are a subset of the configuration management system. Configuration management systems are a subset of the project management information system.

155. D. The final report is created as a result of carrying out activities associated with the Close Project or Phase process. This project artifact summarizes the performance of the project or phase and generally captures the following: summary description of the project or phase, performance against scope/quality/cost/schedule objectives, summary of validation information about the work completed, summary of risks or issues encountered, and summary of whether the end result produced by the project satisfies the business needs that the project was addressing.

156. E. The role of project manager within Agile practices continues to be debated. According to the *Agile Practice Guide*, the project manager role is sometimes called a team facilitator, team coach, Scrum master, or project team lead.

157. A, D. The adoption of Agile practices begins by embracing an Agile mindset. According to the *Agile Practice Guide*, project teams looking to adopt Agile can ask themselves the following questions while developing an implementation strategy: How can the project team act in an Agile manner? What can the team deliver quickly and obtain early feedback about to benefit the next delivery cycle? How can the team act in a transparent manner? What work can be avoided in order to focus on high-priority items? How can a servant-leadership approach benefit the achievement of the team's goals?

158. A, C, D. According to the *Agile Practice Guide*, a servant leader maintains the following characteristics: promote self-awareness; listen; serve those on the team; help others grow; coach versus control; promote safety, respect, and trust; and promote the energy and intelligence of others. This type of style is often used in environments that have adopted Agile practices.

159. B. Common causes of variances are the result of random variances, known or predictable variances, or variances that are always present in the process.

160. C. The formula for ETC when variances are expected to continue is ETC = (BAC − EV) ÷ CPI. First you need to calculate CPI, which is $925 ÷ $925 = $1. Now you can plug in the numbers: ($1,400 − $925) ÷ 1 = $475.

161. A, C, D. Conflict management, decision-making, emotional intelligence, influencing, and leadership are all examples of interpersonal and team skills that a project manager should use to manage a team.

162. B. According to the *Agile Practice Guide*, the burndown chart refers to a graphical representation of the work remaining versus the time left in a timebox.

163. D. Inspection may involve a simple or physical review of the work performed by a contractor. It is structured in nature and is meant to ensure that a mutual understanding exists of the work in progress.

164. A. Deliverables are an input, not an output, of the Manage Project Knowledge process. The remaining options all represent outputs of the process.

165. B. Generally, Agile practices create a culture of transparency. Participating in peer-coding activities, sharing interim deliverables, and revealing failures can be intimidating and frightening for some team members who prefer to perfect their work before releasing it. In this situation, the best approach is to lead by example and demonstrate transparency when making decisions. This will eventually create a feeling of safety and comfort.

166. B. According to the *PMBOK® Guide*, the change log is a comprehensive list of changes submitted during the project and their current status. It captures corrective actions, preventive actions, or defect repair needed. The change log becomes a key document managed as part of the Perform Integrated Change Control process, where change requests are reviewed and a decision on the request is made.

167. C. The Tuckman ladder, also referred to as stages of team development, consists of five stages that teams may go through: forming, storming, norming, performing, and adjourning. In the forming phase, team members do not know each other well and are learning about the project and their roles.

168. E. There are several technical practices that can help teams deliver at maximum speed, several of which come from eXtreme Programming. Examples include continuous integration, test at all levels, acceptance test-driven development, test-driven development and behavior-driven development, and spikes.

169. D. The communications management plan describes how communication throughout the project will be planned, structured, implemented, and monitored for effectiveness. It is a component of the broader project management plan. One of the elements captured within the communications management plan includes the escalation processes.

170. A. Stakeholders have the greatest amount of influence during the early stages of a project's life cycle.

171. A-4, B-1, C-2, D-3. Project managers and other leaders use power to convince others to do tasks in a specific way. The kind of power used depends on their personality, their personal values, and the company culture.

172. D. Earned value management is a performance measurement method. Forecasting is not a performance measurement method. Variance analysis and trend analysis are types of performance review.

173. B. The team is engaged in backlog refinement activities. This encompasses working with the team to prepare stories for the upcoming iteration. Stories should contain sufficient detail for the team to understand the scope of work and how large they are in relation to each other.

174. B, C. The team charter captures and documents the guidelines for how the team will operate together, and it also captures the team values and agreements. Examples of elements addressed in the team charter include team values, communication guidelines, decision-making criteria and process, conflict resolution process, meeting guidelines, and team agreements. The roles and responsibilities and process for acquiring team members are captured within the resource management plan.

175. A, B. A highly predictive (waterfall) life cycle typically has detailed specifications, with requirements defined up front before work begins. A highly adaptive life cycle (Agile) has requirements that are progressively elaborated on, and delivery occurs frequently. Change within a predictive life cycle is constrained, while adaptive encourages change to be incorporated in real time during delivery.

176. D. According to the *Agile Practice Guide*, team members who are not dedicated to an Agile team and who must context switch between tasks lose on average 20 percent to 40 percent productivity.

177. D. According to the *PMBOK® Guide*, corrective action is an intentional activity that realigns the performance of the project work with the project management plan; in other words, it's work that brings the project back in line with the plan.

178. C. The lessons learned register is typically created early on within the project's life and updated at various points throughout the project (i.e., end of a phase). At the end of the project, a final lessons learned session is held to capture information, which will then be archived for future reference.

179. C. Colocation brings team members together in one physical location for the duration of the project or for critical points during the project life cycle. A war room is an example of colocation where team members work in a common meeting room.

180. A. This question lists all the outputs of the Manage Stakeholder Engagement process. The issue log is used more like an action item log in this process.

181. A. The Tuckman ladder, also referred to as stages of team development, consists of five stages that teams may go through: forming, storming, norming, performing, and adjourning. In the norming stage, the team members have come to know each other well and are focused on confronting project concerns versus each other.

182. B, C, D. Burnup charts, burndown charts, lead time, and cycle time provide useful in-the-moment measurements, providing insight into capacity measures and predictability measures. These types of measurements can provide the team with an understanding of how much more work they have and whether they will finish on time.

183. A, C. In this scenario, you are using the eXtreme Programming (XP) approach, which is an adaptive approach to managing projects. XP delivers business value in each iteration and starts with creating story cards. Story cards are like user stories and contain requirements, features, and functionality. The story cards are designed in an incremental fashion. Pair programming involves two developers working on code together.

184. A-3, B-4, C-1, D-2, E-5. There are several motivational theories developed by well-known theorists who explain how individuals are motivated and why they may feel or behave in certain ways.

185. A. The risk register contains the list of risks captured and information about them, such as risk owners, risk triggers, risk response plans.

186. C. Adaptive life cycles are also known as Agile or change-driven life cycles.

187. D. Osmotic communication is a form of polite eavesdropping and is used within the Crystal methodology. It occurs when there are conversations going on in the background but within earshot of the team. Team members overhear conversations and may realize the topic has importance to the project.

188. B. Variance at completion is calculated this way: BAC – EAC.

189. E. Inbound competencies refer to self-management and self-awareness, while outbound competencies refer to relationship management.

190. B. The minimum viable product (MVP) is used to increase the speed of delivery and obtain feedback on a product early. The product contains just enough features or deliverables to obtain feedback; this feedback can then be used for future incremental development of the product.

191. A, C, D. The incremental life cycle approach delivers completed functionality or deliverables at the end of the iteration that the product owner can use immediately. The sponsors or customers are therefore able to gain value more often rather than waiting until the end of the project. This approach is optimized for speed of delivery, releasing a subset of the overall solution as a way of gaining feedback and a better understanding of the requirements.

192. A-3, B-2, C-1, D-5, E-4. The Five-Factor Model, also known as the Big Five personality traits, is a personality survey that identifies five broad dimensions used to describe an individual's personality. The five factors are openness to experience, conscientiousness, extraversion, agreeableness, and neuroticism.

193. D. A charismatic leader is someone who leads by inspiring followers; they create high energy around them and tend to hold strong convictions.

194. A. There are three common roles used in Agile teams: cross-functional team member, product owner, and team facilitator.

195. B. According to the *Agile Practice Guide*, definition of done (DoD) refers to a team's checklist of all the criteria required to be met so that a deliverable can be considered ready for customer use. Acceptance criteria refers to a set of conditions that must be met before deliverables are accepted.

196. B. The minimum viable product (MVP) is used to increase the speed of delivery and obtain feedback of a product early. MVP can satisfy early adopters by making a version of the product available and then use the feedback for future incremental development of the product.

197. A. Agile promotes frequent and transparent communication, particularly when the project environment is subject to ambiguity and/or change. This concept applies to the handling of project artifacts as well. According to the *Agile Practice Guide*, project artifacts should be posted in a transparent manner, with regular stakeholder reviews held to promote communication among stakeholders.

198. D. Configuration status accounting is an activity that is associated with the configuration management system. This activity documents and stores the status of changes and the information needed to effectively manage product information.

199. D. Within Agile there is a concept that describes the degree to which individuals can take on work, according to their depth and breadth. "T" shaped people are considered generalizing specialists who have expertise in an area but can also contribute to other areas. "I" shaped people refers to those who have deep specialization in one domain and rarely contribute to work outside of that domain.

200. B. Data analysis is the only tool and technique of the Control Scope process.

Chapter 6: Full-Length Practice Exam 3

1. B. Expected value can be calculated using a triangular distribution (simple average) or beta distribution (weighted average). The three-point estimating formula that uses a beta distribution is as follows: (Optimistic + Pessimistic + (4 × Most Likely)) ÷ 6. Plug in the values provided to calculate the following: ($25 + $50 + ($35 × 4)) ÷ 6 = $35.8, or 36 when rounded to the nearest whole number.

2. D. Iterative life cycles focus on correctness of solution. For this reason, stakeholder feedback is obtained early and often, such as through prototypes, so that changes can be incorporated into the solution based on feedback and insights received.

3. A. The Expectancy Theory states that employees who believe that more effort will lead to better performance, which will then lead to rewards that they personally value, will continue to be productive. This is a conscious choice; otherwise, if they don't value the rewards, their incentive to be productive is lost.

4. B. Outputs of the Define Activities process include the activity list, activity attributers, milestone list, change requests, and project management plan updates. The question has already indicated that the activity list has already been created, and the milestone list is the only viable option.

5. C. Team-building activities increase team collaboration and social relationships, as well as foster a cooperative working environment. A team benefits from continuous team-building activities throughout the life of the project; it is particularly important during the early stages of a project, when relationships among team members are not yet developed.

6. C. The Determine Budget process establishes the cost baseline for the project and is an output of this process.

7. B. All of the options listed are types of communication. When dealing with complex issues, it is best to use a written format that is formal. Formal written is also the best choice when working with other cultures, communicating over long distances, updating a plan, or dealing with legal matters.

8. B. While the risk management plan covers the details of risk-related reports and formats, it does not cover all of the communication requirements of project stakeholders. This is addressed within the communications management plan.

9. A. While several benefits to virtual teams are included within the various options, this particular project requires a specialized skill set. Since virtual teams widen the resource pool available, with team members potentially located across the globe, it allows for this unique resource need to be met. Without the use of virtual teams, the project may not have been possible, or it may have been very costly due to relocating team members or frequent travel.

10. A, B, D. Daily stand-ups encourage the team to remain self-organized and hold each other accountable for completing work that they have committed to. Whereas iteration-based Agile focuses on accountability, flow-based Agile focuses on the team's throughput.

11. C. Philip Crosby believed that quality is achieved when zero defects are present, and if a defect is present and considered acceptable, then the requirements should be altered to reflect this fact.

12. A, C. Knowledge can be split into explicit and tacit knowledge. Explicit knowledge can be captured and expressed using words, pictures, and numbers; tacit knowledge is more difficult to capture or express, such as beliefs, experiences, and "know-how."

13. D. Level of accuracy describes your rounding precision, and units of measure describes how you will measure resources, for example, days, weeks, months.

14. D. You are currently performing activities associated with the Control Schedule process, which is part of the Monitoring and Controlling process group.

15. B, C, D. There are various Agile suitability filters and/or models available that help determine whether an organization would benefit from adopting Agile approaches. A broad model presented within the *Agile Practice Guide* assesses organizations against three categories: culture (i.e., does the environment support the approach?), team (i.e., is the team of a suitable size?), and project (i.e., are there high rates of change?).

16. C. Internal rate of return is when the present value of the cash inflows equals the original investment; payback period refers to the number of periods (in this case months) that must pass before the initial investment is recouped. While both Project X and Project Revolution have an IRR of 3 percent, project revolution has a shorter payback period.

17. C. Transformational is a form of leadership style where the leader encourages the ideas of others, innovation, and creativity.

18. B. The WBS serves as the basis for estimating costs. It is an input to the Estimate Costs process through the scope baseline, which is part of the project management plan. It contains all the project deliverables and the control accounts associated with work package elements.

19. A, D. While Agile teams vary, typical characteristics include the following: they range in size from three to nine team members, they are colocated, and they are 100 percent dedicated to the team.

20. B. The Five-Factor Model, also known as the Big Five personality traits, is a personality survey that identifies five broad dimensions used to describe an individual's personality. The five factors are openness to experience, conscientiousness, extraversion, agreeableness, and neuroticism. The conscientiousness domain measures where individuals fall on the spectrum of efficient versus careless.

21. A. Prototypes allow for early feedback on the requirements for further refinement and clarification. They are a technique used as part of the Collect Requirements process.

22. D. You are carrying out the Create WBS process. The purpose of the process is to subdivide the project deliverables and project work into smaller, more manageable components.

23. B. Kanban is an agile approach that is often used in manufacturing projects but also makes a presence in the information technology field. Using Kanban, the work is balanced against available resources or available capacity for work. It's a pull-based concept where work progresses to the next step only when resources are available.

24. C. The formula for calculating expected monetary value is probability times impact. Plug in the values to get the following: $10\% \times \$4,000 = \$400$.

25. A-1, B-5, C-3, D-2, E-4. There are several Agile-based approaches that follow iterative or flow-based Agile methods. In addition to the various flavors of Agile, hybrid approaches also exist, such as Scrumban (a combination of Kanban and Scrum).

26. B. The Determine Budget process yields the cost baseline, project funding requirements, and updates to project documents. The project funding requirements represent the total funding requirements and periodic funding requirements of the project.

27. A, B, D. The organizational breakdown structure, bill of materials, risk breakdown structure, and resource breakdown structure all present project information in a hierarchical fashion. The resource assignment matrix does not.

28. B. The quality management plan may describe measurements that fall within a specified range. These are called *tolerable results*.

29. B. The project manager has told the scheduler that the schedule must be compressed by one week. That means that we will use one of two schedule compression techniques: crashing or fast-tracking, both of which are options. When possible, select the lowest-cost option first, which would be fast-tracking.

30. B. If the team maintains a velocity of 60 story points per iteration, it would take seven iterations to complete the remaining 420 story points.

31. A, B, C. Servant leaders engage the team and take on a selfless view by serving others. They do this by approaching their work in the following order: purpose, people, and process.

32. C. Cost baselines and schedule baselines are used to measure performance in the Executing and Monitoring and Controlling processes.

33. A, B, C. The probability and impact matrix is not an input to the Perform Quantitative Risk Analysis process. It is used to prioritize risks, it's defined in the risk management plan, and it's used as a tool and technique in the Perform Qualitative Risk Analysis process.

34. C. The correct answer is that inspection keeps errors from reaching the customer, while prevention prevents errors from occurring.

35. D. A burndown chart is used to track the remaining work to be completed against the backlog. It shows work completed to date by iteration and the forecasted rate at which the team will complete the remaining work over the remaining iterations, based on velocity.

36. B. Requirements are documented through user stories that make up the backlog. The user stories are then prioritized and refined.

37. C. The project budget includes the cost baseline. Option C has it backward.

38. C. To calculate the critical path, you must first draw out the network diagram and then add the duration of each activity that falls within the individual network paths. Figure 6.1 shows the network diagram and the three network paths that exist within it. The following is the duration of each of those paths: A-B-D-F = 17, A-C-D-F = 19, A-C-E-F = 21.

FIGURE 6.1   Network diagram: critical path

39. C. To calculate the early finish of activity D, you would first need to perform a forward pass. To calculate forward pass, draw the network diagram and then follow these steps:

1.   Begin with the first activity.

2.   The calculation of the first activity begins with an early start date of 1. Add the duration of the activity and then subtract 1 to determine the early finish. This is based on the concept of calendar days.

3.   The early start date of the next activity is the early finish date of the previous activity plus 1. Continue calculating the early start and early finish dates forward through all the network paths while following the existing dependencies.

4.   When an activity has two connecting predecessors, the early start date would be the early finish of the predecessor that finishes last, plus 1.

Figure 6.2 shows the network diagram with early start and early finish dates calculated.

FIGURE 6.2   Network diagram: forward pass

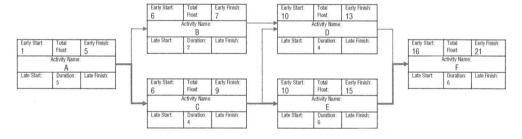

40. A. To calculate the late start of activity C, you would first need to perform a forward pass and a backward pass. To calculate backward pass, draw the network diagram and perform a forward pass and then follow these steps:

1.   Begin with the last activity. The late finish will be the same as the early finish date.

2.   Subtract the duration of the activity from the end date and add 1 to calculate late start. Take this number and subtract 1 to calculate the late finish of its predecessors.

3. Continue calculating the latest start and latest finish dates, moving backward through all the network paths.

4. When an activity has two connecting predecessors, the late finish date would be the late start minus 1 of the activity that follows.

Figure 6.3 shows the network diagram with early start and early finish dates calculated.

FIGURE 6.3   Network diagram: backward pass

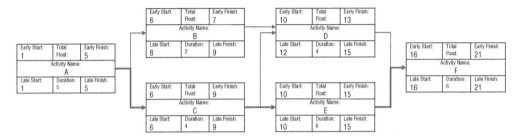

41. A. Total float refers to the amount of time you can delay the earliest start of an activity without delaying the ending of the project. To calculate total float, you would first need to draw the network diagram and then perform a forward pass and a backward pass. Next, subtract either the early start from the late start or the early finish from the late finish (both should give you the same answer). Figure 6.4 shows the network diagram with total float calculated.

FIGURE 6.4   Network diagram: float

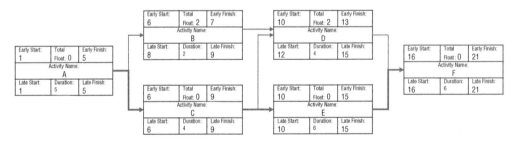

42. A, B, D. Agile PMOs guide the organization in achieving business value. There are multiple types of PMOs; an Agile PMO is value-driven, invitation-oriented, and multidisciplinary.

43. A. Resource leveling involves leveling out resource usage to resolve over-allocation of resources and/or to level out the peaks and valleys of resource usage over time.

44. D. According to the *Agile Practice Guide*, the role of a servant leader is to facilitate the team's discovery and definition of Agile.

45. B. The analogous estimating technique is a form of expert judgment, which uses the actual duration of a similar activity completed on a previous project to determine the duration of the current activity. This means that Alyssa would rely on feedback from the subject-matter expert who noted that in a past similar project it took 13 hours to complete a similar activity.

46. A, C, D. The Plan Procurement Management process can influence the project schedule (and vice versa). The Estimate Activity Resources process, make-or-buy decisions, and the organization's business cycle may have an impact on the Plan Procurement Management process.

47. C. Based on the activities Marysil has already carried out, the next logical step would be to begin implementing the risk responses based on plans documented in the risk register. While some risk responses are implemented when risk triggers occur, others are implemented immediately to avoid or exploit a risk.

48. C. Based on the performance indexes provided, the project is 10 percent ahead of schedule but over budget. Leveling out resource usage is a strategy used to spread out costs over time. This helps in reducing sudden spikes in spending, although it may lead to lengthening the schedule.

49. A, C, D. There are four primary events used by Scrum teams: sprint planning, daily scrum (versus weekly), sprint review, and sprint retrospective.

50. D. Parametric estimating is a quantitatively based estimating method that multiplies the quantity of work by the rate or uses an algorithm in conjunction with historical data to determine cost, budget, or duration estimates. Based on this definition, take 1,320 and divide by 110 to get 12.

51. C. The to-complete performance index (TCPI) is the projected cost performance the remaining work of the project must achieve in order to meet the BAC or EAC.

52. C. There are five types of power that a project manager can utilize. These include formal, reward, penalty, expert, and referent. The question asks for the one that is based on the respect or admiration that others hold for an individual, which is referent power.

53. B, C, D. Only the Arrow Diagramming Method (ADM) uses dummy activities, which are not real activities but instead are meant to show that a relationship between two activities exists. All other statements are accurate.

54. A, D. According to the *PMBOK® Guide*, there are four common project life cycles: predictive, iterative, incremental, and Agile. Hybrid refers to a combination of two or more life cycles.

55. D. The project charter is generated at the start of a project. Before we can move forward in planning or building out the backlog of the project, there is one key activity that a project manager should perform at the start of a project—building out the stakeholder register. This is created as a result of performing stakeholder analysis.

56. C. A CPI of greater than 1 is performing under budget; an SPI of less than 1 is performing behind schedule. Remember that generally an index > 1 is good, an index = 1 is perfect, and an index of < 1 is bad.

57. B. Independent peer review is the correct answer. This type of review ensures that the concepts, the designs, and the tests that are utilized at the beginning of the project were good choices.

58. A. Agile teams often create a team charter as a way of creating a social contract for the team. The team charter identifies team norms and an understanding of how the team is to work together. This social contract captures team values, working agreements, ground rules, and group norms.

59. F. Servant leaders enable teams to be more Agile and play the important role of facilitating the team's success. According to the *Agile Practice Guide*, characteristics of a servant leader include promoting self-awareness, listening, serving the team, helping others grow, coaching versus controlling, promoting safety/respect/trust, and promoting the energy and intelligence of others.

60. C. The matrix diagrams tool includes two-dimensional and three-dimensional diagrams. It is a part of the data representation tools and techniques of the Manage Quality process.

61. C. Halo effect is when a person's strong traits are perceived as an indication of another trait. In this example, it is thought that because Jon is good at his job, he must therefore be a good project manager. But the job of a research technician has different required skills than the job of a project manager. The most common example given is that an attractive person, such as a celebrity, must be intelligent, which is why they are often used in advertising.

62. D. At this point, pre-assignments is a technique already used, and the issue is that a key resource was not pre-assigned and is now unavailable. The best option would be to negotiate with the project managers of the other two projects, along with the resource's functional manager, to open up availability for participation in the project in question. Acquisition may be a potential option, but not until negotiation has been attempted.

63. B. Specification limits and assignable cause are related to control charts and are therefore not the correct answers; trend analysis relates to run chart, also not the answer. That leaves the 80/20 rule, also known as Pareto's Law or the Pareto Principle, which states that 80 percent of problems result from 20 percent of causes. This is exactly what the project manager in this scenario is looking for.

64. A. Incremental life cycles focus on speed through frequent smaller deliveries. This supports a project with dynamic requirements that allow the project team to hand over completed deliverables to the customer that can be used immediately. Other options refer to predictive, iterative, and Agile life cycles.

65. B. Only "formal written" and "informal written" are communication types. Email can be considered to be a formal or informal way of communicating, depending on the contents. In the context of the scenario presented, email is considered to be informal.

66. A, B, D. Risks on a watch list are low-priority risks that are determined to contain a minimal amount of threat but that should be monitored regularly for a change of status as the project moves forward. All other statements are true.

67. B, E. While all options may have contributed to the project issues, a poorly written scope can quickly result in project failure, no matter how good the change control procedures or systems are. A lack of formal project management may have contributed as well but being certified does not guarantee that this type of scenario will not occur. The scope baseline is often used for change control purposes and in making project decisions, which is why a poorly written scope will result in a large number of project changes for projects managed using a predictive life-cycle approach. Given that the project contained high ambiguity, issues may have been reduced by using an adaptive or hybrid life-cycle approach.

68. A. Negotiation is a common technique used by project managers to acquire resources for a project. Ideally, the project manager would have first approached the director of engineering for approval, but at this stage, the best option was to attempt to negotiate with the resource's manager. The project sponsor should not get involved in cases like this unless it is detrimental to the project.

69. B. The best choice is to note the issue within the issue log. The reason for this is that an owner can then be assigned to the issue, and a target resolution date set. This allows for more structured and documented resolution. The issue log is also something that will be archived at a later date within the project files.

70. E. While retrospectives are often held at the conclusion of an iteration or increment, teams can facilitate retrospectives at various key points in a project to gain benefits. This includes situations where the team does not feel that the work is flowing well. While teams are not necessarily limited as to when retrospectives are held, they are typically used after the project work begins.

71. B. Observation and conversation is a technique from the Manage Team process and describes a way for the project manager to monitor the team's progress, accomplishments, and interpersonal issues, and it is therefore the correct answer. 360-degree feedback is a type of project performance appraisal, where feedback is received from all levels of interaction with a team member. This provides information about a team member, but not from the team member themselves. Issue log tracks issues so is not relevant here, and team-building activities seems like a good choice, except that the purpose is to grow relationships among the team, with a focus on establishing cohesiveness, not assessing work attitudes.

72. A. To solve a decision tree, calculate the expected monetary value of each scenario. Expected monetary value can be calculated by multiplying the impact by the probability. Scenario A has a potential implication of –$1,250, and scenario B has a potential implication of –$2,275. Therefore, scenario A is the best choice.

73. D. Knowledge can be split into two types: explicit or tacit. Explicit knowledge can be captured and expressed using words, pictures, and numbers; tacit knowledge is more difficult to capture or express, such as beliefs, experiences, and "know-how."

74. D. The project manager is using the Stacey Complexity Model to plot the degree of certainty about the complexity elements, such as requirements, technical challenges, or team skills. The degrees are measured as low uncertainty or agreement to high uncertainty or lack of agreement. Projects that fall within the complicated and complex quadrants are best suited for Adaptive approaches, while projects that fall within the simple quadrant are best suited for predictive/linear approaches.

75. B. The project charter is typically signed off by the project's sponsor, who is responsible for approving the project. In this case, Nicolas is identified as the sponsor and is therefore the correct answer.

76. B. The concept of continuous improvement centers around the idea that small or incremental improvements within a product or process has the ability to reduce cost and keep consistency of performance. The word *kaizen* in Japan translates to "change for the better."

77. C. The question refers to a key input of the Direct and Manage Project Work process, which is a process that provides overall management of the project work and deliverables. While several inputs are important, without the approved change requests, you cannot complete the activities referenced in the question.

78. B. A retrospective is similar to a lessons learned session in that the team learns from previous work. Retrospectives are a way for Agile teams to learn about and improve the process. Oftentimes, teams will commit to improving one item during the next iteration.

79. D. Interpersonal skills are used by the project manager to build trust, resolve conflict, actively listen to stakeholders, and overcome resistance to change. It is a technique used by the Manage Stakeholder Engagement, Develop Project Team, and Manage Project Team processes.

80. D. A team charter is also referred to as a social contract. This document captures how team members are to interact with one another, including their ground rules, group norms, working agreements, and team values.

81. A. As a project manager, it is your responsibility to contribute to the project management knowledge base, which includes educating others on project management practices. Independent estimates is a tool and technique of the Plan Procurement Management.

82. D. Data analysis is a tool and technique of the Estimate Costs process. There are several techniques that are part of data analysis, such as alternatives analysis. Other techniques include reserve analysis and cost of quality.

83. A. To calculate CPI, use the following formula: $CPI = EV \div AC$. Plug in the values to calculate the following: $1,700 \div 1,950 = 0.87$. A CPI of less than 1 means that the project is performing over budget.

84. C. The transfer strategy involves the transfer of a risk to a third party. In this case, the third party manages and takes responsibility for the risk. Insurance is one example of risk transference.

85. C. Sensitivity analysis determines which risks have the most potential impact on the project and utilizes tornado diagrams. This type of diagram compares the importance of variables that have a high degree of uncertainty to the more stable variables.

86. A-5, B-2, C-1, D-3, E-4. There are five types of conflict resolution technique: withdraw/avoid, smooth/accommodate, compromise/reconcile, force/direct, collaborate/problem-solve.

87. C. This statement describes virtual teams. Virtual teams consist of individuals who are dispersed across various locations and interact primarily through technology, such as video conference, online, chat, telephone, etc. There is minimal to no face time. Colocation is the exact opposite, where team members are physically located in the same place.

88. B. The power/interest grid groups stakeholders based on their level of authority, a reference to power, and, by level of concern, a reference to interest.

89. A. Kaylee has just performed the Implement Risk Responses process and is likely to carry out activities associated with the Monitor Risks process next. Risk audits are a tool and technique used to evaluate the effectiveness of risk responses that have been implemented, and typically occur either through risk review meetings or through dedicated risk audit meetings.

90. A. The question is asking for the most common source of conflict. The correct answer is scarce resources. The other common sources of conflict include scheduling priorities and personal work styles.

91. D. The project is not officially considered to be complete until the customer or buyer signs off. This is a mistake many companies make, which leaves the door open for further requests or conflict as to whether the project was really completed. Formal closure addresses it directly by obtaining agreement from the customer that the deliverables and scope have indeed been met.

92. E. The Agile Manifesto lists four values: individuals and interactions over processes and tools, working software over comprehensive documentation, customer collaboration over contract negotiation, and responding to change over following a plan.

93. B, C, D. The resource management plan describes when and how resource requirements will be met. It addresses things such as staff acquisition, timetable of when the team will be acquired, release criteria, training needs, recognition and rewards, compliance, and safety. It doesn't, however, define the roles and responsibilities, which is a separate output of the human resource management planning process.

94. B. The communications management plan offers the who, what, where, why, and when of communications and reporting. This plan should contain the detailed information of when the report in question is scheduled for distribution.

95. A. Noise is defined as anything that may interfere with getting or receiving the message (such as static). Only noise and medium were official terms provided within the four options, according to the basic model of communication.

96. B. Under organizational process assets, the project management team utilizes the policies, procedures, guidelines, and management systems that pertain to procurement. It's important to understand how the company currently conducts procurement activities, which will aid the project team in compiling a good procurement management plan.

97. C. All options provided are forms of probability distribution. The most commonly used probability distributions are beta distributions and triangular distributions. Since beta is the only one of the two included as an option, it is the best choice.

98. C. Cost-reimbursable, also known as cost plus, is a contract type where the buyer agrees to pay the seller for all actual costs incurred in completing the work, plus an additional amount. Some cost plus contracts pay an additional fixed fee, while others pay an additional award fee or incentive fee. The buyer is the one with the highest risk, since they may have little control over the seller's spending.

99. D. Templates are stored within the organizational process assets. When using templates from previous similar projects, the project manager can create a consistency of results, such as by using portions of activity lists or network diagrams, thereby making more efficient use of their time. It also allows for improved results.

100. C. The project manager is using the Stacey Complexity Model to plot the degree of certainty about the complexity elements, such as requirements, technical challenges, or team skills. This model displays levels of uncertainty from low to high on both the x- and y-axes, or it may show levels of uncertainty on the x-axis and agreement levels on the y-axis. This two-dimensional model shows the progression of the certainty and agreement of complexity elements, which are plotted into categories such as simple or chaotic.

101. D. A fishbowl window is a method of creating a shared virtual workspace to accommodate team members who are dispersed across multiple locations. Individuals can join a live video stream at the start of their workday and close it out at the end of the workday. This method is intended to increase collaboration.

102. C. The sender, who initiated the communication, is the project team member; the receiver of the information is the project manager.

103. D. Notice that Sally took in the facts and made a choice on the spot, without listening to the two-team members or attempting to discuss the choices. This type of conflict resolution technique is known as forcing, where one person makes a decision without taking into account others' feedback. Forcing is also known as directing.

104. D. A RACI is a type of responsibility assignment matrix (RAM), and it stands for responsible, accountable, consult, and inform.

105. B. The answer is cost of conformance to requirements. While quality works toward preventing rework and providing better customer satisfaction, these are results of conforming to the project requirements.

106. B. Pre-assignments occur when individuals have been promised as part of a contract to a customer, or they have been assigned as early as the project charter. In either case, the resource has officially been committed to the project.

107. D. The question provides examples of project management information systems, which is a tool and technique of the Manage Communications process. Information systems are tools used to facilitate communication.

108. F. Projects may follow different project life cycles, depending on the organization and unique needs of the project. According to the *PMBOK® Guide*, typical projects can be mapped to a generic project life-cycle structure: starting the project, organizing and preparing, carrying out the work, and closing the project.

109. A. When managing a project, you should always be aware of the local laws affecting the project, as well as the political climate. By being aware of the political climate, the project team would have planned and taken preventive actions. The question is not necessarily asking you how to avoid the rally but, instead, how to prevent it from affecting the project.

110. D. Gold plating is a term often tied to quality. It involves giving customers extras that are not included in the project scope, meaning that it is a form of scope creep. This can include things like extra features, increasing performance, and adjusting components.

111. C. There are four primary items that the process improvement plan contains: process boundaries, process configuration, process metrics, and targets for improved performance. Therefore, failure rate is the correct answer.

112. D. According to the *PMBOK® Guide*, the 100 percent rule refers to the work breakdown structure including all of the work of the project. The WBS therefore represents all of the product and project work, which can be best described as the scope of the project.

113. D. Mitigation reduces the probability and/or the impact of a risk. Other options describe the transfer, avoid, and enhance strategies.

114. D. According to the *PMBOK® Guide*, business value is defined as the net quantifiable benefit derived from a business endeavor. Benefits may be both tangible and intangible.

115. A. A fixed-price contract, also known as lump sum, is where the seller provides an estimate for the work, negotiates with the buyer, and commits to doing the work at that price. The seller has the greatest risk, because if the estimate was not good, they may end up with little to no profit.

116. C. The question is asking for the project team to get to all the possible causes. There are a few potential answers, but based on the question and options provided, a cause-and-effect diagram is the best choice. This is the diagram that resembles a fishbone and shows how various factors can be connected to potential problems.

117. A. All of the options included are risk attitudes. The names of the risk attitudes are fairly descriptive, making them easy to understand at face value.

118. B. RACI stands for responsible, accountable, consult, and inform. The chart identifies Alfred as being responsible for the Research activity, making him the correct answer. Responsible indicates who will be performing the work.

119. C. A team performance assessment has a goal of increasing the team's performance, while project performance appraisals are feedback given directly to project team members. Team performance assessments are an output of the Develop Project Team process.

120. F. A team charter serves as a type of social contract for the team. According to the *Agile Practice Guide*, the team charter captures team values, working agreements, ground rules, and group norms.

121. C. An influence/impact grid can be split into four quadrants, where stakeholders will be plotted against according to their level of influence and impact. Stakeholders with low influence/low impact are likely to be monitored; stakeholders with high influence/low impact will likely be kept satisfied; stakeholders with low influence/high impact are likely to be kept informed; and stakeholders with high influence/high impact are likely to be managed closely. Tony falls in the latter of the options stated.

122. C. This is a great example of where multiple options appear correct. For example, you can argue that option A is correct, since the description fits a project. However, the best answer is that it is a program. A program is defined as a group of related projects coordinated together. A portfolio also contains a group of projects that have been grouped in such a way as to meet a specific and strategic business objective, but not necessarily because the projects are related. Work package is incorrect, since it refers to a deliverable within a work breakdown structure.

123. F. Cost of quality refers to any related costs resulting from carrying out quality activities. This is considered an investment of time, money, and resources, which technically all boils down to an investment of money. The correct choice is rework.

124. A, B, D. A run chart is a type of quality tool and therefore not a format you would use to display an organizational chart.

125. B. The project manager is responsible for providing project team members with the appropriate level of training needed to perform the work.

126. B. Perquisites is another type of benefits offered; they are often called "perks," making it the correct answer.

127. B. In a start-to-start relationship, the successor activity (activity B) must wait for its predecessor (activity A) to start before it can start. Since both activities are beginning as soon as possible, we can assume that activity B will begin immediately after activity A starts. However, there is a lag of two days, meaning that activity B must wait two days to start after activity A has started. That means that from the moment that A starts, activity B will not be completed until nine days have passed (just add the duration of the activity, plus the two day lag). Since the activities overlap in this scenario, then the duration that has passed for both activities to finish will have been 10 days total.

128. D. The project manager should allow team members to resolve their own conflict. However, when the issue escalates and requires the involvement of the project manager, the best method is to collaborate (or problem-solve) to resolve the issue. This is a recommended conflict resolution technique because it leads to a win-win situation.

129. A-5, B-1, C-3, D-2, E-4. A project manager may leverage various leadership styles to accommodate various situations and organizational norms. There are five leadership styles referenced within the *PMBOK® Guide*: Laissez-faire, transactional, servant leader, transformational, charismatic, interactional. Agile teams favor servant leadership due to its focus on team.

130. C. Based on the question, the VP is clearly a stakeholder of the project, which means that they were not previously identified. If all stakeholders have not been identified, this means that all expectations, needs, and requirements have not been fully documented and resolved, which can create major issues within the project.

131. B. The definition of a project, as defined by the *PMBOK® Guide*, is "a temporary endeavor undertaken to create a unique product, service or result." What the question is testing is whether you recognize the difference between a project and operational work. The definition of operational work is work that is ongoing, repetitive, and meant to sustain a business.

132. A. Minimum viable products (MVP) contain just enough features or deliverables to obtain feedback; this feedback can then be used for future incremental development of the product.

133. A. Rolling wave planning is where work in the near term is planned out in detail, while work in the future is planned out at higher levels of the WBS. While this is a form of progressive elaboration, rolling wave planning is a more specific choice. Progressive elaboration and rolling wave planning are different from scope creep in that they are planned and controlled.

134. B. The correct response is to allow the audit to take place. Audits are not always planned, and the purpose is to increase efficiency and reduce the cost of quality. Discovering existing inefficiencies will highly benefit the team. Audits are a win-win; even if sometimes it feels like an inconvenience, the big picture must remain at the forefront.

135. D. Target benefits refer to the tangible and intangible business value to be gained by the implementation of the product, service, or result. They are typically documented within a benefits management plan that details how and when benefits will be achieved.

136. D. A benefits management plan describes how and when the benefits of a project will be delivered. It captures the timeframe for realizing benefits, both during the project's life span and during post-project closure.

137. D. Osmotic communication is a form of polite eavesdropping and is used within the Crystal method. It occurs when there are conversations going on in the background but are within earshot of the team. Team members overhear conversations and may realize the topic has importance to the project.

138. D. As the sender of the message, the project manager is responsible for confirming that the message was understood correctly and that the information was clear and complete. In this scenario, the project manager assumed that the message was understood.

139. E. There are specific factors considered in the development of roles and responsibilities. They are organizational, technical, interpersonal, logistical, and political.

140. C. Procurement audits are structured reviews that audit the procurement management processes. The idea is to pinpoint what the efficiencies and inefficiencies were within the procurement management processes, which will be documented as part of the lessons learned. This information is important for future procurements, whether for the current project or future projects.

141. C. The correct answer is forcing, which is a type of conflict resolution technique, not a leadership style. There are six primary leadership styles: laissez-faire, transactional, servant leader, transformational, charismatic, and interactional.

142. A. The accuracy level of One Sigma is 68.27 percent.

143. A. The EAC formula for this question is BAC ÷ CPI. First, calculate CPI, which is EV ÷ AC: 145 ÷ 138 = 1.05. Plugging in the numbers from the question, you get 200 ÷ 1.05 = 190.

144. A. Brainstorming is when individuals are brought together to generate and collect ideas on a variety of topics, such as requirements.

145. D. Kanban is based on lean-thinking principles and helps the team stay organized; it keeps team members collaborating and everyone informed. A flow-based agile approach such as Kanban pulls work from the backlog according to the team's capacity to perform the work.

146. C. The project manager applies general management skills to coordinate and harmonize the group of stakeholders toward accomplishing the project objectives. General management skills is a technique of the Manage Stakeholder Engagement process.

147. D. The Agile Manifesto identifies 12 principles that describe the Agile approach. It came about through a group of software developers who came together in 2001 to formalize the Agile approach.

148. D. The internal rate of return (IRR) is the discount rate when the present value of the cash inflows equals the original investment. If basing project selection on the IRR, choose the project with a higher IRR value.

149. C. Colocation refers to team members working out of the same location physically. Creating a war room is a method of colocation.

150. A. Virtual teams are team members located outside of the physical office where the project is primarily taking place.

151. D. It's clear that the project manager did not check the resource calendars when creating the schedule. Resource calendars contain working and nonworking days of resources. This includes holidays, vacations, and when resources are idle.

152. D. Team-building activities build trust among the project team, allowing them to work in a more efficient and cohesive manner.

153. D. This refers to a milestone list that contains all the project's milestones. It also notes whether a milestone is optional or mandatory. A milestone is a significant point or event in the project, and as the project progresses and the work is underway, the milestone list can be used as a benchmark to measure progress.

154. B. The correct answer is continuous improvement. The word *kaizen* means to change for the better in Japanese.

155. A. It is impossible, and sometimes inefficient, to plan out a project to perfection. There are too many moving parts and factors, regardless of the similarity that projects may have to others managed in the past. A good project manager understands that change is inevitable, which is why project maintenance, varying project life cycles, and overall project management is so important.

156. D. In this question, you're taken to the Plan Human Resource Management process. What Sue is doing is adding value to the project. Networking is a form of informal interaction with others as a way of understanding political and interpersonal factors that impact the project and developing industry relationships and partnerships (if done within the company, it would be building of relationships and partnerships internally).

157. B. The stakeholder management plan, which is created out of the Plan Stakeholder Management process, identifies the strategies needed to effectively engage stakeholders. The plan is based on the stakeholder analysis completed as part of creating the stakeholder register. While the project management plan is also technically correct, it is not the best answer as a more specific option was available.

158. A-4, B-3, C-1, D-2. The Crystal method is actually a family of methodologies that are designed to scale to the project needs. It examines three factors to determine which Crystal methodology to use: criticality of the project, priority of the project, and number of people involved.

159. D. The top three sources of conflict include scarce resources, scheduling priorities, and personal work styles.

160. B. Cost-reimbursable contracts are a higher risk to the buyer. This is because the buyer reimburses the seller for the seller's actual cost, plus an additional amount, and depending on the type of cost-reimbursable contract will determine whether this additional fee is capped. For this reason, this contract is typically used when the buyer can describe the work but not how to go about the work.

161. D. Organizational process assets contain historical information from past archived projects, lessons learned, templates, policies, procedures, and other valuable information. In this case, the project manager is using a previous schedule management plan as a template and tailoring it for use by the current project. This is recommended practice and prevents having to re-invent the wheel for every project. Instead, the effort is placed on increasing the efficiency and refining existing practices and templates.

162. A. The lowest level of the WBS is the work package level. The next step from there would be to decompose the work packages into the activity lists. The activity list, however, is not considered to be part of the WBS itself. Planning packages and control accounts are placed within the WBS but are not the lowest levels.

163. C. Alfred is using an information management system, which captures, stores, and distributes information to stakeholders of the project.

164. A. At the beginning of a project ambiguity is at its peak. Stakeholders have a great deal of input into this. As the project progresses and work is underway, the cost of change increases and the volume of change begins to decrease. As this is the case, stakeholders are most likely to get their requests for inclusion and changes approved during the initial phase of the project.

165. C. The question is referring to pre-assignments, which can be negotiated within the contract, can be included in the project charter, or can be a result of a project that revolves around a staff member's expertise. Pre-assignments is used as a tool and technique of the Acquire Team process.

166. A. This question involves applying the communication channels formula, which is: $n(n-1) \div 2$. Plugging 24 in place of the n results in 276.

167. C. The *PMBOK® Guide* defines risk as an uncertain event or condition that, if it occurs, has a positive or negative effect on a project's objectives. A workaround is put into action for an unidentified negative risk that has occurred. An issue can be described as a negative risk or event that is occurring in the present. A trigger, or risk trigger, is an event that signifies a risk is about to materialize.

168. C. Notice that the constraint impacts the sequence of events of the project, since the project manager must work around the deadline of providing the necessary parts before the vendor can begin, based on a contractual requirement. Dependencies that result from a physical or contractual requirement are known as mandatory dependencies, or hard logic.

169. B. To answer this correctly, you'd need to recall Maslow's Hierarchy of Needs pyramid and the five steps within the pyramid. The question asks for the highest level, which according to the pyramid is self-actualization.

170. C. A milestone has a duration of zero; it is a significant point or event in the project, such as the completion of a deliverable.

171. D. Attending an expo does not translate to spying on the competition and is an example of networking. On a smaller scale, examples of networking include informal conversations, committee gatherings, luncheons, and so on. In this scenario, Bob is being proactive through his actions.

172. C. Of the options provided, the project management office (PMO) would be the best choice. The PMO is responsible for providing project managers with training and resources. They also have archived organizational process assets, which would help in this scenario, along with training. Offering to manage the project with him is implying that you will take on part of his project and responsibility, which is an incorrect answer. Not offering any type of assistance is a poor choice, since part of our responsibility as project managers is to encourage and educate other project managers, although not at the expense of your own projects.

173. A. The correct choice is observation and conversation. This is a technique that allows the project manager to observe the attitudes of team members toward the project and better gauge what is going on. The project manager also gets direct feedback from team members.

174. B. Negotiation and staff assignments don't pertain to where a team member is located. That leaves virtual team and colocation. Virtual team includes project team members who are located at different locations, often never even meeting face to face. This can include working from home offices, from a remote location in general, and at different company sites. Colocation is when project team members are brought to work together at the same physical location. Based on these descriptions, virtual team is the correct choice.

175. D. The risk manager is utilizing the expert judgment technique. This involves subject-matter experts who are internal or external to the project and who validate the data and techniques used to conduct the process.

176. B. Reports are considered formal written, since they are an official report of the project, and they are delivered in written format.

177. A. The correct choice is fringe benefits, which are those benefits provided to all employees.

178. B. The theorist responsible for the 14 Steps to Quality Management is W. Edwards Deming.

179. A-4, B-1, C-3, D-2. There are four project life cycle categories: predictive, iterative, incremental, and Agile. The life cycle selected to manage a project is driven by various factors, one of which is life-cycle goal.

180. A. The minimum viable product (MVP) is used to increase the speed of delivery and obtain feedback of a product early. The product contains just enough features or deliverables to obtain feedback; this feedback can then be used for future incremental development of the product.

181. B. Referent power is based on the respect or admiration that others hold for an individual.

182. C. It's often thought that the project manager or functional manager is responsible for resolving this type of conflict. But in actuality, these individuals should be brought in only to provide assistance or to address the conflict in a formal manner. The best option is that the project team members resolve the conflict on their own, directly.

183. C. Conflict management is not a form of feedback; 360-degree feedback is a formal type of feedback, as opposed to observation and conversation. 360-degree feedback is a type of appraisal, whereas team performance assessment focuses on the team's performance.

184. A. Money already spent refers to sunk costs. Opportunity cost refers to money lost when selecting one project over another, equaling the value of the project that was passed up. Direct costs are costs that are directly attributed to the work on the project. Fixed costs are costs that remain the same throughout the project, such as rentals.

185. A. Negotiations and project staff assignments take place within the Acquire Project Team process, the second process within the Project Resource Management Knowledge Area.

186. C. Gold plating is when additional functionality is added that is outside of the project scope. Sometimes this is done with good intentions, but it is not considered acceptable, no matter what the intent is. If the addition was not a part of the project requirements, quality is not considered to have been met.

187. B. Joseph Juran is connected to the concept that the results produced should be fit for use by the customer.

188. A. Exploit is a strategy used when the organization is interested in making sure that the risk occurs, as well as increasing the impact of the positive risks. Exploit is the exact opposite of avoid, which seeks to eliminate the possibility of the risk occurring. The primary difference between exploit and enhance is that exploit applies changes to ensure that the opportunity will occur, which may or may not include an increase in the impact, while enhance only increases the likelihood and/or impact of the opportunity occurring.

189. D. Quality metrics determine what to measure and what the acceptable measurements are.

190. B. There are three types of organizational structures: functional, matrix, and project-oriented.

191. D. Empathy, influence, and creativity are forms of interpersonal skills, also referred to as soft skills. Interpersonal skills itself is part of general management skills. It is thought that the project manager can decrease issues and increase cooperation by understanding how project team members are feeling, knowing what their concerns are, and being able to follow up on existing issues.

192. B. Defining what acceptable behavior looks like may have taken care of this issue from the start. Even though John felt that Nick's issue was not an immediate priority, all issues should be allowed to be brought to the table or through the outlined procedures.

193. C. The correct answer is poor quality. Remember that quality also looks to remove waste and non-value-added processes. It looks to improve processes and make sure that project requirements are being met.

194. C. The project charter is created to formalize a project. Following the start of the project, identification and analysis of stakeholders come next.

195. C. Benchmarking takes the current project and compares it to other projects, using the previous projects as the point of comparison.

196. B. As the sender of the information, the project team member is responsible for confirming that the project manager understood the information and that the information is complete and clear. On the other end, the project manager also failed to meet the responsibilities of a receiver, which are to make sure that they understood the information correctly and that it was received in its entirety.

197. D. The resource management plan is a component of the project management plan. It outlines the training needs, safety needs, and compliance of the project. As an extra note, it also contains details of how the project team will be acquired, managed, and released.

198. B. 360-degree feedback is a type of project performance appraisal, where feedback is received from all levels of interaction with a team member. This provides information about a team member but not from a team member. Next, observation and conversation come together as a technique from the Manage Project Team process. It's a way for the project manager to monitor the team's progress, accomplishments, and interpersonal issues and is therefore the correct answer. Issue log simply tracks issues so is not relevant here, and team-building activities seems like a good choice, except that the purpose is to grow relationships among the team so the focus is on establishing this cohesiveness and of working together, not of assessing work attitudes.

199. D. A face-to-face meeting is the preferred method for dealing with stakeholders. There is nothing within the question to indicate that a one-on-one meeting with stakeholders is required, which makes "an in-person meeting" the best and most efficient choice.

200. D. PERT stands for program evaluation and review technique and uses a weighted average of the following three estimates: optimistic, pessimistic, and most likely. PERT analysis is used as part of the three-point estimating tool and technique within the Estimate Activity Durations and Estimate Costs processes.

Index

Q

R

Online Test Bank

Register to gain one year of FREE access to the online interactive test bank to help you study for your PMP certification exam—included with your purchase of this book! All of the chapter review questions and the practice tests in this book are included in the online test bank so you can practice in a timed and graded setting.

Register and Access the Online Test Bank

To register your book and get access to the online test bank, follow these steps:

1. Go to bit.ly/SybexTest (this address is case sensitive)!
2. Select your book from the list.
3. Complete the required registration information, including answering the security verification to prove book ownership. You will be emailed a pin code.
4. Follow the directions in the email or go to www.wiley.com/go/sybextestprep.
5. Find your book on that page and click the "Register or Login" link with it. Then enter the pin code you received and click the "Activate PIN" button.
6. On the Create an Account or Login page, enter your username and password, and click Login or, if you don't have an account already, create a new account.
7. At this point, you should be in the test bank site with your new test bank listed at the top of the page. If you do not see it there, please refresh the page or log out and log back in.

Printed and bound by CPI Group (UK) Ltd, Croydon, CR0 4YY
13/07/2022
03135859-0001